The Duxbury Press Series on Public Policy

Charles O. Jones, University of Pittsburgh
General Editor

An Introduction to the Study of Public Policy, 2nd edition
  Charles O. Jones

The Domestic Presidency: Decision-Making in the White House
  John H. Kessel (Ohio State University)

Public Policy and Politics in America
  James E. Anderson, David W. Brady (University of Houston)
  and Charles L. Bullock, III (University of Georgia)

Understanding Intergovernmental Relations
  Deil Wright (University of North Carolina)

Introduction to Budgeting
  John Wanat (University of Kentucky)

*Politics and the Bureaucracy: Policymaking in the Fourth Branch
of Government*
  Kenneth Meier (University of Oklahoma)

Forthcoming

Policy Analysis: An Interdisciplinary Approach
  Duncan MacRae, Jr. and James Wilde (University of
  North Carolina)

Of related interest

A Logic of Public Policy: Aspects of Political Economy
  L. L. Wade (University of California, Davis) and Robert
  L. Curry, Jr. (California State University, Sacramento)

Democracy in America: A Public Choice Perspective
  L. L. Wade (University of California, Davis) and R. L.
  Meek (Colorado State University)

Politics, Change, and the Urban Crisis
  Bryan Downes (University of Oregon)

POLITICS

AND THE

Policymaking
Branch of

Duxbury Press

BUREAUCRACY:

in the Fourth Government

KENNETH J. MEIER

University of Oklahoma

North Scituate, Massachusetts

Politics and the Bureaucracy: Policymaking in the Fourth Branch of Government was edited and prepared for composition by Lucretia Lyons. Interior design was provided by Joanna Prudden Snyder, and the cover was designed by Oliver Kline.

Duxbury Press
A Division of Wadsworth Publishing Company, Inc.

Library of Congress Cataloging in Publication Data
Meier, Kenneth J   1950–
    Politics and the bureaucracy.

    Includes bibliographical references and index.
    1.   Administrative agencies—United States.
2.   United States—Politics and government.   3.   Policy sciences.   4.   Bureaucracy.   I.   Title.
JK421.M39   353.01   78–15232
ISBN 0–87872–208–4

Printed in the United States of America
1 2 3 4 5 6 7 8 9 — 83 82 81 80 79

For my Mother and Father

Contents

⤜ List of Figures ⤛

⤐ List of Tables ⤏

6   1

6   0

4   6

3   6

6   1

6

5   3

——————

    16

30

Bureaucracy is like sin: we all know something about it, but only those who practice it enjoy it. Ordinary people tend to be against both, and experts on the subjects tend to become obsessed, so that some see bureaucracy everywhere, as fanatical clerics see sin up every back alley. If you hold that all sex is sin, you simply mean you wish you had never been born; if you believe all bureaucracies are degenerate you are simply registering a protest against modern society. (Brian Chapman, "Facts of Organized Life," *Manchester Guardian Weekly*, January 26, 1961, p. 20.)

Kenneth J. Meier believes that, like sin, bureaucracy is inevitable in any complex society. However, it is precisely because he does *not* accept the degeneracy of all bureaucracies that he has taken the trouble to write this book. Acknowledging the phenomenal growth of government administration in the past forty years, Professor Meier well advises us that it is time to understand the impact and effects of this expansion.

This book achieves demanding goals. In addition to providing a working knowledge of what a bureaucracy is, how it is organized and how it works, primarily at the federal level, Meier wants the student to understand how powerful the permanent apparatus of government can be. But more than that, he seeks to provide a basis for estimating the conditions for bureaucratic abuse of authority and reviews the techniques for controlling these abuses. Finally, Professor Meier attempts something that

Foreword

one seldom finds in texts of this type: He proposes "a rough blueprint for a more responsive and more competent bureaucracy." Whether or not one agrees with his nostrums, the reader will find them stimulating and evocative of further thought on this important subject.

In a continuation of the remarks cited in the opening of this foreword, Brian Chapman points out that "much of the heat engendered by bureaucracy is really the reflected glow of a fire in another quarter . . . attacks on bureaucracy are really inarticulate protests against the modern state." Professor Meier would, I believe, agree with this statement. Certainly one effect of reading his book is an improved understanding of the modern state, thus making possible more articulate protests and reforms. *Politics and the Bureaucracy: Policymaking in the Fourth Branch of Government* is a lively and well-written book. I am confident you will profit from reading it.

Charles O. Jones
University of Pittsburgh

During the past forty years, the federal bureaucracy has grown from a small subordinate institution to a separate fourth branch of government. Limiting and structuring the impact of this bureaucracy is perhaps the major political issue facing the US today. Other policy problems, such as energy, inflation, food production, et cetera, are all affected by the federal bureaucracy. Nearly all that government does is filtered through the bureaucracy. Every program, policy, and proposal at some stage is influenced by a portion of the bureaucracy.

Since the growth of bureaucratic power is a recent phenomenon, this book attempts to explain the reasons for this growth. Yearly bureaucratic gains are not the result of evil bureaucrats seeking to extend their political influence but rather a function of the needs of modern government. Demands for public services have reached the stage where the Congress, the president, and the courts cannot meet the demands without relying on bureaucracy. Nearly all public policy, according to Theodore Lowi, has degenerated into instructions to bureaucracy. Foreign and defense policies, long the domain of individual actors, have become an area of bureau influence. Yielding to bureaucracy and its influence, however, is not inevitable. Fairly effective mechanisms and procedures can be devised to limit or structure bureaucratic policymaking.

The chapters of this book elucidate the mechanisms and procedures for controlling bureaucracy. Chapter 1 introduces the concept of bureaucratic power while chapter 2 introduces the reader to the federal bureaucracy. Chapter 3 explains why government bureaus develop political power. Chapter 4 discusses the policymaking process when bureaucracy

Preface

uses its power. With chapter 5 the focus shifts to bureaucratic responsibility with a discussion of public expectations of bureaucracy. Chapters 6 and 7 evaluate the normal approaches to controlling bureaucracy. In chapter 8 I offer prescriptions for a more responsive and competent bureaucracy.

Several people contributed to the formation of this volume and deserve my deepest appreciation. My greatest debt is to David Brady. Without him this would be just another unpublished manuscript. Scott Harris sharpened my perspectives on many issues included in this book despite his failure to even read the manuscript. Randall Ripley, Jeremy Plant, Charles O. Jones, John Wanat, and several anonymous reviewers offered comments on portions of this manuscript that improved it greatly. My students, both at Rice University and Syracuse University, have my gratitude for patiently listening as this text evolved in their classes. I also owe a debt of appreciation to Pat Stermer whose excellent typing made my proofreading a joy. Any errors of omission or commission are solely my responsibility.

POLITICS
AND THE
BUREAUCRACY

CHAPTER ONE

When James Burnham published *The Managerial Revolution* in 1942, he argued that control in society had passed from the hands of political officials to a technological elite of managers.[1] The Burnham trend paralleled the development of the modern nation state and has continued to the present. Since midcentury, however, the functions government is expected to perform have shifted radically. No longer is government that governs least assumed to be that which governs best because that government could hardly be termed government at all. Collecting taxes, maintaining law and order, and dispensing justice to the contractually and criminally aggrieved have become minor portions of government. The eclipse of limited government by "positive" government has added functions to the nation state totally foreign to nineteenth century and early twentieth century governments. In the past few years the American national government has entered fully armed to do battle in the fields of protecting the environment, planning and coordinating the current and future energy needs of the nation, regulating the health and safety of the nation's work force, and attempting to protect the unorganized consumer from the disadvantages of the market place.

The growth in positive government has added to another trend—the growth in the major instrument of positive government, bureaucracy. For each new function the federal government has undertaken in the recent past, a corresponding bureaucracy has evolved from the enabling legislation. With the advent of President Lyndon Johnson's Great Society programs, the Department of Health, Education and Welfare grew from a budget of $5 billion in 1963 to $181 billion in 1978. To coordinate the

Bureaucracy

nation's energy policies the Office of Emergency Preparedness was dusted off and charged with new functions. When this office appeared inadequate, the Federal Energy Office (FEO) was formed within the executive office of the president. Even this effort pales when the grandson, the Federal Energy Administration, followed by the great grandson, the Department of Energy, were created and instructed to solve the nation's energy crisis. Concern for workers' health and safety gave rise to the Occupational Health and Safety Administration (OSHA), and the needs of the consumer were entrusted to the Consumer Product Safety Commission. Other examples in the recent past are too numerous to mention. When faced with acute crises, chronic problems, or even apathy, the positive state responds and the response usually entails a bureaucracy.

Bureaucracy has grown not only in size and the quantity of resources it consumes but also in a qualitative sense as well. Few aspects of a citizen's life are immune to the tentacles of government bureaucracy. Today's citizen awakes in the morning to a breakfast of bacon and eggs, both certified as fit for consumption by the United States Department of Agriculture. The breakfast is rudely interrupted by a long distance phone call, the cost of which is determined by either state or federal regulatory commissions. As our citizen drives to work, his car's emissions are controlled by a catalytic converter mandated by the Environmental Protection Agency. As our citizen stops for gasoline, he pays the price that is partially determined by policies set by the Department of Energy. To take his mind off the numerous bureaucracies impinging on his life the bureaucratic man turns on his radio. The station is licensed by the Federal Communication

and Politics

Commission, and all advertisements broadcast are subject to the rules and regulations of the Federal Trade Commission. When our citizen arrives at work, perhaps with a bureaucracy like a university, he climbs stairs (inspected by OSHA) in a building built with federal monies to a job financed in large part by the Office of Education.[2]

Although our hypothetical person has been awake only a few short hours, at least nine federal, state, and local bureaucracies have affected his life. The normal citizen in the United States works in a government bureaucracy (one of every six workers) or in a private bureaucracy that is regulated unobtrusively or obtrusively by a government bureaucracy, eats bureaucratically inspected food, wears bureaucratically regulated clothes, plays in bureaucratically sanctioned places and ways, and will probably be buried in a bureaucratically approved manner. No part of any person's life is left untouched by the entity called bureaucracy.

This chapter will discuss the phenomenon of administrative power. First, the dissatisfaction with bureaucracy in the United States will be analyzed. Second, this dissatisfaction will be traced to the phenomenon of administrative power. Third, the use of administrative power by four federal government bureaus will be discussed in detail. Fourth, "administrative power" will be explicitly defined as the term will be used in the book.

⤫ Bureaucracy: A Favorite Target ⤫

The growth of the bureaucratic state has not been without dissent. In a nation that subscribes to the notions of individual liberty and limited government, the growth of bureaucracy is viewed at best as a threat to freedom, at worst as un-American. Bureaucracy has become a favorite target of both the politicians and the citizens. In 1975 then President Ford attempted to make the size and responsiveness of the bureaucracy a political issue. He attacked several regulatory agencies including the Civil Aeronautics Board and the Interstate Commerce Commission as inefficient and harmful.[3] The war on bureaucracy was extended to other agencies such as the Food and Nutrition Service, which was charged with incompetence and uselessness.[4] Ronald Reagan, Gerald Ford's opponent for the Republican nomination in 1976, proposed cutting federal spending by $90 billion. When opposition to Reagan's proposal surfaced, he retreated to the safety of anecdotes about bureaucracy and rhetoric about the abuse of the positive state. Alabama Governor George Wallace never failed to receive resounding cheers from his audience when he promised that if elected he would throw all the pointy-headed bureaucrats and their briefcases into the Potomac. The bureaucracy often dismissed such criticism in the past as crazed rumblings of the right. But from the center of the political spectrum former

Vice-President Nelson Rockefeller denounced bureaucratic red tape in a series of meetings across the country.[5] From the left Senator William Proxmire rates press coverage with his revelations about National Science Foundation studies of bisexual frogs and drunk fish, and the waste generated by the Defense Department.[6] President Carter's election in 1976 was, in part, a response to his pledge to reorganize the federal bureaucracy and to make it more effective and more efficient.

The politicians have been joined, or more probably led, by private citizens in denouncing government and bureaucracy. The nation's businesses have traditionally blamed the bureaucracy for stifling initiative, for rising prices, and for any other ills the economy might have. Charles Polliod, President of Goodyear, stated "Production, innovation, and efficiency are inhibited (by the bureaucracy) . . . the taxpayer foots the bill for the expanding network of federal regulators, estimated to number 63,000 at a cost of over $2 billion." [7] Although elite debate over politics often does not penetrate to the mass level, bureaucracy and its evils are universally understood. Fully 77 percent of the population, as indicated by public opinion surveys, feel that government bureaucracy has grown too large.[8]

Analysis of these criticisms of bureaucracy would reveal that these criticisms possess a common core, the belief that bureaucracy is inefficient. Bureaucracy hinders the effective operation of the market mechanism that efficiently allocates resources; therefore, the impact of bureaucracy will always be deleterious.

◢◣ Criticism and Rhetoric ◢◣

Within every criticism of bureaucracy there is a kernel of truth indicating that something is wrong with the bureaucracy. Only the idealist would be so foolish as to contend that government bureaucracy is without sins and is an unmixed blessing for modern society. The contemporary criticism, however, must be classified more as rhetoric than conclusive evidence for two reasons.

Efficiency: A Nonmeasurable Proposition

First, the contention that bureaucracy, specifically government bureaucracy, is inefficient is essentially an untestable proposition. If efficiency is defined as delivering goods and services at the least possible cost, then efficiency only has meaning in comparative terms; that is, is organization A more efficient than organization B? In the private sector efficiency comparisons are sometimes possible because many firms produce the same items. Those that produce an item at less cost can be termed more efficient. Government bureaus, for the most part, cannot be compared to any other organizations or among themselves because each bureau produces a unique product. For example, only the Department of Defense "produces" a national defense. As a result, descriptions of government bureaucracy as inefficient rarely have solid foundations.

The perception of government bureaucracy as inefficient is often based more on assumption than fact. The critic of bureaucracy often un-critically accepts the assumption of the classical economic theory that competition leads inevitably to efficiency through efficient allocation of scarce resources. Applying this assumption the critic reasons, "if there is no competition to force efficient production, the organization must be ineffi-cient." [9] To support the claim of inefficiency the critic usually cites an extreme case study that everyone accepts as ludicrous. The critic cites past mistakes made by the bureaucracy or denounces red tape—namely, addi-tional requirements that the bureaucracy has imposed on the citizen. Never are we given any indication of the extent of the condemned behavior, its frequency, or whether the bureaucracy has taken corrective action. These examples of bureaucratic mistakes demonstrate little because all large scale formal organizations either public or private make mistakes. Ford Motor Company's decision to produce the Edsel rivals the publicized De-fense Department weapons failures. Sperry Rand, in the early 1950s, con-cluded no market existed for computers, a forecasting error as large as any produced by government bureaucracies. A widely discussed example of public versus private enterprise is the National Broadcasting Company's effort to develop a new logo, an abstracted N, which cost the company $750,000. The Nebraska Educational Television Network, a government bureaucracy, developed the same logo before NBC did for under $100. These examples do not prove that Ford, Sperry Rand, or NBC are ineffi-cient; they only show that large scale organizations occasionally make mis-takes. Without some information as to the frequency of the mistakes, judgments as to efficiency cannot be made. Most of the measures of effi-ciency that can be applied to public sector bureaucracy are ambiguous. Therefore, the "bureaucracy is inefficient" hypothesis is not testable.

Second, in some instances measures are available to judge the effi-ciency of the bureaucracy, but these measures are applicable to only a small portion of the activities that governments perform and may involve assum-ing that efficiency is a bureau's only goal. The Postal Service, some defense procurement, the government printing office, and on the local level sanita-tion and street repair are some government activities that can be assessed in terms of efficiency. To make this assessment, however, we must assume that the primary goal of these organizations is to deliver the service as efficiently as possible. Anyone with any experience in government, or for that matter, experience with the pre-Nixon Post Office will agree that many times the goal is maximum service rather than efficient service. More efficient postal delivery could be achieved by shifting the tasks of the small post offices to large mechanized centers where economies of scale could operate. Efficiency could probably be increased if the Postal Service merely assigned every citizen within a hundred mile radius a post office box in a single building and made the citizen pick up his own mail. The cost of delivering mail under these circumstances would be greatly reduced while the number of items "delivered" would remain constant. By definition this type of service is more efficient. Clearly, the public would not passively accept this "efficiency" when the cost is such decreased service.

If efficiency is a difficult concept to apply to the few areas of government that perform quasi-private functions, such as delivering the mail, then for most governmental functions the concept is irrelevant. How does one measure the efficiency of health research, of environmental protection, or even of occupational safety in an unambiguous manner? Efficiency is a foreign term in these and other areas of government because the tasks we demand that government perform are more complex than the tasks we demand of the private sector. The objective of building Chevrolet Vegas must pale before the goal of curing cancer; protecting environments is much more complex than designing a computerized payroll system; developing new forms of energy is not amenable to the same standards of profit measurement that the production of tires is. Since the goals and objectives of public programs are more complex and require different and possibly more sophisticated expertise, the public sector rarely has the regularity and predictability of private sector operations.[10]

∾ Administrative Power as Political Power ∾

The argument that the public is dissatisfied with bureaucracy because it is inefficient is not well documented. Dismissing the complaints against bureaucracy, however, would be too hasty. While the bureaucracy may not be peopled with incompetents anxious to infringe on the economic and political freedoms of the American people, neither are they neutral angels without political objectives of their own.

To understand the criticism of bureaucracy as it exists in American society, bureaucracy and its functions in the society must be examined. What does bureaucracy do to cause three-fourths of the population to reject it? Bureaucracy, in the case of our hypothetical bureaucraticized citizen, impacted on all aspects of life. Bureaucracy regulates our behavior;

it redistributes our income; it distributes benefits of society; in short, bueaucracy allocates societal resources.

Authoritative Power

The impact that bureaucracy has on our lives is authoritative. In most
cases it is perceived as legitimate and backed up by the coercive power of
the state. By authoritatively allocating values bureaucracy is engaging in
politics of the first order. As a political institution, the bureaucracy is not
immune to the frequent vocal criticism levied at all American political
institutions. Recent public opinion polls (see table 1–1) convincingly
demonstrate that all government institutions, and bureaucracy is no exception, lack the confidence of a large number of people. This lack of confidence is probably related to bureaucracy's need to make hard political
choices that often result in denial of benefits and assessment of costs to
certain individuals. The bureaucracy's exercise of political power, therefore,
naturally leads to public criticism.

To the person used to viewing bureaucracy as a neutral instrument
for implementing other's political choices, the concept of bureaucracy as
a political power is a difficult one. The following four cases are included
to demonstrate the political nature of bureaucracy in a variety of different
policy areas.

Case Study 1: Administrative Power and Federal Housing.   The
Federal Housing Administration (FHA) is an agency within the Department of Housing and Urban Development whose goal is to improve the
quality of housing in the nation through construction and rehabilitation.[11]
In 1937 Congress assigned FHA the goal of improving housing but left the
method of implementing the goal to FHA discretion. The approach used
by the FHA was to set standards for acceptable housing. To enforce those
standards, FHA offered to underwrite mortgages for houses meeting those
standards. In effect the FHA offered positive benefits for compliance with
their own housing standards.

Before 1967 the FHA required that all mortgage loan guarantees
be economically sound. The value of the house underwritten must have a
market value high enough to compensate the government's loss if the
homeowner defaulted. Within these narrow bounds the FHA program was
a spectacular success, millions received the loan guarantees necessary to
purchase homes making the single family dwelling the norm for middle
class American families. As a result of the agency's fiscally conservative
management, the loan default rate was less than one-half of 1 percent.

Although the FHA's method of implementing congressional hous-

TABLE 1–1   Assessment of Specific Leadership Being in Touch with People's Needs

Leaders of:	Really Know What People Want %	Mostly Out of Touch %	Not Sure %
Medicine	69	21	10
Television News	66	24	10
Banks	64	24	12
The Press	59	29	12
Colleges	55	34	11
Local Government	47	40	13
State Government	46	41	13
Organized Labor	45	39	16
Law Firms	45	38	17
Organized Religion	44	40	16
Major Companies	39	50	11
The Military	38	44	18
The U.S. Supreme Court	38	43	19
The White House	35	51	14
The Executive Branch of the Federal Government	34	50	16
Congress	34	54	12

Source: Harris Survey, "Public Feels Leaders Out of Touch," *Houston Post*, October 18, 1975, p. 3d.

ing policies is clearly an exercise in political decisionmaking, the implications of this policy demonstrate more clearly the FHA's influence on national priorities. In order to limit the losses from defaulted mortgages, certain localities in every city were redlined, that is, designated as areas where mortgages would be poor risks due to the nature of the neighbor-hood and other factors. Unfortunately, for some residents, most of the inner city and ghetto areas of the nation were redlined so that no federal mortgage guarantees were available in these areas. Because federal mortgage guarantees lowered housing costs by eliminating the hazards of default, permitting FHA loan guarantees in the "economically sound" areas only hastened the exodus to the suburbs by the white middle class. The lower cost of housing in the suburban areas contributed to the inner city decay by denying the financial support necessary to undertake rehabilitation through increased ownership.

The actions of the Federal Housing Administration were redistrib-utive in every sense of the word. Housing benefits were redistributed from the poor and minorities in the cities to the middle class in the suburbs through selective granting and denial of benefits. The program served to redistribute income from other social needs to housing but only to the portion of the housing market used by the middle class. Money available for loans was wisely invested by banks in completely safe FHA loans rather than a myriad of other uses.

This redistribution was the status of housing policy prior to 1967. With the creation of the Department of Housing and Urban Development (HUD) in 1965 the Federal Housing Administration was transferred to HUD. The transfer of the fiscally conservative FHA to the social welfare conscious Department of Housing and Urban Development had a pro-found impact on the goals of FHA. FHA was charged with correcting some deficiencies of its past policies; FHA was to house the nation's poor.

With this new goal the implementation of the policy was left to the FHA since the complexities of housing policies were beyond the ken both of the executives in HUD and the congressmen overseeing the area. The FHA moved to eliminate the practice of redlining inner city areas. Unfortunately, the new goal of the agency was counter to the standard operating procedures of the lower level agency personnel. Newspapers re-ported case after case of FHA appraisers estimating the market value of houses from their car because they were afraid to appraise ghetto housing. The results were disastrous. Through both fear and corruption thousands of shoddy houses worth at most a few hundred dollars were each appraised for thousands.[12] Purchasers were found for these houses which required only a down payment of a few hundred dollars. When the inadequacies of the house became known to the owner and the costs for repairs exceeded the resident's ability to pay, the house was abandoned. With abandonment came default and the Federal Housing Administration became the proud owner of a defective house with no market value.

The redistributive nature of the post–1967 FHA policies is evident. The FHA used its discretion and adopted an implementation strategy that increased inner city deterioration. The poor, the intended beneficiary of the policy, suffered the most since the amount of housing declined (in many cases after the FHA failed to resell a house, it was destroyed). The beneficiaries of the policy were the real estate brokers who were able to sell the house and the banks who were able to make risk-free investments at the expense of the government.

Case Study 2: Bureaucracy and the Cuban Missile Crisis. National security policy, especially during a crises such as the Cuban missile crisis, is a policymaking area where we expect bureaucracy to be subservient.[13] Power in such situations ought to pass to the president and his close circle of advisers. The Cuban missile crisis, in fact, had at least two characteristics that Richard Neustadt deemed necessary for the exercise of presidential power: there was clear presidential involvement and the other actors had no doubts about the president's ability to act.[14] In addition, the bureaus involved, the Central Intelligence Agency and the armed services, are hierarchically structured organizations designed to quickly carry out presidential orders.

When the president and his advisers learned with certainty that the Soviets placed missiles in Cuba, they narrowed their choice to two options—a surgical air strike against the missiles and a blockade of the island. Although one would expect the armed services to be neutral in questions of military strategy, this was not the case. The United States Air Force argued that a surgical air strike was not feasible. To be effective and to be certain of success the air force argued that they must bomb all missile sites, storage depots, airports, and artillery batteries. Since that option was clearly beyond the risks the president was willing to assume, the advice of the air force effectively foreclosed one option of the president.

With the decision for the blockade, the initial details were left to the discretion of the navy. The navy, to assure the safety of its mission, initially established the blockade out of the range of the Cuban Air Force five hundred miles from Cuba. The president, feeling this gave the Soviets too little time to think and react, requested the ships to be moved closer to the Cuban coast. When the navy balked at the suggestion, the secretary of defense, Robert McNamara put the request in the form of a direct order.

Although the decision makers felt their order had been implemented, when the first ships were intercepted it was clear that the navy had followed its own conscience. The first ship was intercepted some five hundred miles off the coast of Cuba. To avoid the appearance of direct disobedience, Graham Allison presented evidence that the navy permitted at least one ship to slip through the blockade.[15] Clearly, in the Cuban missile crisis the air force and navy exercised political power. The air force through its advice foreclosed one option of the president, the navy chose to ignore an order of the secretary of defense and in the process increased the risk of a confrontation. However political power is defined, increasing the risks to national security must be included as an exercise of that power.

Case Study 3: Medicine and Bureaucracy.   The National Institutes of Health (NIH) is a fairly autonomous bureau within the Department of Health, Education, and Welfare charged with the goal of "improving the health of the American people." The National Institutes of Health is composed of ten research institutes specializing in different diseases and four other more general units. Unlike many other areas of government, Congress and the president (the "political" branches of government) pay a great deal of attention to the line items in the NIH budget because the individual institutes are listed as separate programs. As a result the "political" branches of government affect NIH priorities or rather can affect NIH priorities when Congress is not overwhelmed by the polished lobby of doctors and scientists NIH has cultivated. In theory, Congress decides whether health research monies ought to be invested in cancer research, heart research, or general medical research.

Within each institute, however, the priorities and research approaches are decided by administrators and their scientific peers. Congress lacks the knowledge to carefully scrutinize the activities of the National Cancer Institute (NCI). The priority NCI places on different cancer research is clearly an allocation of resources that dearly affect the American people. Whether most research concentrates on lung cancer, a disease of the old, or leukemia, a disease of the young, has implications for every citizen. The National Cancer Institute by allocating $600 million a year from tax money to private and public research institutes according to priorities it decides is exercising political power.

Although NCI's discretion is unchallenged, it is limited to a relatively narrow area—cancer research. The National Institute of General Medical Sciences, on the other hand, has a broader mandate. General Medical Sciences spends some $200 million annually on genetics, pharmacology, and three or four other areas of research. The areas are broad and amenable to significant discretion in terms of what research ought to be pursued. Congressional and executive supervision of that discretion is virtually nonexistent as is evidenced by the Institute's status in the budget. Only 12 lines in an unwieldy 1,000 page budget are devoted to the National Institute of General Medical Sciences.

The National Institutes of Health provides another example of the exercise of political power because the agency is allowed to set and implement the nation's health research priorities with little scrutiny by the political branches of government. To be sure the general health priorities are set by the president and Congress, but the priorities are set with the advice of the experts in the National Institutes of Health. In addition, the political priorities that are established are fairly broad so that NIH is free to pursue its own priority list within the general political priorities.

Case Study 4: The Federal Trade Commission-Bureaucratic Activism. The Federal Trade Commission (FTC) was created in 1914 as an independent agency charged with maintaining "strongly competitive enterprise as the keystone of the American economic system." The FTC is given several tools to pursue this goal including anti-trust law, consent decrees, cease and desist orders, and informal bargaining; but the FTC is given little guidance as to where to act or what specific policies to follow.

For a long time the FTC was regarded as an agency with little life or power, but in recent years the FTC has revitalized and vigorously pursued its policies of fostering competition in the market place and protecting the American consumer from fraud. A simple list of the activities undertaken by the FTC in 1975 will demonstrate the policymaking influence of the Commission.

The FTC in 1975 set standards for the rights of a purchaser who buys on installments, and the FTC increased the liabilities of a "holder in due course" (a person who purchased a buyer's IOU from a retailer). The FTC ruled that mail order firms must fill orders within 30 days of purchase or offer the consumer a full refund on the merchandise. Going beyond normal market place regulation the FTC proposed standards for funeral home operators including advance notice of the costs involved in a funeral. In other actions in 1975 the FTC proposed rules on selling used cars by requiring that actual mileage, nature of prior use, extent of major repairs on the automobile, and the full extent of the warranty be disclosed to the buyer of the automobile. The FTC also proposed regulations on advertising for hearing aids, investigated the optical industry for restraint of trade, prohibited Warner-Lambright from making unproven claims that Listerine prevents colds, started proceedings to permit advertising by doctors, and began an investigation of real estate dealers in an effort to establish some standards. These were only the actions of the FTC that caught the attention of the media.

The Federal Trade Commission's actions are clearly exercises of political power by an administrative agency. In each of the actions listed above some of the resources of one group of citizens were redistributed to other groups or the behavior of a group of citizens was restricted. The FTC has favored the consumer in recent years and placed severe constraints on the behavior of the sellers. FTC's actions have been done without clear guidelines from Congress stating what the FTC should accomplish in the general area of consumer protection. The decisions made by the FTC are occasionally appealed to the courts or through the political process to

Congress, but even the initial decision by the FTC to start investigation is an act of administrative power because a business must expend substantial resources just answering the FTC's charges.

The four case studies show not only the exercise of administrative power but also the breadth of policy areas that are affected by administrative power. Theodore Lowi contends that all policy can be divided into four policy types—distributive policy, redistributive policy, regulatory policy, and constituent policy (these types are discussed in detail in chapter 4).[16] Our cases present evidence of bureau power in each of the four areas of policymaking—the Federal Housing Administration operates in a sphere of redistributive policy; the Federal Trade Commission is a regulatory policy actor; the Department of the Navy is in constituent policy; and the National Institutes of Health's policies are distributive.

Our cases indicate that administrative power is not necessarily harmful to everyone in the state. For every FHA policy that may pursue objectives in the narrow self-interest of its clientele, a FTC policy may seek a broader consumer interest despite organized opposition. For every navy admiral who may directly disobey an order of the secretary of defense, a medical researcher in NIH may spend long hours trying to anticipate new public health problems before they occur. The objective of the citizen in a state where bureaucracy exercises a great deal of political power, and the United States is such a state, should not be to condemn and destroy bureaucratic power but to structure it so that the benefits of bureaucracy (see chapter 5) can be attained without some of its deleterious effects.

ᖇᖇ Administrative Power: A Difficult Term ᖇᖇ

Until now we have been imprecise in our definition of administrative power, equating it with the exercise of political choice by the bureaucracy. To be a useful concept, administrative power must be defined more carefully. Administrative power is the ability of a bureaucracy to allocate scarce societal resources. Administrative power, in this definition, is nothing more than political power exercised by governmental bureaucracies as they determine, in Lasswell's words, who gets what, when, and how. Administrative power, and political power for that matter, has two requisites—resources and discretion. The *sine qua non* of administrative power is access to resources—to money, personnel, and other tools necessary to make and carry out political decisions. A bureau, therefore, is more powerful than another bureau when it extracts more resources from its environment. The needed resources include trained personnel, money, and legitimate control over a policy area or set of decisions. The extraction of resources aspect of administrative power is equivalent to Katz and Kahn's definition of organizational effectiveness.[17]

Having access to resources or rather having the ability to extract resources is not sufficient to create a powerful bureaucracy. The National Institutes of Health and the Social Security Administration are both successful in extracting resources from their environments, but the Social Security Administration is rigidly bound by rules and legislation passed by Congress designed to restrict SSA's discretion.[18] To become powerful an agency must have discretion, the ability to make decisions concerning agency activities. Discretion without resources, however, is only a moderate form of power because an agency will not have the money, personnel, or authority to enforce any decision it makes.

Resource extraction and discretion in the use of resources after extraction are two distinct dimensions of administrative power. Agencies can have a great deal of resources with little discretion as the Social Security Administration has or agencies can have few resources but a great deal of discretion as the Internal Revenue has, or can have both as in the case of NIH, or can be so unfortunate as the Selective Service Commission in the mid 1970s as to have neither (see table 1–2).

This chapter discusses the phenomenon of administrative power. The public displeasure with bureaucracy is noted and tied to the growth of bureaucracy as a powerful institution. The policymaking power of bureaucracy is illustrated through case studies of the Federal Housing Administration, the Cuban Missile Crisis, the National Institutes of Health, and the Federal Trade Commission. The chapter concludes with a definition of administrative power. Chapter 2 presents a descriptive background of the federal bureaucracy so that the reader has a core of knowledge essential for understanding the remainder of the book. Chapter 3 discusses the reasons why some bureaus develop political power and others do not.

TABLE 1–2   *Dimensions of Administrative Power*

Autonomy	Resource Extraction	
	High	Low
High	NIH	IRS
Low	SSA	Selective Service

The discussion centers on the political environment of federal agencies. Chapter 4 examines the policymaking process in the bureaucracy in an attempt to determine the different reasons that permit different agencies to affect public policy. With chapter 5 the focus shifts to control of administrative power. Chapter 5 discusses the public's expectations of bureaucracy on the two major dimensions, responsiveness and competence. Chapters 6 and 7 examine a series of proposals for controlling the political power of bureaucracy. The final chapter, chapter 8, presents some new proposals for checking the ill effects of administrative power.

Notes

1. James Burnham, *The Managerial Revolution* (New York: John Day, 1942).

2. My students are fond of noting that all this contact with bureaucracy at so early an hour of the day will produce a painful headache. The remedy is, of course, two aspirin regulated by the Food and Drug Administration.

3. David Burnham, "Ford to Seek Curb on Power of C.A.B.," *New York Times*, February 6, 1975, p. 1. "Ford Plan Revealed for Regulatory Reform," *Houston Post*, May 14, 1976, p. 8c.

4. "Ford Asks Drastic Cut for (Food) Stamps," *Houston Post*, October 23, 1975, p. 1.

5. Fred Bonavita, "Rocky Says People Tired of Red Tape," *Houston Post*, November 12, 1975, p. 1.

6. See for example "National Science Foundation Grants Assailed," *Washington Post*, March 2, 1975, p. A14.

7. "Tire Chief Urges Cut in Red Tape," *Houston Post*, November 10, 1975.

8. The poll conducted by Citicorp, the parent corporation of National City Bank of New York, was cited by Treasury Secretary William Simon in Gerald Egger, "Bureaucratic Monster Runs Wild, Simon Says," *Houston Post*, October 5, 1975, p. 17c.

9. The perceptive reader will note that the critic's logic is fallacious. The critic assumed that if there is competition, then there will be efficient allocation of resources. Observing a basic fact of government bureaucracy, that there is no competition, the critic concludes the bureaucracy must be inefficient. The critic has denied the antecedent, one of the most elementary logical fallacies.

10. Many economists argue that government should be limited to performing the services that private industry cannot perform or cannot perform at a profit. Simply, that definition of the area that government should concen-

trate in a tacit recognition of the great difficulties with the measurement efficiency of the public sector.

11. The information in this case study is taken from Harold Wolman, *The Politics of Federal Housing* (New York: Dodd Mead, 1971) and Brian D. Boyer, *Cities Destroyed for Cash* (Chicago: Follett Publishing Co., 1973).

12. The charge of corruption has been documented by Boyer, several investigations by newspapers and Congressional committees. By May of 1973 116 indictments had been handed down in cases involving the FHA program naming some 250 people in over 300 charges. Despite the low priority placed on these cases by local prosecutors 46 convictions were returned by May 1973.

13. Graham Allison, *Essence of Decision* (Boston: Little, Brown, 1971).

14. Richard Neustadt, *Presidential Power* (New York: John Wiley and Sons, 1960).

15. Graham Allison, "The Power of Bureaucratic Routines," in *Bureaucratic Power in National Politics*, ed. Francis Rourke (Boston: Little, Brown, 1972), p. 94.

16. Theodore Lowi, "Four Systems of Policy, Politics, and Choice," *Public Administration Review* 32 (July/August): 298–310.

17. Daniel Katz and Robert L. Kahn, *The Social Psychology of Organizations* (New York: Wiley, 1976).

18. Allen Schick, "Toward the Cybernetic State," in *Public Administration in a Time of Turbulence*, ed. Dwight Waldo (Scranton: Chandler, 1971), pp. 214–233.

O f all the institutions of American government, bureaucracy is by far the most obscure. The president, as a visible actor, is constantly subject to media and public attention whether his activities are official or private. Congress also has high visibility even if only as a focal point for opposition to the president. Even the courts periodically rate public attention when they rule on significant cases. Although bureaucracy directly affects the lives of many citizens (chapter 1), it rarely receives the public attention that other political institutions receive.

Because this general knowledge about the bureaucracy is lacking, this chapter describes the federal bureaucracy in order to provide a foundation for the arguments in later chapters. This chapter examines several characteristics of American bureaucracy including the organization of the federal government (the types of departments, agencies, and other organizations that comprise the federal bureaucracy), the size of government bureaucracy, the government's personnel system (the different types of government employees and how they are recruited to government), and the role of state and local bureaucracies in the federal system.

❧ The Organization of the Federal Government ❧

In theory the organization of the federal government is relatively simple. The United States government has three co-equal branches—the executive, the legislative, and the judiciary. The bureaucracy is officially responsible

American

to the president so that he can take care that the laws of the nation are faithfully executed (see figure 2–1). In reality the federal bureaucracy, despite its formal subordinate status, is a relatively autonomous policy-maker. Both the president and the Congress, partly in response to bureaucracy, have developed bureaucratic organizations of their own. This section will outline the major organizational features of the federal bureaucracy and then discuss the political bureaucracies of the president and Congress.

Departments

The first level of organization below the president is the 12 executive departments each headed by a cabinet secretary (see table 2–1). Not only do the departments conduct the more important policy activities but they contain over 60 percent of the federal employees. The departments were established by Congress over a period of 190 years with the department structures and functions existing as a product of the political forces present during their creation.

Departments Performing Essential Government Functions. The Departments of State, Treasury, and War were created in 1789 as the three essential functions of government.[1] Both State and War Departments were initially perceived as presidential departments because they performed the functions of diplomacy and national defense where the president was intended to be the dominant force. The Department of the

Bureaucracy

TABLE 2–1 *Estimated Size of US Government Executive Departments, 1978*

Department	Personnel	Budget ($ millions)
Agriculture	84,000	$ 17,727
Commerce	29,800	4,385
Defense	933,500	117,747
Health, Education and Welfare	145,100	181,265
Housing and Urban Development	17,400	9,529
Interior	56,000	4,002
Justice	55,100	2,533
Labor	20,800	25,134
State	22,800	1,355
Transportation	73,100	15,798
Treasury	112,500	62,612
Energy	19,100	10,087

Source: The Budget for the US Government.

Treasury, on the other hand, was initially perceived as a congressional department closely related to Congress' power to tax. Currently the State Department performs functions similar to those in its early days; the State Department conducts the nation's diplomacy and coordinates a variety of US programs that affect other nations. The Treasury Department through its bureaus collects the nation's taxes, prints the nation's money, finances the national debt, and dispenses revenue sharing funds to the states. The War Department went through a variety of organizational permutations; in its last major reorganization the Department of Defense was created by merging the Department of War and the Department of the Navy.

Departments Reflecting the Needs of a Growing Nation.   Congress created two departments to reflect the growing needs of the nation, the Department of Justice and the Department of the Interior. In the first cabinet President Washington had an attorney general, but in the early years of government the attorney general was simply a lawyer hired to serve

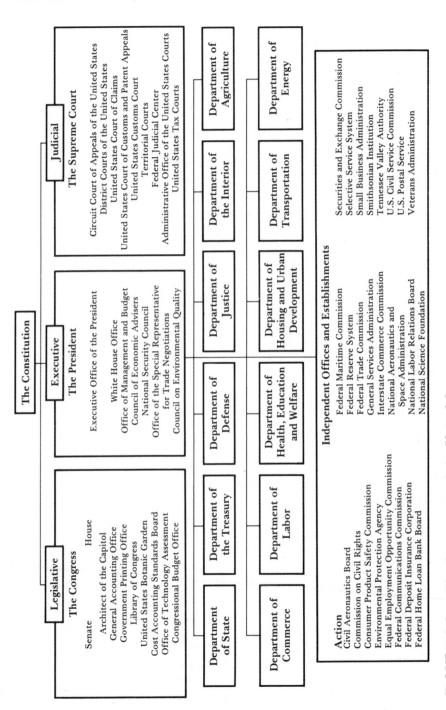

FIGURE 2–1   *The Government of the United States.*
Source: Redrawn from *The U.S. Government Manual,* USGPO, 1977, p. 28.

the government. As the legal needs of the nation grew so did the attorney general's tasks, and in 1870 Congress created the Department of Justice. The Department of Justice is comprised of several legal units that represent the United States in court on legal matters concerning antitrust, criminal law, civil law, civil rights, tax law, and land and natural resources law. The Department also contains the nation's federal law enforcement agencies (for example, the FBI), the immigration service, and the federal prisons.[2]

Another federal department created in response to growing national needs was the Interior Department.[3] Creating an Interior Department was a major political issue from 1789 to 1849 because the states feared that a federal department on the order of the British Home Department would interfere with states' rights. Proposals to create a Department of the Interior were either proposed or debated in Congress several times before 1849. The Interior Department was created in 1849 by combining other departments' programs that covered internal affairs such as patents, public lands, and Indian programs. Currently the department no longer has jurisdiction over patents but has added parks, recreation, and some natural resources programs. Soon after the creation of the Department of the Interior it developed strong ties to interest groups interested in public lands, recreation, and reclamation. This interest group pressure brought about the clientele ties that became a blueprint for the next three departments established.

Clientele Departments.   The clientele departments are the Departments of Agriculture, Commerce, and Labor. These departments were not created to serve the needs of government but in response to interest pressure. The U.S. Department of Agriculture (USDA), created in 1862, was the first of the clientele departments. USDA began as a research department developing new agricultural techniques. During the New Deal the department was transformed into a subsidies and regulation department designed to limit farm production and raise farm income. Currently the bulk of USDA programs are in marketing agricultural goods either in domestic or in foreign markets and in distributing food (food stamps and foreign food aid).

The Commerce Department was established in 1903 and at one time may have been the dominant department of the federal government. During the 1920s the Commerce Department was a major force in shaping domestic policies of economic development. With the rise of labor unions and the growth of government in other areas, the Commerce Department has lost its great influence. Today Commerce contains several diverse programs including promoting business, the Census Bureau, and the Patent Office.

The Department of Labor was originally part of the Department of Commerce but was separated from Commerce in 1913. The current Labor Department monitors worker health and safety, employment standards, unemployment compensation programs, and programs to create additional jobs.

For several decades after the creation of the Department of Labor no new departments were established.[4] Government expansion during the New Deal either took place inside current department organizations or in the form of independent agencies as will be discussed in the next section.

Departments Reflecting Pressing National Needs. The remaining four federal departments were all established to respond to a pressing national need or to recognize the priority of certain problems. The Department of Health, Education and Welfare (HEW) was created out of the Federal Security Administration and other programs to signify the priority of these functions. The present HEW operates programs that distribute funds for education, health research, health care (medicaid, medicare), welfare, and social security.

The Department of Housing and Urban Development (1965) reflected President Lyndon Johnson's commitment to urban problems. The department administers the federal mortgage guarantee programs, the public housing programs, as well as the programs designed to address the problems of urban life. The Department of Transportation, an agency including most federal government transportation programs (railroads, airline safety, highways, Coast Guard), was established in 1967 to emphasize the need for comprehensive approaches to transportation problems. Finally, the Department of Energy was created in 1977 in response to growing concern about the nation's energy shortage and President Carter's request for a unified approach to energy problems. The department contains research, development, and regulation functions for most forms of energy.

The Department Bureaus and Agencies. The twelve executive departments of the federal government are not monolithic units. Each department is composed of several other bureaus and agencies that perform the department's specialized functions. In some departments such as the Department of Housing and Urban Development, the department controls the bureaus and agencies closely so that they operate with little autonomy *vis-à-vis* the department. Other federal departments are not really departments at all; they are holding companies. In a holding company department, power resides at the bureau and agency level. The Department of Health, Education and Welfare (HEW) is a good example of a holding company. Some of the units in HEW, such as the Office of Education or the Public Health Service, were in existence long before the Department was created. These bureaus have their own clientele, were established by legislation different from the law that established the Department, and in some cases (the Office of Education) may even aspire to become a cabinet level department.

A good example to illustrate the nature of department agencies and bureaus is the US Department of Agriculture. As the organization chart of the Department shows (see figure 2–2), the first level of organization under the secretary of agriculture is the assistant secretary level. In USDA the assistant secretary for International Affairs and Commodity Programs is in charge of an administrative apparatus designed to monitor the actions of the bureaus under the unit. The bureau level in this unit is one level down —the Agricultural Stabilization and Conservation Service, the Federal Crop Insurance Corporation, the Foreign Agricultural Service, the Office of the General Sales Manager and the Commodity Credit Corporation. These bureaus and agencies actually administer the programs and make the policy choices.

The assistant secretary is a political appointee. In theory bureau chiefs, as determined by law, are either civil servants or political appointees. In practice, however, many political slots are filled by nonpartisan individuals. During the Nixon administration approximately 38 percent of the bureau chiefs were politicians filling appointed positions.[5] These men and women had long records of service in the Republican party. Their average age was 51 and they were appointed initially as a bureau chief or held at most one other position in the agency before assuming the top spot. The politician's average career was less than four years in the agency.

Three of every ten bureau chiefs were career civil servants although many held positions that were designed as political appointments. The civil servant was slightly older (56) than the politician. Unlike the politician, the civil servant entered the federal service at a young age spending an average 23 years in the agency. Despite the longer career of the civil servant, the average civil servant bureau chief, during the Nixon administration, had been a bureau chief only five years.

The remaining bureau chiefs, some 32 percent, may be termed professionals. The professional pursues a scientific or technical career outside of government. After establishing themselves as reputable professionals, these individuals are appointed to top level bureau positions, moving up to bureau chief in a few years. Professionals (average age 51) tend to head bureaus with research or scientific missions such as the National Institutes of Health.

The Independent Agencies

The Federal government has approximately 60 agencies, similar in size and influence to department agencies and bureaus. These agencies are inde-

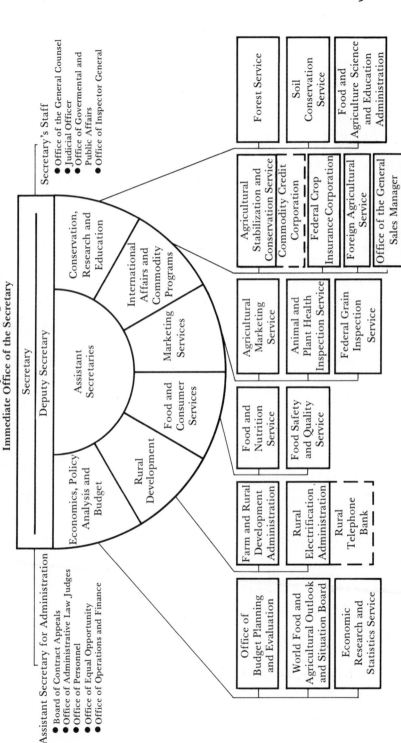

FIGURE 2–2   Organization Chart for US Department of Agriculture

pendent of the 12 major departments and report directly to the president. An independent agency may be fairly large as is the Veterans Administration, which has more permanent employees than all but one of the executive departments (Department of Defense). Most independent agencies, however, are small; the American Battle Monuments Commission or the Federal Maritime Commission, for example, each have less than 400 employees (see table 2–2).

Agencies are established outside the jurisdiction of the executive departments for a variety of reasons. Franklin Roosevelt created several agencies outside the executive departments because he felt the departments

TABLE 2–2   *Selected Major Independent Agencies of the Federal Government, 1978*

Agency	Employees	Budget (in millions)
Environmental Protection Agency	9,700	$ 6,135
General Services Administration	36,200	303
National Aeronautics and Space Administration	23,700	4,331
Veterans Administration	205,500	17,938
Civil Service Commission	7,100	11,303
Panama Canal	13,500	4
Small Business Administration	4,600	511
ACTION	1,981	168
Federal Trade Commission	1,622	58
Equal Employment Opportunity Commission	2,220	72
Interstate Commerce Commission	2,076	62
National Foundation on the Arts and Humanities	587	351
National Labor Relations Board	2,404	88
National Science Foundation	1,385	825
Smithsonian Institution	3,733	122

were tied to old ways of approaching policy problems. Other independent agencies were created to avoid the clientele pressures in departments with strong clientele ties. Others still including the independent regulatory commissions (for example, the Federal Trade Commission) were made independent to avoid presidential control. Still other agencies such as the National Aeronautics and Space Administration were made independent because their function did not fit within any of the departments.

The Government Corporation

Government corporations are located in a gray area where the distinction between government and business blurs. Government corporations are created to operate a government-owned economic enterprise. To isolate the corporations from politics, they usually are headed by boards or commissions with bipartisan membership and long terms of office. The isolation from politics, in theory, allows the corporations to employ efficient businesslike procedures. The corporations have separate personnel systems, can borrow money, can undertake projects without approval of Congress, and can even operate at a profit. Some government corporations go so far as to sell stock and accord their stockholders certain rights that private sector shareholders also have (for example, the Federal National Mortgage Administration and COMSAT).[6] Government corporations exist in a variety of areas. The Tennessee Valley Authority operates power systems, reclamation projects, and a variety of other enterprises in the Tennessee River Valley. The Federal Deposit Insurance Corporation operates a system of insuring deposits for national banks and savings associations from loss due to failure, robbery, or other misfortune. The Postal Service operates the nation's mail system with some assistance via governmental subsidies. Government corporations may be either independent agencies as are the Postal Service, Tennessee Valley Authority, and Federal Deposit Insurance Corporation or within a department as are the Commodity Credit Corporation and the Federal Crop Insurance Corporation (U.S. Department of Agriculture).

Government corporations closely resemble other institutions that are either private or public sector organizations. Federally Funded Research and Development Centers (FFRDCs) are private research centers established throughout the country funded by the federal government to conduct government research.[7] These institutions may run solely on federal money as some of the FFRDSs do or may combine federal money with private money as do some Health Maintenance Organizations designed to deliver preventative, prepaid health care.

The difference is small between FFRDCs or the Postal Service and private corporations that rely on government to provide most of the demand for their products. Some corporations, such as Grumman or Lockheed, receive such large percentages of their income in federal government contracts that they cannot be considered private organizations. In fact, by comparison the Postal Service receives less of its operating funds from the federal government than does Lockheed Aircraft. Because these companies have argued that they perform a role not unlike federal labs, they want government to have the responsibility to see that they do not suffer financial collapse. In these cases the distinction between government organizations and private organizations is not clear. This book does not deal with the problems of private sector bureaucracy even though their problems are as pressing as the problems of the public sector bureaucracy.[8]

When the terms "agency" and "bureau" are used in the remainder of this book, they will refer to the department agencies, the independent agencies, and the government corporations. Departments will be referred to only by the term "department." These four organizational forms are the dominant forms of government organization, but they do not exhaust the total governmental units. Other forms include the federal advisory commission, minor boards, commissions, and committees.

The Advisory Committee

When proposing massive government reorganization President Carter noted that there were nearly 2,000 federal agencies, but many of the organizations that he was counting were federal advisory committees. In terms of the definitions provided here, only approximately 150 agencies and bureaus exist on a permanent basis. Federal advisory boards numbered approximately 1,500 in 1976.[9] The function of these advisory boards is to provide advice, expert or political, to government departments and bureaus on topics of concern to the agency. They are found in various areas from business and agriculture to the National Science Foundation and the National Endowment for the Humanities. Advisory committees are useful to the president for patronage reasons (he can reward loyalists by appointing them to these boards) and useful to agencies because they can provide organized feedback from their clientele.

Boards, Committees, and Commissions

The federal government has over 120 boards, committees, and commissions established either by Congress or the President for a specific purpose. These are not really agencies since they are usually staffed by temporary personnel, do not have any program responsibilities, are extremely small, or have only the power to recommend action. The Commission on Federal Paperwork was a newsworthy unit in 1976 and 1977 when it published a series of recommendations on how to eliminate many government forms currently in use. The Harry Truman Scholarship Fund is administered by the Harry S. Truman Scholarship Foundation. There is even one committee that exists to encourage federal employees to purchase US Savings Bonds. The bulk of these committees, boards, and commissions are relatively unimportant and will not be discussed in this analysis.

The Political Bureaus of the President and Congress

Both Congress and the president have institutionalized; they have developed a system of supporting bureaucracies. These "political" bureaus are not just staff agencies designed to answer letters, but actual agencies that assist their sponsors in policymaking activities. This section discusses the political bureaus of the president and Congress because these units are often used to control the remainder of the federal bureaucracy.

The bureau nearest the president is the White House Office; it provides staff assistance to the president. The White House Office contains the president's congressional lobby, the press secretaries, and the president's special assistants. Within the executive office are a series of bureaus designed to assist in policymaking activities. The first among equals is the Office of Management and Budget (OMB). OMB prepares the federal budget and evaluates legislation to determine if it is in accord with the president's program. President Nixon added to OMB the responsibility for federal management improvement and bureaucratic oversight. President Carter lodged his government reorganization team in OMB.

On roughly the same level, the presidency has two policy councils. The National Security Council, an influential agency under McGeorge Bundy and Henry Kissinger, advises the president on a wide range of foreign policy and defense issues. The Council of Economic Advisors and its staff provides assistance in broadly defined economic matters.

The executive office also contains a group of lesser bureaus. In 1976 these units included a unit for trade negotiations, the Council on Environmental Quality, the Office of Telecommunications Policy, the Council on International Economic Policy, the Federal Property Council, the Office of Drug Abuse Policy, and the Office of Science and Technology Policy. These units advise the president and assist in formulating policies in their specialized area. The president's bureaucracy also includes one nonstaff agency, the Central Intelligence Agency, the key intelligence agency for the US government.

The size of the president's political bureaucracy is difficult to determine. Although the 1977 federal budget lists 1,604 people exclusive of the CIA and the foreign assistance programs, this figure is augmented by detailing. The president can request other executive agencies to "detail" personnel temporarily to these agencies. Detailing has been used extensively to increase the president's policymaking resources.

The congressional bureaucracy is more bewildering than the president's. Congress and its staff are the fastest growing bureaucracy in Washington D.C. Each member of Congress has a personal staff whose size depends on the size of the member's district/state and the member's access to funds. The personal staff is augmented by committee staffs, which serve the committee members. A reasonable estimate of total personal and committee staff is about 16,000 people.

Congress supplements these staff members with a group of information-gathering bureaus. The Library of Congress and particularly the Congressional Research Service provides general information on current policy issues. The Congressional Budget Office (CBO) was established in the Budget Reform Act of 1974 to perform the same budget analysis for Congress that OMB performed for the president. The General Accounting Office performs both accounting and performance audits for Congress. The Office of Technology Assessment provides scientific advice to members of Congress.

Congress also has several bureaus that perform nonpolicy functions. The Government Printing Office prints not only Congress' heavy volume of documents, but also many other bureaus' publications. The Architect of the Capitol maintains the buildings and grounds of Congress and plans its physical expansion. Even the Botanic Gardens is located as a congressional agency. The information bureaus and the nonpolicy bureaus have some 21,000 employees although many perform routine blue collar functions.

ᕬ The Size of the Bureaucracy ᕬ

The size of the federal bureaucracy is subject to more misinformation than any other aspect. Common perception holds that the federal bureaucracy is growing rapidly and threatening to engulf us all. Although the budget of the federal bureaucracy is growing by leaps and bounds, the number of people employed by the federal government is not. Current estimates of total federal civilian employment are 2.85 million people (400,000 are part time). Although 2.85 million people is not a small number of people, the size of the federal bureaucracy (see figure 2–3) has not changed dramatically over the past 30 years. The present federal bureaucracy is 10

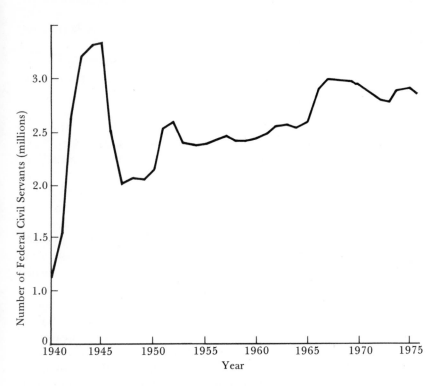

FIGURE 2–3   Growth of the Federal Bureaucracy 1940–1976.
Source: Based on data in U.S. Statistical Abstract, 1940–1976.

percent smaller than the bureaucracy was in 1967, and fully 25 percent smaller than it was at the end of World War II.

Despite this lack of growth, the US bureaucracy is large compared to those of other nations. On a per capita basis the US federal bureaucracy is twice the size of the English central bureaucracy and four times that of the German federal government.[10] Only the massive Soviet bureaucracy surpasses the American bureaucracy in size.

Although the US federal bureaucracy has generally decreased in size since World War II, it fluctuates somewhat in response to environmental conditions. During wars, recessions, and other crisis-level events, the bureaucracy grows as government attempts to deal with these problems. During quiet periods the bureaucracy goes through a period of fasting with gradual reductions in size.

The bulk of the federal bureaucracy is not located in Washington, D.C., but rather is decentralized throughout the nation. Of the 2.85 million civilian employees, only 350,000 or 12 percent work in the Washington metropolitan area. The relatively small number of capital city bureaucrats can best be understood in comparison. The 350,000 federal bureaucrats in Washington is only 50,000 more than the number of federal employees stationed in the state of California and fewer than the number of people who are employed by New York City (415,000).[11]

Unlike many other nations, the decentralized bureaucracy represents the American preference for decentralized government. In 1816 only 11 percent of the civil service resided in Washington, D.C. This percentage has remained fairly constant until today when 7 of every 8 federal employees work outside the nation's capital.

The number of federal civil servants is, in fact, dwarfed by the number of state and local bureaucrats in this country. Since 1950 the federal bureaucracy has grown 35 percent to include 2.85 million people. The 50 state bureaucracies have grown 209 percent to include 3.3 million people. The local government bureaucracies have ballooned 174 percent to 8.8 million people.[12] The total federal civilian bureaucracy is now smaller than the combined size of the state and local bureaucracies of California, New York, and Texas.

Figure 2–4 shows the relative decline in the size of the federal bureaucracy compared to the growth of the state and local bureaucracy. One of every three bureaucrats worked for the federal government in 1950 (over half worked for the federal government in 1945) while less than one in five bureaucrats in 1975 were employed by the federal government. If current trends continue, by the year 2000 less than one in ten bureaucrats will be employed by the federal government.

☙ The Federal Personnel System ❧

The people who serve in the public service have a great deal of impact on the decisions made by the bureaucracy. The methods of recruiting bureaucrats will be discussed because public service selection processes influence the type of bureaucrat hired. Public servants come to their positions through a variety of different government personnel systems, each system designed to meet different needs of government. The competitive civil service supplies the bulk of federal government personnel. The Civil Service was created in 1883 in response to the evils of the spoils system which led in part to the assassination of President Garfield by a disappointed office seeker.[13] The merit principles of the Civil Service system gradually spread to most of government. Several federal agencies, however, do not use the competitive civil service but rely on similar principles by using their own merit system. These separate merit systems provide more specialized

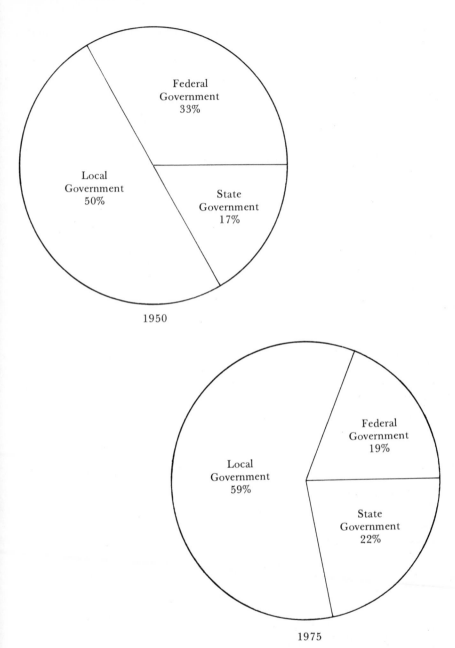

FIGURE 2-4   *Relative Size of Federal, State, and Local Bureaucracies*

TABLE 2–3   *White Collar Pay Table: Federal Civilian Salaries Effective*
              Oct. 1, 1976

	1	2	3	4
GS–1	$ 5,810	$ 6,004	$ 6,198	$ 6,392
2	6,572	6,791	7,010	7,229
3	7,408	7,655	7,902	8,149
4	8,316	8,593	8,870	9,147
5	9,303	9,613	9,923	10,233
6	10,370	10,716	11,062	11,408
7	11,523	11,907	12,291	12,675
8	12,763	13,188	13,613	14,038
9	14,097	14,567	15,037	15,507
10	15,524	16,041	16,558	17,075
11	17,056	17,625	18,194	18,763
12	20,442	21,123	21,804	22,485
13	24,308	25,118	25,928	26,738
14	28,725	29,683	30,641	31,599
15	33,789	34,915	36,041	37,167
16	39,629*	40,950*	42,271*	43,592*
17	46,423*	47,970*	49,517*	51,064*
18	54,410*			

personnel than does the competitive civil service. The excepted service provides for patronage employees and other personnel hired on a noncompetitive basis. The executive schedule provides the political leadership for the government bureaucracy. Each of these four personnel systems—the civil service system, the separate merit systems, the excepted service, and the executive schedule—has characteristics that affect the role bureaucracy plays in the policy process and, thus, merits fuller discussion.

5	6	7	8	9	10
$ 6,586	$ 6,780	$ 6,974	$ 7,168	$ 7,362	$ 7,556
7,448	7,667	7,886	8,105	8,324	8,543
8,396	8,643	8,890	9,137	9,384	9,631
9,424	9,701	9,978	10,255	10,532	10,809
10,543	10,853	11,163	11,473	11,783	12,093
11,754	12,100	12,446	12,792	13,138	13,484
13,059	13,443	13,827	14,211	14,595	14,979
14,463	14,888	15,313	15,738	16,163	16,588
15,977	16,447	16,917	17,387	17,857	18,327
17,592	18,109	18,626	19,143	19,660	20,177
19,332	19,901	20,470	21,039	21,608	22,177
23,166	23,847	24,528	25,209	25,890	26,571
27,548	28,358	29,168	29,978	30,788	31,598
32,557	33,515	34,473	35,431	36,389	37,347
38,293	39,419	40,545*	41,671*	42,797*	43,923*
44,913*	46,234*	47,555*	48,876*	50,197*	
52,611*					

* The rate of basic pay for employees at these rates would be limited by section 5308 of title 5 of the United States Code to the rate for level V of the Executive Schedule which, under the adjustment would become 39,600.
Source: US Civil Service Commission.

The Career Civil Service

Containing 61 percent of all civilian federal employees, the career Civil Service system is governed by the Office of Personnel Management (OPM) and the Merit System Protections Board (MSPB). The OPM has a large staff (approximately 7,000 people) that administers civil service exams, handles employee grievances, and performs other personnel functions.[14] The MSPB monitors merit system violations. The career Civil Service is based on the merit principle; individuals are tested to determine if they can perform civil service jobs and are promoted on the basis of past performance.

The Civil Service contains two different merit systems. Blue collar employees are hired under the OPM's wage board schedule based on local wages in the private sector. Because the wage board employees are not policymaking personnel for the most part, they will not be discussed here. The more important system is the General Schedule (GS) for clerical, administrative, and professional personnel. The General Schedule has 18 grades from GS1 to GS18 and within each grade are steps based on seniority, time in grade, or the scarcity of the person's skill (see table 2–2). The lower four grades of the general schedule are for clerical personnel, the clerks, administrative aids, and secretaries that perform the day-to-day nonpolicy tasks of government. Grades 5, 7, and 9 are the professional entry level grades. A college graduate normally enters the civil service at GS5; if the graduate has a good undergraduate record or a high score on the PACE exam he or she might enter at the GS7 level. A job applicant with a needed masters degree or a Master of Public Administration degree would normally expect to enter at GS9. Grades 6, 8, and 10 are normally reserved for executive secretaries; most professional personnel skip these grades with two grade promotions such as from GS9 to GS11. Grades 11, 12, and 13 are the Civil Service's midlevel management positions. Grades 14 and 15, the entry levels for the higher civil service, contain those persons marked for bigger and better things. GS16, 17, and 18 are the supergrades, some 10,000 elites who hold most of the policymaking positions in the federal government.

The General Schedule contains a broad cross-section of the American people. The two groups compare favorably in terms of region of origin, occupation, education, income, social background, and race.[15] For many of these characteristics the American people and the civil service are exact replicas of each other. The differences are slight. Civil servants, for example, are slightly better educated and have slightly higher status occupations than the rest of the American people. If the American people and the civil service differ on any significant dimensions, it is partisanship. As would be expected civil service employment appeals more to Democrats than to Republicans. Republicans with their strong beliefs in smaller government are more likely to be attracted to private sector employment.[16]

The Separate Merit Systems

Thirty percent of federal employees work for agencies that require specially trained personnel. For those agencies, Congress has established separate merit systems administered by the individual agency. The largest of these separate merit systems is the one governing the US Postal Service; five of every six persons under separate merit systems work for the Postal Service. Other agencies with separate merit systems include the Department of State for its foreign service officers, portions of the Public Health Service, the Veteran's Administration for scientists and doctors, the Tennessee Valley Authority, the Federal Bureau of Investigation, the Panama Canal Company, and the portion of the Department of Energy that was once the Atomic Energy Commission. Separate systems are established to make public employment more attractive to professionals, to give the agency some freedom in hiring and firing employees that the civil service system does not permit, or to provide for greater employee screening before and during employment.

Each agency with a separate merit system establishes its own personnel procedures, thus making each merit system somewhat different. Frederick Mosher, however, has discovered some similarities in these special merit systems.[17] In these agencies employment is usually considered a career rather than a short period of employment. People joining the FBI or the Department of State are expected to remain with the agency until retirement. To insure adequate promotion opportunities, which are considered to be almost automatic, these organizations permit little lateral entry (hiring at other than entry levels). Often the systems have an up or out promotion system whereby an individual passed over for promotion is involuntarily retired.

The Excepted Service

The excepted service is often considered the patronage position of the public service. In reality few members of the excepted service are patronage appointments despite the absence of competitive entry procedures and merit system principles governing these positions. The excepted service includes four separate groups, schedule A, schedule B, schedule C, and the noncareer Executive Assignments (NEA).[18]

Schedule A includes those jobs where recruiting personnel through competitive civil service procedures is not practical and the positions are not of a "policymaking" nature. Approximately 100,000 persons are included under schedule A. The major occupation in schedule A is attorneys because the Office of Personnel Management is prohibited by law from spending any funds to examine or rate attorneys for public employment. All attorneys are hired by the individual agencies through noncompetitive procedures; that is, attorneys apply and the agencies select those they wish to hire without any specific comparative criteria. Also included under schedule A are chaplains, undercover narcotics agents, and certain seasonal workers that the federal government employs.

Schedule B includes additional jobs where recruiting personnel through competitive civil service procedures is not practical and where the positions are not policymaking positions. The difference between schedule B and schedule A is that schedule B employees in order to be hired must take a noncompetitive exam while schedule A employees do not have this restriction. Relatively few people are hired under schedule B (approximately 1,700). Good examples of schedule B personnel are Treasury Department bank examiners and air force communications intelligence personnel.

Schedule C includes some 1,200 positions at GS15 and below, which the president uses for patronage purposes. President Eisenhower created the schedule C system in response to several problems inherent in the 1950s Civil Service.[19] In 1952 a great majority of the Civil Service had not been appointed through competitive exams but were hired a variety of ways including partisan preference and were later "blanketed in" (designated as civil servants without taking any exams). Since the civil servants were likely to be Democrats, President Eisenhower created schedule C so that he could appoint Republican loyalists to lower level bureau positions. Despite their patronage origins, schedule C employees have valid administrative functions in a nation that demands a responsive public service. Schedule C employees can provide information to the political officials that is "nonbiased" so that the President can determine if programs are working and if bureaucratic information is accurate. Agency heads appoint schedule C personnel at their own discretion without any Civil Service restrictions.

Noncareer executive assignments are people who perform jobs similar to schedule C personnel but at a higher level. Noncareer executive assignments (NEAs) include some 600 policymaking positions at the GS16, 17, and 18 levels. A noncareer executive assignment person will usually either head a small bureau or more likely serve on a staff unit that reports directly to the secretary. The agency head appoints noncareer executives, but the person's qualifications must be approved by the Office of Personnel Management.

Executive Schedule

The executive schedule includes those positions of a policymaking nature that the president appoints either with or without senatorial confirmation.

Approximately 700 positions are in the executive schedule, and these positions have a pay schedule separate from the rest of the public service. The executive schedule has 5 salary levels. Level 1 is reserved for cabinet secretaries and their equivalents; Level 2 positions are usually held by department undersecretaries or heads of major subcabinet agencies such as the Department of the Army. Levels 3, 4, and 5 are used for agency head positions with the exact level based on the size and prestige of the agency. Normally the chairman of a regulatory commission would be a level 3 while the head of a bureau or independent agency would be a level 5. The status of these different rankings is reflected by J. Edgar Hoover's successful efforts to acquire a level 2 position to head the Federal Bureau of Investigation despite the fact that its size merited no more than a level 3 position.

Dismissals

No discussion of the federal personnel system would be complete without a discussion of the termination of federal employees. Although civil servants leave the public service at approximately half the rate of persons who leave the private sector, a large number of employees do leave the public service.[20] Office of Personnel Management figures show that 604,000 people left government service in 1976; only 89,000 of these were retirements. Some 212,000 people voluntarily quit; 209,000 people were fired including 22,000 dismissed without appeal. Another large group of people (56,000) were dismissed because their jobs were eliminated in reductions in force (RIFs), and 36,000 were suspended or placed on extended leave without pay.[21] Despite the federal service's image as a safe place to work, federal employees can be dismissed from their positions.

ᑭ State and Local Bureaucracies ᑫ

Although this book focuses on federal bureaucracy, the important role of state and local bureaus in the policy process must be discussed. As stated earlier, state and local bureaucracies have grown rapidly while the size of the federal bureaucracy has increased only slightly. The reasons for this growth and the importance of state and local bureaus to federal policy-making are related to the nation's federal system.

State and local government bureaucracies have grown because federal policy encourages that growth. An important implementing procedure for many federal programs is to provide federal money but to have state and local governments actually implement the programs.[22] This permits the federal government to use its ability to collect resources and its national scope to attack problems yet avoid the political embarrassment of a growing federal bureaucracy. The pattern of federal funds with state administration developed as early as the Department of Agriculture. The Department of Agriculture gave federal grants to local colleges and local governments to develop agriculture research and to disseminate that research through the county extension agents.

Much federal policy, including most federal redistributive programs, (see chapter 4) is designed to include state implementation. An example of this policy is federal Aid to Families with Dependent Children; states determine within limits the amount of benefits, eligibility, and other policy questions. The Food Stamps program is another federally funded program with the actual distribution of food stamps conducted by local employees. Highway construction, medicaid, and some public health care programs are also administered in this manner.

State and local bureaucracies are often miniature federal bureaucracies in form and substance. These bureaus are generally organized functionally just as the federal government is. Most states have a variety of independent agencies that report directly to the governor, similar to federal independent agencies that report directly to the president. All states and many localities have independent merit systems that range from more comprehensive than the federal system to token efforts covering only a small percentage of employees.

State and local bureaucracies are also subject to the same influences that affect the federal bureaucracy. Agencies, such as the Texas Railroad Commission that regulates the state's oil industry, set policy and develop clientele support among those it regulates. Although generalizations about the relative influence of state and local bureaucracies are difficult to make, they are probably less powerful than federal bureaucracies because they are weaker on the dimensions that contribute to bureau power (see chapter 3). Despite the present status of state and local bureau influence, the impact these bureaus have on public policy is likely to increase as a result of federal policies. In programs where the federal government grants money to the states with restrictions attached to the use of the money, the federal bureau in charge of the program usually grants the money directly to a state bureau charged with administering the program at the state level. Often these state agencies receive more money from the federal government than they do from the state legislature. Given this situation the state bureau naturally develops close relationships with the federal bureau that controls its funds. The result is that such state bureaus gain resources from the federal government and gain autonomy in the use of those resources because their funds are not subject to the control of the state governor or legislature. State governments lose control of the actions of state bureaucracies as a result, and the bureaus are able to develop independent power bases just as federal bureaus do. According to former

North Carolina Governor Terry Sanford, who terms this relationship vertical functional autocracies, the federal bureau to state bureau relationships weaken state government by isolating state bureaus from political control. Sanford believes the independence of state and local bureaucracies created by the federal relationship is one of the major dangers facing state governments today.[23]

～ Summary ～

This chapter serves as a descriptive introduction to the federal bureaucracy so that the reader will have an adequate background to understand the remaining chapters. The common misperceptions about the size of the federal bureaucracy were fully discussed. The federal bureaucracy is not growing rapidly, in fact, depending on the base year, may not be growing at all. The recent growth in bureaucracy has taken place at the state and local levels where the size of these bureaucracies have doubled in the past twenty-five years. The growth of state and local bureaucracies is a function of federal policy that emphasizes the use of federal funds and state administrative organizations to combat public policy problems.

This chapter also discusses the organization of the federal government and the federal personnel system. The federal government is organized functionally into twelve departments. Each was created to meet different needs at different points in the nation's history. Despite the functional organization bias of the federal government, several other organization forms exist at the federal level. Many independent agencies were created to avoid the biases and problems of department organizations. A variety of third sector institutions—government corporations, advisory boards, et cetera—blur the normal distinction between the public sector and the private sector. These organizations operate with the powers of government and the flexibilities of business.

The federal personnel system is designed to meet the goals of merit performance and political responsiveness. The bulk of federal employees enter through the merit system either by competitive or noncompetitive exams and are promoted on the same basis. A small percentage of employees enter via patronage procedures to guarantee a cadre of public servants loyal to the president.

～ Notes ～

1. Good descriptions of the formation of federal executive departments can be found in Paul P. Van Riper, *History of the United States Civil Service* (Evanston, Ill.: Row, Peterson and Co., 1958); Leonard D. White,

The Jacksonians (New York: Macmillan, 1954); Leonard D. White, *The Federalists* (New York: Macmillan, 1948); Leonard D. White, *The Jeffersonians* (New York: Macmillan, 1951); Leonard D. White, *The Republican Era* (New York: Macmillan, 1958). A good brief summary that this section relies heavily on is Martin Diamond, Winston Fisk, and Herbert Garfinkel, *The Democratic Republic* (Chicago: Rand McNally, 1970), pp. 255–262.

2. The nation's court system is separate from the Department of Justice and located under the judiciary.

3. The Post Office Department was created in the nineteenth century in response to governmental needs, but it was changed to a government corporation in the 1970s and will be discussed in the government corporation section of this chapter.

4. The Defense Department was created in 1947 by consolidating the Departments of War and Navy.

5. These statistics were developed from a data set used in Kenneth J. Meier, "Bureaucratic Power: The Impact of Clientele, Expertise, Leadership, and Vitality" (Paper presented at the Annual Meeting of the American Political Science Association, Washington, D.C., 1977).

6. Michael E. McGill and Leland M. Wooten, "Management in the Third Sector," *Public Administration Review* 35 (September/October, 1975): 446.

7. W. Henry Lambright, *Governing Science and Technology* (New York: Oxford, 1976), pp. 163ff.

8. Some of these questions are considered in Mark Nadel, *Corporations and Political Accountability* (Lexington, Mass.: D. C. Heath, 1977).

9. Ibid. President Jimmy Carter reduced the number of advisory boards to approximately 700 in 1977. See Jean Conley and Joel Havemann, "Carter Prepares to Push Reorganization," *National Journal* 9 (December 3, 1977): 1875.

10. Samuel H. Beer et al., *Patterns of Government* (New York: Random House, 1973), p. 753.

11. U.S. Bureau of the Census, *Statistical Abstract of the United States: 1976* (97th ed.), Washington, D.C., 1976, pp. 252, 288.

12. The year 1950 was chosen to avoid biasing the case. This was a year between the Second World War and the Korean War when the size of the federal bureaucracy had reverted to somewhat normal size. The argument here could be better made with other years such as 1946, but that would artificially influence the argument.

13. A good discussion of the merit system's development can be found in Frederick C. Mosher, *Democracy and the Public Service* (New York: Oxford University Press, 1968).

14.   Civil Service Commission chairman Alan K. Campbell proposed in 1977 that the agency be split into two agencies, one to administer the merit system and one to hear employee grievances. The reorganization proposal cleared Congress in August 1978.

15.   Kenneth J. Meier, "Representative Bureaucracy and Administrative Responsiveness" (Ph.D. diss., Syracuse University, 1975).

16.   Milton C. Cummings et al., "Federal and Non-Federal Employees," *Public Administration Review* 27 (1967): 393–402.

17.   Mosher, *Democracy and the Public Service*: 138–146.

18.   U.S. Civil Service Commission, *The Federal Career Service* . . . *At Your Service* (Washington: U.S. Government Printing Office, 1973).

19.   Mosher, *Democracy and the Public Service*, pp. 85–86.

20.   U.S. Civil Service Commission, *Federal Civilian Manpower Statistics* (Washington: U.S. Government Printing Office, 1975), p. 27.

21.   The separation figures are from the Civil Service Commission's records as cited by Stan Bernard, NBC-TV's "Federal File" correspondent as cited in *The Federal Times*, November 7, 1977, p. 2.

22.   Daniel Elazar, *American Federalism: A View from the States* (New York: Thomas Y. Crowell, 1972).

23.   Terry Sanford, *Storm Over the States* (New York: McGraw-Hill, 1967), p. 80.

Accnding to chapter 1, bureaucracy often exercises the political power normally reserved for others in the American polity. The existence of administrative power raises two immediate questions. First, why do bureaucratic organizations take over political functions and exercise the power that in traditional political theory is granted only to the "political" branches of government? Second, given the general causes of administrative power, why do some agencies such as the US Army and the National Institutes of Health have political power and some agencies such as the Bureau of Public Debt and the Selective Service system struggle along without it?

This chapter discusses these two questions. Before controlling bureaucracy can be discussed (see chapters 6–8), knowledge about how bureaucracy in general and how specific bureaus acquire resources and autonomy is necessary. First, a framework for assessing bureau power in relation to bureau environments will be presented. Second, using this framework the general causes for the development of bureaucracy as a political institution will be discussed. Third, the reasons why specific bureaus are able to act relatively autonomously within their own policy sphere will be examined.

A Framework for the Study of Bureaus

Examining a bureau in isolation reveals little about the actual operation of the bureau and why it acts as it does. Many students of bureaucracy believe that organizations can only be understood in terms of their environ-

Bureaucratic Power

ment and relationships with that environment.[1] Since we wish to understand the causes and consequences of bureaucratic power, a framework relating the bureaucracy to the relevant environmental factors must be constructed.

An open systems model for analyzing bureaus is presented in figure 3–1. Although the model is clearly an oversimplification of reality, it illustrates the major environmental influences on a bureau. The bureau receives from its environment a series of inputs that can be classified generally as demands and supports. The model postulates that the proximity of the inputs to the organization is crucial in the bureau's power setting. Level 1 inputs from the environment have little impact on bureau power but rather establish the conditions necessary for bureaucracy to exist. A nation's culture, economics, history, and technology combine to favor the development of bureaucracy. Max Weber argued that the development of bureaucracy was related to the emergence of the money economy and that bureaucracy often formed by routinizing the charisma of a dominant leader.[2] The impact of these level 1 factors on bureaus are relatively remote and will not be considered specifically in this analysis since they should be common to most developed or developing nations of the world. Our concern is with the more proximal factors.

The environmental influences in level 2 are more specific than those in level 1. An examination of level 2 influences will be useful in determining why bureaucracy gains political influence at the expense of the other political institutions of a nation. The reasons for the development of powerful public bureaucracies are political and technical rather

and Its Causes

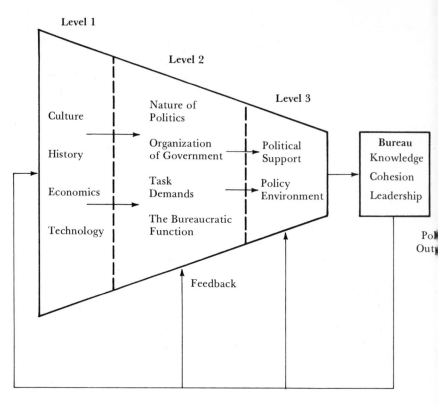

FIGURE 3-1   The Environment of a Bureau

than historical, economic or cultural; not a surprising observation since public bureaucracy is a creature of politics that is designed to accomplish certain types of tasks.

Briefly, the four factors (each to be discussed) in the environment that contribute to bureaucracy assuming political functions are (1) the nature of politics—what questions are considered in the realm of politics and what questions are the sphere of professionals, administrators, and so forth; (2) the organization of government—how is political power distributed in the state and among the governmental institutions; (3) task demands—what types of tools are necessary to perform the tasks of government effectively; and (4) the nature of the bureaucratic function.

Level 3 environmental inputs are factors which determine whether a specific bureau has political power. These factors may be divided into two types, the environment of the bureau and the internal characteristics of the organization. The relevant portions of a bureau's environment are its political support and its policy environment. The political support for a bureau is the support a bureau has with all the people, both citizens and government officials, that deal with the bureau or are affected in some way by the operation of the bureau. The policy environment of a bureau concerns the type of public policy—regulatory, distributive, redistributive, or constituent—that the bureau administers. The policy environment affects both political support and a bureau's internal sources of power. Internal factors can be divided into three types: (1) leadership—the effectiveness of the agency chief in performing the bureau's defined task; (2) knowledge—the information and expertise over which the agency has a monopoly; and (3) cohesion—the commitment of the bureau's personnel to the organization and its goals.

To some extent the distinction between level 2 and 3 inputs to the bureau is artificial. Each of the level 2 inputs influences the level 3 inputs and, thus, is indirectly related to bureau power as well as the transfer of political functions to the bureaucracy. The organization of government, the nature of politics, and the function of bureaucracy, for example, combine to determine the political support for the bureau. The task demands of government policy and the bureaucratic function determine the knowledge of the bureau. Leadership is a function of the organization of government and the nature of politics while cohesion should be directly related to the task demands of government policy. The distinction between level 1 and level 2, although partially artificial, is heuristically valuable since level 2 inputs can effectively explain the transformation of bureaucracy into a political institution and level 3 inputs contribute directly, not through other factors, to the enhancement of bureau power.

A final point about the model in figure 3–1 is in order. The bureau makes decisions and policies, and delivers goods and services; these actions feed back into the environment. In this way the bureau affects the nature of the environment it occupies so that a bureau not only responds to its environment but over time can shape the environment that influences its power base. The Department of Agriculture, for example, was active in forming the American Farm Bureau Federation, giving the department a cohesive, strong clientele; the department could then cite Farm Bureau demands as evidence of public support. Thus, the open systems aspect of bureaus is very important; bureaus interact with the environment; and both the agency and the environment differ as the result of the interaction.

ᓚ Why Bureaucracy Has Become a Policymaking Institution ᓗ

Bureaucracy has grown to its present position as an equal to Congress and the president for four reasons. The four reasons within the environment

that contribute to bureaucracy assuming political functions are: (1) the
nature of politics—what questions are considered in the realm of politics
and what questions are in the sphere of professionals, administrators, and
others; (2) the organization of government—how is political power distributed in the state and among the governmental institutions; (3) task demands—what types of tools are necessary to perform the tasks of government effectively; and (4) the nature of the bureaucratic function.

The Nature of American Politics

The nature of American politics by determining what questions will be
resolved by the political branches of government contributes to bureaucratic power. Early twentieth century government recognized a politics-
administration dichotomy, which meant that policy questions were decided by Congress; and the sole function of bureaucracy was to neutrally
apply policy made elsewhere.[3]

The growth of the positive state contributed to the demise of the
dichotomy, if indeed it ever was a valid description of American politics.
The people and political elites demanded the government take action on
the economy, on safety, on competition, and a variety of other problems.
Congress, faced with a demand for action and the lack of expertise to
adequately design public policy to remedy the perceived ills, turned to
bureaucracy.[4] The bureaucracy was delegated difficult public problems
with little or no guidance as to what standards to apply when considering
solutions. The Interstate Commerce Commission was instructed to regulate interstate commerce using the standard of public convenience and
necessity. The Department of Energy is charged with resolving the nation's
energy crisis with the only requirement that its programs be "equitable."
If regulating interstate commerce or determining future energy questions
involves political choices, then administrative agencies are forced to decide
political questions.

The nature of politics in the United States blurs the distinction
between political and administrative functions. Congress is no longer the
dominant arbitrator of policy questions but shares this power with the
federal bureaucracy and others. Congress gains in this process. When setting other policymaking mechanisms in action, Congress can receive better
decisions because the bureaus have access to more specialized knowledge
than does Congress. The courts have sanctioned this situation with a series
of court rulings upholding the delegation of legislative authority to administrative agencies even under vague standards.[5]

Today "political" questions in the United States differ from "administrative" questions only by who decides them. Political questions are decided by Congress and the president while administrative questions are decided by bureaus. In content, political and administrative questions do not differ. During a brief two-week period in August 1975 Congress considered legislation designed to prevent the Department of Justice from intervening in a school busing case, considered banning DES as a cattle feed additive, and considered refusing to pay Occupational Safety and Health Administration officials for inspecting firms of less than five employees. These questions are similar to common administrative questions; in fact, each piece of legislation cited was introduced to overrule an administrative decision. In most practical situations congressional action and administrative action deal with many of the same problems, even though the scope of congressional lawmaking can be greater than the scope of administrative discretion (I cannot conceive that a bureau could decide the nation should have a social security system and then legitimately adopt one).

As Sheldon Wolin notes, the United States, by permitting political abdication of policymaking, has sublimated political issues into professional, technical, and administrative questions.[6] Since the American people perceive politics as basically corrupt and evil, the removal of policy from the political institutions has some public approval. Many people argue that the sublimation results in better policy. This argument appears frequently in the history of the nation; the merit system was created to remove personnel functions from the evils of spoils system politics; city manager government was established to free the city from the corruption of politics. A contemporary example is the nation's school systems. The subjects and values taught in the nation's school system are of vital concern to the government because they establish the deep diffuse support necessary to permit the government to continue in operation.[7] But the mere suggestion that government, particularly the federal government, should have a say in what is taught in the nation's schools would be met with vocal and perhaps violent opposition. If a professional administrator decides curriculum content, however, that is permissible despite the fact that the end result is the same. The public's preference for decisions by administrators, professionals and technicians rather than by politicians undermines the legitimacy of politics. Politicians no longer have public support to be the major arbitrator of political questions.

The nature of American politics, therefore, contributes to the transformation of bureaucracy into a political institution in two ways. First, the political branches of government acquiesce in the exercise of policymaking by bureaucracy. Second, bureaucratic policymaking is accorded legitimacy, legitimacy that is in many cases denied to popularly elected institutions. Together these factors strengthen the hand of bureaucracy in the policy process.

The Organization
of Government

The second reason why bureaucracy has attained a powerful position in American politics is the organization of American government. If any ideal other than private property was sacred to the founding fathers, it was the concept of limited government. Since the founding fathers felt that everyone was subject to the corrupting temptations of positions of power, the power that any one person could exercise was severely limited. Government at the federal level was fragmented by the separation of political power into executive, legislative, and judicial branches with each branch given the means to act as a check on the other two. The actions of Congress and the courts in checking Richard Nixon's Watergate activities underscore the founding father's hope that no branch of the federal government can rule without considering the objections of the other branches.

In dividing political power the fragmentation at the national level was aided by federalism with the federal and state governments exercising different powers (see chapter 2). The federal government must rely on the states to implement many of the policies it desires even though the federal government currently dominates the federal-state relationship.[8]

If the formal fragmentation of American government was not sufficient, informal mechanisms have developed that further limits each of the political actors. Courts by adopting the concept of judicial self-restraint have limited their role in the policy process. Presidents have specialized in defense and foreign policy, areas where their impact is likely to be greater. The emergence of the United States as a world power means presidents spend most of their time on foreign policy to the neglect of domestic policy, a pattern that held even for such a domestic advocate as Lyndon Johnson. Congress discovered that its size made action difficult, if not impossible, and divided itself into tens of committees and hundreds of subcommittees, all more or less independent of the Congress as a whole. Congress ceased to be a single actor and became 535 actors pursuing different goals.

Politics, the unifying force in English government and in some American cities (for example, Chicago) that are formally fragmented as much as the nation, is not a unifying force in American national government. Despite their increasing concern with political issues, American parties are broker parties; that is, they are broad coalitions more concerned with winning office than enacting specific policies. Without the discipline necessary to purge mavericks and deny party nominations, the parties remain only loose coalitions incapable of unifying the fragmented American policy process.

Subsystem Politics.   Fragmentation permits subsystem politics —a triumvirate of a bureau, committee and interest groups—in specialized areas that, in normal political times, can act without interference from other political actors. The reason is the nature of American politics insures that bureaucracy has some role in determining political questions. After a policy question is shifted from a "political" to an "administrative" area, organized groups and other people interested in the policy area do not abandon their advocacy and return home simply because the arena has become an administrative one. Interest groups remain to develop relationships with bureau policymakers. The bureaus and interest groups are monitored by congressional committees and subcommittees that parallel bureaucratic organization. Long term bureau-subcommittee relationships develop because most substantive committees and subcommittees are usually staffed with members of Congress who have a direct interest in the agency they oversee.[9]

Together Congress, interest groups, and bureaus have all the necessary resources to satisfy each other's needs. Bureaus supply services or goods to organized groups but need resources to do so. Congressional committees supply the bureau with resources but need electoral political support to remain in office and political support to win policy disputes in Congress. The interest group provides the political support that the member of Congress needs, but the interest group needs government goods and services to satisfy members' demands. The result is a triparte relationship that has all the resources necessary to operate in isolation from politics if no great crises occur. The subsystem therefore can continue to satisfy each member's demands only if extensive political interest is not focused on the policy area. If the subsystem's activities become important to the public, as the food production subsystem's did in 1973, when high food prices mobilized public protests, then the president and other members of Congress have incentives to intervene in the subsystem. The best interests of all subsystem participants, therefore, demand that they resolve all their disagreements within the subsystem and limit the scope of any conflicts.

Bureaucracy, therefore, has opportunities to exercise political power because American government is fragmented. This fragmentation, by preventing any one set of political actors from exercising central control over all policy areas, permits the development of self-sufficient subsystems. Subsystems create semipermanent relationships that permit a bureau to aggrandize resources and autonomy and, thus, insure its survival.

Task Demands

A third reason why public bureaucracy has enjoyed a position of political power in the United States is the task demands of public policy. Public policy is no longer so simple that legislative decrees are self-implementing. The complexities of modern public policy demand functions that can only be performed by large scale formal organizations. No other institution can rival bureaucracy in its ability to perform the tasks of positive government.

The first task demand of current public policy is the ability to organize large tasks. In a nation of more than 200 million people, few public policies are small scale. Making air travel safe requires traffic controllers at thousands of airports monitoring millions of flights. Maintaining a social security system means that every month millions of checks must be processed and tens of millions of accounts credited. Bureaucracy has several characteristics that permit it to effectively organize large tasks. The hierarchical nature of bureaucratic authority means that thousands of individuals can be coordinated indirectly by a few top personnel. If the Department of the Army is any indication, bureaucratic organizations can expand almost indefinitely. Bureaucracies also have continuity; permanent employees perform the same tasks day after day, year after year. As the bureaucracy becomes accustomed to its tasks, it develops standard operating procedures and short cuts for effectively handling problems; bureaucracy becomes more effective as time passes. Bureaucracies also have permanence which combined with continuity gives bureaucracy the advantage of time. Unlike the president who must conduct foreign policy in the morning, tax policy in the afternoon, and regulatory policy after dinner, a bureaucracy can concentrate on a single problem or series of problems. The bureaucracy, as a result, is under no pressure to solve a problem immediately; it can nibble away at the problem until an adequate solution is found.

A second task demand of government is the need for expert knowledge when dealing with public policy problems. The average person does not have the knowledge and training to understand the intricacies of tax policy, the limits of health care research, or the technicalities of weapons development. Compared to other political institutions, this task demand is best met by bureaucracy because the large size, continuity, and permanence of bureaucracy permits specialization. Specialization allows the bureaucracy as an entity to know more about a public policy than any individual or institution that lacks its size, continuity, and permanence (that is, everyone else). Despite years of concentration even the House Ways and Means Committee must occasionally defer to the tax experts of the Internal Revenue Service. That any collection of individuals knows more about government bonds than the Bureau of Public Debt is difficult to believe.

Specialization also means many bureaucrats are highly trained professionals—tax experts, doctors, scientists, accountants, et cetera. Fifty-eight percent of the federal government's white collar employees are classified as professionals by the Office of Personnel Management.[10] Professionalization becomes another source of influence because, as politics becomes sublimated into administration, politicians will defer to experts.[11] Although the present deference is much less than it was in the 1950s post-H-bomb awe, it still exists.

A third task demand of public policy contributing to bureaucratic influence is the need for fast, decisive action. Policymakers want swine flu vaccines to be distributed as quickly as possible, schools to be desegregated with all deliberate speed, and safe air transportation now. If a bureaucracy is hierarchically structured and if the bureaucracy has norms of obedience and discipline, then it possesses the ability to act quickly. Although bureaucracy is often cited for its slow procedures, too many counter examples exist to condemn all bureaucracies as slow. The CIA quickly and quietly carried out a "secret" war in Laos. A change in the tax code's withholding provisions can be implemented within days, a change in the length of unemployment compensation in even less time. Although the bureaucracy may not be able to quickly make decisions, it can implement them quickly.

The task demands of public policy, therefore, increase the bureaucracy's influence in the policy process. The need to perform large tasks, the need for expert knowledge, and the need for fast, decisive action are all needs that bureaucracy is designed to meet. Because it holds a quasimonopoly on tools to meet these needs, bureaucracy may be the only way to deliver the goods and services demanded by the population.

The Nature of Bureaucracy's Function

Bureaucracy gains political power relative to other institutions of government because of the nature of the bureaucratic function. Although bureaucracy is involved in all stages of the policymaking process—writing legislation, adopting policy through rulemaking, and in evaluating policy—the primary function of bureaucracy is to implement public policy. Most astute analysts of public policy have given up the idea that implementation is unimportant; it contains the roots of additional power.[12]

The initial reason implementation contributes to the power base of all bureaucracy is that law or policy statements can never be so specific as to cover all future applications. The function of bureaucracy is to fill in the gaps of official policy and filling in the gaps means the exercise of discretion. Congress has passed laws prohibiting deceptive advertising, but the

Federal Trade Commission must decide if a given commercial is deceptive. Congress provides pensions for disabled persons, but the Social Security Administration must define "disabled" and decide if a given person is disabled. According to Theodore Lowi, administrative discretion is increasing because our laws are less specific than they were in the early twentieth century.[13] As a result, policy implementation decisions have a greater impact on the discretion of public policy. As the eminent expert on administrative law Kenneth Culp Davis notes, discretion when exercised by administrators tends to reallocate values from civil liberties to property rights.[14] Implementation of policy is just policymaking on a smaller, though not less important, scale.

During the implementation process, changes in the policy environment also require bureau discretion. The Department of Agriculture in the 1960s was charged with maintaining farm income by decreasing the supply of farm goods. With the Soviet grain purchases resulting in commodity shortages, the department's priorities changed to increasing production.

A special case of changes in the policy environment after a policy has been established is the discovery of new information. If the National Cancer Institute discovered a radical new cure for cancer tomorrow, we would expect them to pursue this cure with new research rather than awaiting political action. When effective performance requires changes in policy as the result of new information, discretion should be given to people in the bureaucracy. If Congress or the president had to personally change policies whenever the environment changed, they would be swamped with detail. Congress and the president set priorities, and they hope that bureaucracy will consider them. To adjust public policy to environmental change, bureaucracy must be granted discretion; and discretion is a key to administrative power.

Another reason for discretion in policy implementation is the uncertainty of political forces. An interest group may desire some action but be uncertain about specifics. In that case giving discretion to an agency permits the interest group to bargain with the agency and try out several policies without lobbying Congress for changes. In other circumstances with unsettled political forces Congress or the president may wish to take some action on a problem but have no preferred solution (for example, 1973-1977 energy policy), so they establish an agency charged with solving the problem subject to congressional review. Discretion with *post hoc* review provides both action and flexibility.

Implementing public policy, the task of bureaucracy, is not a simple process. Other political elites and possibly even the public are not satisfied if implementation is the strict application of a detailed law. They expect and demand implementation that includes flexibility, creativity, and responsiveness to changes in needs. Only if the bureaucracy is granted discretion can it perform in accord with expectations.

Clearly Weber is correct; bureaucracy is a power instrument of the first order.[15] Bureaucracy has become a power force in American politics because the nature of politics thrust bureaucracy into policymaking, because the organization of government requires bureaus to acquire power or disappear, because the task demands of current policy require qualities that bureaucracy monopolizes, and because the bureaucratic function, policy implementation, requires discretion. Several factors basic to the American political process, therefore, contribute to the strengthening of bureaucracy and demand that bureaucracy be a coequal political institution.

The Sources of Bureau Power

Although bureaucracy in general has become a powerful political institution, individual bureaus vary a great deal in the influence they have over public policy. Powerful agencies such as the Defense Department, the Environmental Protection Agency, and the National Institutes of Health have both resources and autonomy; but other agencies such as the Selective Service System, the Arms Control and Disarmament Agency, the American Battle Monuments Commission, and the Bureau of the Mint have neither. The level 2 (see figure 3–1) political and technical environment of American politics that permits the growth of bureaucracy as a political institution also affects whether or not an individual bureau has power. Bureau power is a function of the policy environment, public support, the bureau's special knowledge, the cohesion of bureau personnel, and bureau leadership.[16]

The policy environment of a bureau actually interacts with the other four causes of bureau power, determining which of them are significant. Because the policy environment has such a significant impact on all these factors and also affects the policymaking process within a bureau, discussion of the policy environment will be deferred to chapter 4. The remainder of this chapter discusses the political support, knowledge, cohesion, and leadership of government bureaus.

The Bureau's Political Support

A bureau's political support is its relative balance of support to opposition among people and groups who are affected by the bureau's actions.[17] Because a bureau's clientele can provide political support that other policymaking elites need to perform effectively in office, public support can be a source of bureau power. A political elite who opposes a bureau's position must bear the wrath of the bureau's supporters. Many political elites will also respond to the bureau's supporters for nonelectoral reasons. Groups supporting or opposing bureaus are perceived as representing legitimate interests that government ought to satisfy. American political elites do not respond to the merchant marine because they fear the electoral consequences of that small group, but rather because the maintenance of a US shipping capability is a valid political interest worthy of representation.

Bureaus develop public support in response to three level 2 environmental conditions that make bureaucracy a political institution. The nature of American politics, by sublimating political questions into administrative ones, makes the bureau decide questions of major concern to interest groups. The organization of American government, with its fragmentation and subsystems, forces bureaus to come to terms with their clientele because neither Congress nor the president can give the support necessary for a bureau to impose its wishes on their clientele. Finally, the nature of the bureaucratic function also facilitates the development of a positively balanced power setting by allowing the bureau to exercise discretion in policy implementation, discretion that can be used to build political support.

A bureau's public support ranges from diffuse support for the bureau's function to very specific support for individual programs. This section will examine the various sources of public support beginning with the most diffuse and proceeding through the more specific.

Public Opinion. On the diffuse end of the support continuum is the general public opinion concerning the agency and its function. In most cases the specific bureau will arouse few negative or positive feelings with the American public at large; the Agricultural Marketing Service, for example, evokes no strong feelings one way or the other. The public opinion most relevant to the agency, however, is the public opinion concerning the general function that the agency performs, for example, agriculture, foreign aid, defense, health, et cetera. The public regard for an agency's function affects the value other political elites place on the agency and, thus, its relative position of power. Defense spending provides a good example of this phenomenon.

Figure 3–2 shows public opinion on defense spending and the growth of the Defense Department's budget. Beginning in the late 1960s public opinion turned against defense spending, and defense budgets suffered a decline. After several years the public returned to its previous position of opposing cuts in the defense budget, and the defense budget began to grow again. Although many other factors affected the Defense Department budget in the 1960s and 1970s, general trends in public opinion and defense spending were often similar.

A bureau basking in the warm glow of diffuse public support

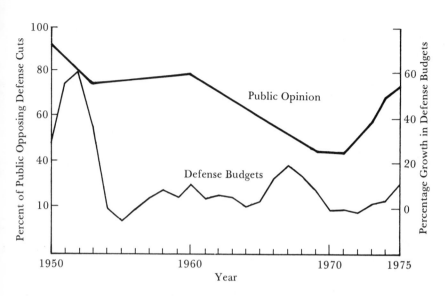

FIGURE 3–2   *Defense Budgets and Public Opinion.*
Source: Data obtained from Budgets of US Government, 1950–1975.

should be able to press its claims for resources with more authority. Table 3–1 presents the national spending priorities of the American people for 1976. These figures suggest that those bureaus able to tie their programs to crime control, health care, drug abuse control, or environmental protection should fare relatively well. Agencies with functions broadly defined as urban problems, education, and possibly minorities have moderate diffuse support. Finally, bureaus in the foreign aid, space exploration, defense, and welfare business face a generally hostile public.

Although favorable diffuse support can be used to extract resources from other political elites, public opinion is fickle; it changes, sometimes rapidly. An agency dependent on the whim of the public is in a precarious position. For example, the public strongly supported the US space program in the early 1960s, but by 1965 and more so by 1971 the space program's public support had dissipated. The drastic nature of public opinion swings is shown by the overwhelming support for increased defense expenditures (63 percent) in 1950 compared to the small support for defense expenditures in 1969 (8 percent). Given the transitory nature of public support, a bureau is well advised to seek more specific support to insure its continued survival.

Clientele Support.   Bureaus can gather specific support from their clientele—the people who directly benefit or suffer from the programs that the bureau administers. The Department of Agriculture, for example,

TABLE 3-1   *National Priorities—Do You Feel What We Spend on the
Following Areas Is Too Little, About Right, or Too Much?*

	% Too Little	% About Right	% Too Much
Space	9.4	28.7	61.9
Environment	57.4	32.8	9.8
Health	62.6	32.3	5.8
Urban	48.3	29.7	22.1
Crime	69.3	22.4	8.4
Drugs	63.0	28.8	8.1
Education	51.8	38.4	9.7
Minorities	29.4	43.4	27.2
Defense	25.8	45.0	29.2
Foreign Aid	3.1	18.6	78.3
Welfare	13.9	23.4	62.6

N = 1484
Source: Data taken from NORC General Social Survey, 1976. National
Opinion Research Center, Chicago.

has the support of the American Farm Bureau; the Department of Defense, the defense related industries; the National Institutes of Health, the researchers it funds. Since clientele may be either supportive or hostile, it behooves the bureau to have more support than opposition. Favorable clientele support means some of an elected policymaker's constituency benefit from bureau programs and feel they are worthwhile. A rational elected official will respond by granting the bureau more resources or permitting it to operate with greater autonomy.

Although clientele are, all things considered, better to have than not, clientele vary in their contribution to a bureau's political support. Clientele groups range in size from the gigantic American Federation of Labor-Congress of Industrial Organizations (AFL-CIO) to the relatively small American Soybean Producers. All things considered the larger a bureau's clientele is, the more weight clientele support is given in allocating resources. Size implies that the clientele can influence, more or less effectively, electoral consequences (in terms of votes and contributions) for other political elites. In addition, the larger a specific clientele group is, the easier the group can argue that its demands are broad enough to be considered a public interest rather than a narrow private interest. Despite the difficulties in defining the concept "public interest," the ability of a group to tie its demands to this concept is beneficial for the agency.

Clientele also vary in their geographical dispersion. If a clientele is centered in only one part of the country, then its demands can be treated as a local interest, thus limiting the group's access to other political elites. The Bureau of Reclamation, for example, serves a Western clientele; the National Aeronautics and Space Administration's clientele are concentrated in Texas, Maryland, Florida, California, and Ohio. In contrast to these narrow bases, the Department of Defense engages in significant activity in most of the nation's congressional districts, and the Department of Labor's clientele is organized in most areas of the country. Dispersed clientele are only helpful, however, if they are dispersed in the United States; having foreign nations or citizens as clientele is a weak position for a bureau, no matter how dispersed they are.

The more cohesive a bureau's clientele is, the more value the clientele has in developing the bureau's power base. A cohesive clientele is one that is organized, self-conscious (that is, recognizes that it has common interests), and receives tangible benefits from the bureau. A small, well-organized, cohesive clientele is always better than a large, unorganized clientele because the former has the motivation and ability to mobilize support for the bureau. As a result, producer interests will normally contribute more to the power base of a bureau than consumer interests or any other similar broad but unorganized group.

Clientele groups vary by how intensely committed to a bureau they are, and this variation affects the political support of a bureau. If an interest is intensely committed to the bureau, then the clientele interest will be more loyal and aggressive in advocating the bureau's interest. Ideally, loyalty and commitment can be best assured if the clientele has only one bureau that can meet its demand. In such circumstances the interest is placed in a dependent position *vis-à-vis* the bureau. The railroads had this relationship with the Interstate Commerce Commission (ca. 1950), as does the US Merchant Marine with the Federal Maritime Commission. With this commitment, the bureau can expect the clientele to strongly advocate and never criticize.

Bureaus can augment their political support if the public in general and other political elites in specific hold the bureau's clientele in high esteem. The impact of professional clientele such as doctors and scientists is impressive, especially when compared with such clientele as welfare recipients and convicts. Since professional groups also tend to be well organized, the impact of prestigious groups is multiplied.

Finally, the structure of a bureau's clientele contributes positively to the bureau's political support. If the bureau's clientele is organized into a single group, the bureau probably depends on the clientele more than the clientele depends on the bureau. If the clientele group withholds its support, the bureau is left with little specific public support. As a result, the group exercises a *de facto* veto power over bureau actions; and the bureau's rivals may perceive such a bureau as the captive of a narrow interest and deny it resources or autonomy. A bureau is much better off if its clientele are organized into several groups with no single group dominating. Multiple groups permit the bureau to be flexible, playing one interest's demands against the other's. The bureau can avoid being captured by interest groups because no matter what decisions it makes, some of the groups will support it.

The ideal clientele for a power-seeking bureau is one that is large, geographically dispersed throughout the nation, well-organized, intensely committed to the organization, valued in the eyes of the nation, and organized into several groups rather than a single group. The more a bureau is able to build political support composed of these elements and is able to maintain a positive rather than a negative evaluation by such clientele, the greater the political support of the bureau will be.

Richard Fenno, in his study of congressional budgeting, has shown that clientele support is related to a bureau's ability to extract resources.[18] Bureaus with strong public support are able to continually expand their resource base by receiving larger appropriations from Congress. If an agency's support is used to extract resources from other political elites, then developing even more specific (as opposed to diffuse) support is an asset. Since the best lobbyist an agency can have is a member of Congress, the legislature is an ideal place to cultivate political support. Members of Congress may be enticed to testify for a bureau if the congressman's constituents are served by the bureau. The Agricultural Research Service, for example, is very effective in getting members of Congress to advocate research programs that affect their district.

Support for a bureau among members of Congress is beneficial, but the bureau does not need political support from just any member of Congress. If the bureau can develop good relations with strategically placed members of Congress, then it fares well at the hands of Congress. The leadership of the substantive committee that oversees the agency is important because the committee authorizes bureau programs. Members of the appropriations subcommittee for the agency are vital since they have final say over the resources the agency receives.

Since substantive committees are staffed according to the interests of members' constituencies, substantive committee support for the bureau is usually forthcoming. Substantive committee members are usually advocates for the bureau. The appropriations subcommittee, however, is usually staffed with people who see their role as guardian of the public purse.[19] These members of Congress view agency claims with a great deal of skepticism. If the bureau can convince the appropriations subcommittee leadership that it is a well-meaning, efficient organization, then it can benefit many times over. Fenno has noted that legislative support for a bureau is directly translated into support for the bureau's budget; favored agencies are successful in avoiding cuts in their budget, that is, they receive a high percentage of the money that they request.

Support for a bureau's programs can also be generated within the executive branch of government. Executive branch support resembles political support in general because executive branch support may be either specific or diffuse. The best type of political support in the executive branch is presidential support, but the president can rarely give specific support to a bureau, and requests for specific aid from the president will place the bureau in the president's debt. The president can, however, give diffuse support to the bureau by advocating general priorities that favor the agency's function, as President Johnson did for poverty programs. More specific support must come from other members of the institutionalized presidency, specifically bureaucrats in the Office of Management and Budget (OMB). OMB is an agency that has developed into a first-rate power broker as the result of presidential confidence and its strategic location. It acts as a budget and legislative clearinghouse; all bureau proposals for additional legislative authority must be cleared by OMB. Of course, OMB also compiles the budget and makes decisions on resources often with little direct presidential guidance. John Wanat, a perceptive student of federal budgeting, found OMB was the locus of most important budget decisions.[20] As a result, support in OMB is a resource that all bureaus desire.

Executive branch support can also be generated among other government bureaus. For example, the power base of NASA could have been increased in the late 1960s if NASA were more effective in gaining support from the Department of the Interior, USDA, the Weather Bureau, and other agencies for its manned space program. These agencies' desire for cheaper unmanned satellites for their earth-resources and weather-prediction programs contributed to a lower priority for manned space. Another example is support for the Selective Service system by the Department of Defense (DoD), the prime user of the Selective Service. When DoD's need for the Selective Service disappeared with the volunteer army, the once mighty Selective Service collapsed. Support among other executive agencies is important for all bureaus but especially so for those bureaus whose clientele is defined as other federal agencies (for instance, the Gen-

eral Service Administration or the Office of Personnel Management).
Without support among government units these federal agencies have no
power base at all.

In summary, the development of a bureau's clientele is necessary
to augment bureau power and insure organizational survival. Specific support is necessary to gain resources and autonomy in the use of resources,
the necessary components of bureau power. Diffuse support is valuable
since it facilitates the bureau's gaining specific support. Since diffuse support is constantly changing, the rational bureau seeks to develop as much
specific support as possible.

Internal Sources of Bureau Power

If organization theory provides a lesson for the study of bureaucracy and
politics, it is that organizations do not passively respond to their environment. As an open system a bureau not only responds to environmental
pressures, the bureau reacts with the environment and shapes those pressures. Implied by this reasoning is that the internal workings of a bureau
can further the development of a positive bureau power setting. This
section examines three internal characteristics of a bureau that affect
the political power the bureau can exercise—knowledge, cohesion, and
leadership.

Knowledge.   Information is a source of power for bureaus simply because other political elites are concerned with delivering services as
effectively as possible. For this reason they cannot afford to press projects
against unanimous expert advice. Although knowledge usually results in
greater bureau autonomy, if knowledge produces superior performance, it
can also help an agency extract needed resources.

Bureaus are more likely to possess unchallengeable knowledge than
are other political institutions for five reasons. First, a bureau's organizational size permits specialization beyond the capabilities of other political
institutions. Concomitant with specialization is a second factor, the ability
of bureaucrats to concentrate their full time and energies on a single subject. The advantages of specialization and concentration are heightened by
a third factor, the generalist nature of other political elites who are politicians not well-trained scientists, doctors, or other professionals. Since politicians lack independent verification of administrative information that
they use, the power of bureaucratic knowledge is strengthened even more.
Finally, the influx of professionals into bureaucracy adds the weight of
scholarly reputation to bureaucratic advice. Deference to professional ad-

vice is a long standing American tradition. In combination, these five factors limit the control politicians can exercise over bureaucratic policymaking.

The task demands of public policy provide a favorable soil for
knowledge to develop into a bureau power source.[21] Policy task demands
require that technical expertise be applied to complex policy problems to
the advantage of bureaus that possess technical knowledge. In addition,
the nature of the bureaucratic function, implementation, provides additional knowledge to bureaus. Day-to-day bureau operations provide the
administrators with insight into policy problems that cannot be gained
from a casual inspection of program budgets once a year. This understanding places political elites at a relative disadvantage because they are unable
to refuse bureaucrats who can cite countless reasons why a favored program is not feasible.

Just as all clientele support is not equally beneficial in building a
bureau's power base, neither is all knowledge. Knowledge gained from
large numbers of professional employees is especially valuable. Every
agency has some professionals—some lawyers, social scientists, planners, or
natural scientists. The key, however, is the extent to which the mid and
upper levels of the organization are dominated by scientists, engineers,
doctors, social scientists, and other professionals. The greater the penetra-
tion of professionals, the more likely professional reasons will be presented
to the outside world to justify the agency's decisions, justifications that are
difficult to counter.

A second aspect of knowledge that varies by bureau is the degree
to which the public holds the agency's specific profession in high esteem.
Many agencies are dominated by professionals, but reactions to these professionals differ. While the nation and its political elites trust medical
doctors and defer to scientists, lawyers and accountants are respected only
as long as they remain in their specialization; and, except for economists,
social scientists are rarely trusted. The more prestige a profession has both
within and outside the government, the more members of that profession
are allowed to regulate their own affairs. Many states have quasi-private
professional organizations passing on the qualifications, ethics, and mem-
ership of the profession. The same relationship holds in the policy process; the more prestige the profession has, the more the profession is
allowed to designate part of public policy as a professional matter and the
more the profession is deferred to in that area. The argument that professionals should be allowed to regulate their own conduct has been translated
into policymaking autonomy.

The third dimension of knowledge contributing to the power of
professionals and experts is the possession of technical knowledge that a
layman cannot master. Open heart surgery, nuclear sciences, and other

techniques impress the normal citizen with their complexity and their requisite skills. Not all professionals, however, have power through lay ignorance. The scientists who conducted the drug research on cyclamates were closely questioned. Not only were other scientists offering conflicting information, but the lay politician can understand injecting chemicals into rats even if he or she does not understand why it is done. Technical knowledge that the layperson cannot master is divisible into three categories. The bottom category includes all the tasks where a layperson can understand the entire process. In cases such as the processing of social security checks, the bureaucrat's power position is not enhanced. The two remaining categories include a middle category in which the layperson knows what the professional does but not how the task is performed, and the top category where neither the professional nor the process is understood. Lawyers and bridge builders are examples of the middle category; the politician cannot understand how the experts do these things but has a fair idea what they do. Professionals in the middle category have influence as long as the topic is within their area of expertise. Atomic scientists, nuclear medical specialists and weapons technologists fall into the top category. Since these professionals are far removed from the everyday experiences of the politician, their expert advice, if unchallenged, will be accepted uncritically.

Finally, the production of tangible benefits aids the professional in aggrandizing power for his agency. Mystery about the methods of science adds to bureau policymaking autonomy only if the mysterious actions produce tangible benefits. After all, while the actions of Zen Buddhists are understood by few members of Congress, Congress has not permitted Zen monks to decide national security issues. If methods are mysterious and benefits lacking, the political elite is likely to believe such behavior is one of the deleterious consequences of being an egghead. Something useful that the political elite can see, feel, or appreciate—for instance, bombs, planes, or miracle drugs,—must result from the process.

The best combination of knowledge variables for an agency desiring to build resources and autonomy includes a high percentage of experts in the bureau who belong to a highly esteemed profession, who use techniques that lay people cannot understand, and who produce tangible results. Under such conditions the contribution of knowledge to the power base of the agency is maximized.

Cohesion.   The second internal bureau characteristic contributing to a bureau's power base is agency cohesion. Cohesion may be defined as the commitment of bureau members to the organization and its ideals.[22] If the organization is dominated by members who truly believe in the ends of the organization, the bureau can easily motivate its members.

People who strongly identify with an organization will see their job as more than a weekly paycheck. They are quite willing to work the long hours necessary to improve bureau performance. Problems of high turnover which require the bureau to commit resources to recruitment and training rather than its prime function are less severe in cohesive, vital organizations.

The reason why cohesion contributes to agency power is related to the task demands of public policy. Public policy problems, as noted in chapter 1, are complex and defy easy solutions. Public policy in such areas as crime control, health care, and defense require creativity, dedication, and long hours to produce solutions. Cohesion makes a bureau a more effective policymaker because it promotes better employee performance, and a reputation for effectiveness is an asset in power politics.

Some agencies, the early Peace Corps and the Marine Corps, for example, clearly benefit from cohesive forces. If an agency performs a function that excites the general public or some portion of it, the agency can attract well-qualified people because it offers an identity as well as a job. Thousands of the best and brightest university products in the early 1960s turned down well-paying jobs to work in the Peace Corps. After the agency is stocked with zealous, talented people, it must only structure its tasks to take advantage of normally withheld energy. If the agency is organized creatively, it should be more effective on effort alone.

Taking advantage of cohesion and zeal often requires that the agency create an ideology for its members, an ideology that serves as a perceptual screen on the world and that ties the member closely to the organization's goals. The Forest Service does this by rotating their personnel, stressing its goal of protecting wilderness for future generations, and creating "saints" such as Gifford Pinchot.[23] The marines attempt to instill the same pride and cohesion by building identification with the corps. "The Marines are looking for a few good men" is more than a recruiting slogan to the marines. ACTION is trying hard to recapture the vigor of the Peace Corps with its ad campaign, "Don't crawl under a rock, join ACTION."

Nowhere is the impact of a bureau's function clearer than in shaping the cohesion of an organization. Some organizations by their nature cannot use normative appeals. This prevents building agency power by announcing "the GAO is looking for a few good accountants" or "Don't crawl under a rock, be a letter carrier."

Although cohesion is a difficult and elusive term to apply to agencies, some agencies do have the ability to motivate their members with appeals to common goals. With this additional commitment, the agency can ask for and get better performance out of its employees. Performance and the reputation for performance is an invaluable asset to a power seeking bureau.

Leadership.   If vitality is a difficult term to grasp, then leadership is an impossible term. Similar to such qualities as the public interest which we know to have some influence yet cannot precisely define, leadership has an impact on a bureau's power base. Leadership contributes to agency power both as a result of the organization of American government and through the nature of politics. The fragmentation resulting from the organization of government makes the bureau leader a politician in the classic sense. The bureau chief must build a coalition, seek resources to placate the coalition, and implement programs that please the clientele, other political elites and members of the agency. The nature of politics makes leadership a factor because the sublimation of politics provides the leader with opportunities to aggrandize political power by making policy and allocating scarce societal resources.

Clearly case studies indicate that leadership can be a vital factor in augmenting agency power. Compare the difference in respect for the FBI when it was run by a power broker such as J. Edgar Hoover to its diminished respect under L. Patrick Grey. Although bureau chiefs vary in their ability to effectively build organizations, leadership is also situational. Sargent Shriver drew rave reviews as a dynamic leader in the popular Peace Corps, but as director of the nation's poverty program he was dwarfed by the task.

Bureau leaders can build agency power by affecting both internal and external variables. Internally, a good leader can develop vitality and expertise. The ability of Clark Clifford or Elliot Richardson to motivate agency personnel offers a sharp contrast to the impact that John Powell had on the morale of the Equal Employment Opportunity Commission. A bureau chief who loses the confidence of bureau personnel soon sees the agency's influence dissipate. In the mid 1970s IRS employees who felt Donald Alexander's leadership was not "nonpartisan" enough leaked information damaging to the commissioner and undercut both Alexander and the position of the agency. A bureau chief can also increase a bureau's reputation for expertise either because the bureau chief is a respected authority, as was the AEC's Glenn Seaborg, or because the bureau chief professionalized agency staff as J. Edgar Hoover did for FBI crime labs.

Externally, the leader may build power through a variety of strategies. The leader may cultivate congressional allies as Melvin Laird did for the Department of Defense, but his successor, James Schlesinger, failed to do. Frances Knight, former director of the State Department's passport office, had the reputation in Washington for developing strong congressional ties by doing favors for members despite the general function of her bureau.

Fenno's study of the federal budget indicates congressional confidence in bureau leadership safeguards resources by allowing the bureau to avoid budget cuts. Bureau chiefs with strong ties to clientele groups can build an agency's power base by tying the beneficiaries closer to the agency. Earl Butz, as Secretary of Agriculture, had strong support from the American Farm Bureau whereas Clifford Hardin never won their confidence. EPA Administrator, Russell Train, has insured his agency's survival by opening lines of communication to both industrial and environmental groups and as a result winning support in both camps. Finally, leadership is important because an administrator's reputation for brilliance is an aid that helps any agency. Robert McNamara, in the early 1960s, and, later, Elliott Richardson were perceived as good administrators; McNamara's agency benefited and Richardson's might have if he remained in one agency for an extended period. Others who lack this reputation, such as William Saxbe as Attorney General, Thomas Kleppe in the Small Business Administration or Donald Johnson in the Veterans' Administration, added little to their agency's base of power.

ᒼᔑ Summary ᔑᒼ

The growth of bureau power is a function of both individual bureaus and the environment in which they operate. Bureaucracies in general become policymaking institutions in response to four environmental conditions. The nature of American politics defines normally political questions as the responsibility of administrative agencies. The organization of government disperses political power, thus permitting bureaucracy to coalesce with others to form powerful policy subsystems. The task demands of public policy require an institution that can concentrate expertise on specific problems as bureaucracy can. Finally, the bureaucratic function, implementation, has within it additional opportunities for discretion and power.

Individual bureaus, however, vary a great deal in political influence. One environmental factor and three internal factors permit individual bureaus to become powerful institutions. First, the political environment of the bureau provides specific and diffuse support for both the bureau and the programs it administers. Second, the bureau's ability to store and process information that other political elites do not have places it in a relative advantage in policymaking. Third, the cohesion of the organization contributes to power by improving agency performance through motivation of agency personnel. Fourth, positive agency leadership is necessary to exploit the environmental opportunities for building powerful bureaus. Powerful bureaus do not develop because bureaucrats conspire to bureaucratize American life. Rather powerful bureaucracies develop in response to environmental demands. Those agencies blessed with a favorable environment and the internal characteristics to exploit that environment become power brokers of the first order.

~~~ Notes ~~~

1.   Charles Perrow, *Complex Organizations* (Glenview, Ill.: Scott, Foresman, 1972); Donald P. Warwick, *A Theory of Public Bureaucracy* (Cambridge: Harvard University Press, 1975); Daniel Katz and Robert L. Kahn, *The Social Psychology of Organizations* (New York: Wiley, 1966); Francis Rourke, *Bureaucracy, Politics and Public Policy* (Boston: Little, Brown, 1976).

2.   H. H. Gerth and C. Wright Mills, *From Max Weber: Essays in Sociology* (New York: Oxford University Press, 1946).

3.   Woodrow Wilson, "The Study of Administration," *Political Science Quarterly* 2 (1887): 197–222; Frank J. Goodnow, *Politics and Administration* (New York: Macmillan, 1900).

4.   Congress turned to bureaucracy for reasons other than insufficient expertise. If a question was politically sensitive, delegating it to a bureau shifted the pressure from Congress to a bureau. Congress also delegates authority because it is unsure about the direction policy ought to take. The bureau can try several alternatives with Congress retaining a veto over final policy.

5.   Kenneth Culp Davis, *Discretionary Justice* (Urbana: University of Illinois Press, 1971).

6.   Sheldon Wolin, *Politics and Vision* (Boston: Little, Brown, 1960).

7.   David Easton and Jack Dennis, *Children in the Political System* (New York: McGraw Hill, 1969).

8.   Daniel Elazar, *American Federalism: A View from the States* (New York: Crowell, 1972).

9.   For a fuller discussion of subsystem politics see Douglas Cater, *Power in Washington* (New York: Random House, 1964); and J. Leiper Freeman, *The Political Process* (New York: Random House, 1965).

10.   United States Civil Service Commission, *The Federal Career Service* (Washington: US Government Printing Office, 1973).

11.   To be sure Congress and the president can hire experts to advise them in an effort to counter bureaucratic advantage, but the number rarely equals that of the bureaucracy.

12.   Charles O. Jones, *An Introduction to the Study of Public Policy* (North Scituate, Mass.: Duxbury Press, 1977).

13.   Theodore Lowi, *The End of Liberalism* (New York: Norton, 1969).

14.   Davis, *Discretionary Justice*.

15.   Gerth and Mills, *From Max Weber*.

16. The following discussion draws heavily on Francis Rourke, *Bureaucracy, Politics, and Public Policy* (Boston: Little, Brown, 1976). The analysis contains Rourke's four determinants of bureau power—constituency support, expertise, leadership, and vitality although the variables have been regrouped and integrated into the general model presented earlier in the chapter.

17. The definition of a bureau's power setting is taken from Anthony Downs, *Inside Bureaucracy* (Boston: Little, Brown, 1967).

18. Richard Fenno, *The Power of the Purse* (Boston: Little, Brown, 1966), especially Chapter 8.

19. See Fenno, *The Power of the Purse* and Aaron Wildavsky, *The Politics of the Budgetary Process* (Boston: Little, Brown, 1964).

20. John Wanat, "Bases of Budgetary Incrementalism," *American Political Science Review* 68 (December 1974): 1221–1228.

21. The variable under consideration is designated as knowledge rather than expertise, as Rourke terms it, to distinguish power as the result of professionalism and ability to do a task well from power as information others do not possess. J. Edgar Hoover's access to information about congressional leaders, for example, is knowledge but can hardly be characterized as expertise. Few will deny such information did not augment the FBI's power. Possession of information *per se* is the variable that affects bureau power. The possession of information as the result of specialization or professionalization is a special case.

22. The reader should be aware that while vitality is defined as commitment to the organization and that this commitment is a source of power, the cause of both of these is the performance of a function that excites the community. Commitment is the key variable, however, because agencies within limits can develop more or less commitment among their employees whereas the degree to which their function excites the general public is fixed.

23. Herbert Kaufman, *The Forest Ranger* (Baltimore: Johns Hopkins University Press, 1960).

CHAPTER FOUR

P ublic policy is a purposive course of action followed by an actor or set of actors (usually affiliated with the government) in dealing with a problem or matter of concern.[1] Although public policy definitions are usually vague, a distinguishing characteristic of public policy is that government actions are reinforced by the coercive forces of government. Only government can *legitimately* demand action or inaction on pain of fine, imprisonment, or even life.

According to Theodore Lowi, understanding the coercive force of government and how that force is applied is essential to understanding the formation and implementation of public policy.[2] The coercive power of government may be either remote or immediate. If government coercion is remote, then the sanctions of government are absent or indirect; that is, the costs of public policy are borne by general tax revenue, if at all, so that the direct cost of the goods or services to the individual is minimized. Immediate coercion takes the form of penalties directly assessed for violating policies, direct levies to fund programs such as fines for polluting, or a user-tax for highway construction.

Coercion in public policy may also be applied either directly to the individual or work through the environment. For example, given a law prohibiting fraudulent advertising, coercion may be applied directly to individuals by punishing those who violate the law. Direct coercion implies that government officials act directly against an individual. Environmental coercion, on the other hand, changes the environment of the individual without direct contact. Federal Reserve Board policies, for example, affect

Bureaucracy and

investments and savings by changing environmental conditions such as the volume of money and interest rates. Thus, Federal Reserve policies "coerce" people into acting in prescribed manners, but the coercion does not directly touch the individual.

Lowi combines these two dimensions of coercion into a two-by-two typology of public policy.[3] Where government coercion is immediate and acts directly, the policies are usually regulatory. Where government coercion is immediate but acts through the environment, the policies are redistributive. Where coercion is remote and the coercion directly affects the individual, the policy is distributive. Remote coercion acting through the environment results in constituent policies. This grouping of public policy will help illustrate the impact of bureaucracy on public policy. The remaining sections of this chapter discuss these areas of policy in depth focusing on the bureaus that operate in each area and the ways they influence public policy.

Before proceeding, one difficulty with Theodore Lowi's typology must be noted. Most agencies perform functions in many different areas of public policy simultaneously.[4] For example, the Environmental Protection Agency was established as a regulatory agency to protect the nation's environment, but it acts as a distributive agency when it allocates sewage treatment grants to cities and performs redistributive functions when industrial externalities (the costs of pollution) are transferred from urban dwellers to factory owners. The multifunctional nature of many government agencies means that the impact of bureaucracy on public policy is

Public Policy

more complex than the following discussion reveals. Despite this difficulty, the four policy types have some similarities that are helpful to understanding bureaucracy and the policy process.

∼ Regulatory Policy ∼

Regulatory policy uses immediate coercion to prevent individual conduct from transcending acceptable bounds. People are prohibited from selling unsafe drugs, from competing unfairly in the market place, or from polluting the air and water. Regulation has been a part of the government's repertoire of responses to policy problems since 1887 when the Interstate Commerce Commission (ICC) was created. Although most government regulatory activities are conducted by police and law enforcement agencies, modern regulation dates from this first attempt to protect the consumer from the pitfalls of modern capitalism.

As nineteenth-century laissez-faire capitalism matured into oligopoly, trusts, and monopoly, American consumers felt the impact of such monopolist practices as rate discrimination, exorbitant prices, and defective goods. Charged with protecting the consumer from the practices of large corporations, a new form of bureaucracy, the independent regulatory commission, was created. What began as a single attempt (the ICC) to regulate rail transportation spread to foods (the Food and Drug Administration), airlines (the Civil Aeronautics Board), securities (the Securities and Exchanges Commission), banks (the Federal Reserve), and a host of other areas. At times regulatory agencies were created not in response to popular pressure but in response to industry demands for protection from the major hazard of competition, failure. The Federal Communications Commission for example was created in response to broadcasters' demands for regulation.[5]

The United States does not have a comprehensive regulatory system. The current system was jerry-built in response to individual problems without concern for an overall regulatory system. Despite that lack of planned development, however, American regulatory policies fall into four distinct types of regulation.

The Scope of
Regulatory Policy

At the state and local levels the dominant form of regulation is legal regulation of criminal activity. Although our federal system generally relegates the law enforcement function to local government, several bureaus in the

Department of Justice perform law enforcement functions at the federal level. The Federal Bureau of Investigation (FBI) serves as a national police force; the Immigration and Naturalization Service (INS) and the Customs Service regulate the entry of persons and goods into the United States; the Drug Enforcement Administration (DEA) enforces narcotics laws while the Bureau of Alcohol, Tobacco and Firearms regulates three of America's legal vices.

A second set of regulators are the myriad federal agencies that regulate American business to insure that it is competitive and equitable. These agencies were established to check fraud, unfair practices, and monopolistic actions in areas such as air travel (Civil Aeronautics Board), nonair transportation (ICC), securities (SEC), the shipping industry (the Federal Maritime Commission), stockyards (the Packers and Stockyards Administration), commodity exchanges (the Commodity Futures Trading Commission), and labor relations (the National Labor Relations Board).

A third more modern area of regulation is regulating access to public goods. In its own interest the public, with government as its agent, can create a monopoly or permit a business to use a resource that belongs to people in general. The nation's air, water, and communications spectrum are good examples of public goods where access must be regulated. If everyone who wanted to broadcast radio and television signals were permitted to broadcast them, for example, the resulting interference would reduce all transmissions to mere noise and prevent coherent communications. Government regulation attempts to limit access to public goods in order to provide maximum possible benefits. A similar process occurs in pollution regulation, where a public good, clean air and water, is monitored by the Environmental Protection Agency (EPA) to rectify the past lack of regulation.

The fourth area of regulation is public health and safety. Public concern raised by Sinclair Lewis, Ida Tarbell and other muckrakers mobilized the government in the early twentieth century to regulate the quality of food and drugs. Since this early foray into the area of health regulation, government has attempted public health and safety regulation in a wide variety of areas. Regulatory agencies monitor health and safety by inspecting animals (the Animal and Plant Health Inspection Service), airlines (the Federal Aviation Administration), consumer products (the Consumer Product Safety Commission), and workplace conditions (the Occupational Health and Safety Administration).

Given the numerous areas of federal regulations, the size of the federal regulatory effort is not surprising. Nearly two hundred thousand employees work for some thirty agencies at a cost of $8 billion a year to regulate the nation's businesses, its safety, its health, and its public goods.[6]

Little of a citizen's life is unaffected by regulation, either from benefits of effective regulation or from costs added to consumer goods to comply with the edicts of federal regulators.

Despite the scope of federal regulation, regulation is an invisible process for most citizens. If the Federal Aviation Administration increases airline safety and prevents airplane hijackings in the US, the effort is almost unnoticed. The same can be said for such agencies as the Animal and Plant Health Inspection Service or the Department of Housing and Urban Development's Office of Interstate Land Sales. Only in controversial areas such as environmental protection, worker safety regulation, and possibly transportation are agency actions visible; and in those cases usually only the people directly affected by the regulation notice it.

Regulatory Policymaking

Regulatory agencies affect policy through the normal mechanisms of policy implementation (see below). Another policymaker, in this case usually Congress, sets general guidelines on regulatory policy, and agencies expand these general guidelines into specific policy actions. Since most regulatory agencies are not known for policy initiation, they usually act within the parameters established by congressional policy. Given a general congressional policy instructing an agency to regulate some phenomenon in the "public interest, convenience, or necessity" or to prevent "unfair competition," regulatory agencies may influence policy content through the processes of rulemaking, adjudication, or law enforcement.

Rulemaking.   Rulemaking is a quasi-legislative process whereby an agency issues rules with the force of law that apply to all persons under the agency's jurisdiction; these rules specify more clearly the public policy that was vaguely announced by Congress. Rulemaking follows a legislative-like procedure as required by the federal Administrative Procedure Act. Agencies must give notice of possible rules to be issued, must allow interested parties to be heard, and must publish final rules in the *Federal Register*.

An excellent example of agency rulemaking is the Federal Trade Commission's attempt to require all cigarettes and cigarette advertising to carry the now common health warning that cigarette smoking is hazardous to one's health.[7] After the 1964 Surgeon General's report linking cigarette smoking with cancer and other health problems, the Federal Trade Commission (FTC) published proposed rules that would restrict cigarette advertising and require health warnings on cigarette packages. Not only did the FTC's statutes not authorize it to make rules concerning cigarette advertising, but there was some question about the FTC's authority to issue any rules. Tobacco growers and manufacturers, however, were able to prevent FTC action by pressuring Congress. Congress passed the Cigarette Labelling and Advertising Act of 1965, which required only a weak warning on packages and prohibited any FTC action on advertising for four years. The continued willingness of the FTC to issue rules in this area resulted in Congress enacting several stronger laws banning radio and television advertising and requiring the health warning on all other forms of advertising.

Adjudication. Despite the twenty-three thousand pages of federal rules issued by regulatory agencies (seventeen pages of rules for every one page of statutes), critics contend that regulatory agencies eschew rulemaking for adjudication.[8] Adjudication is a quasi-judicial process where each individual suspected of violating the law is charged and administratively tried to determine violations. Rules of procedure for adjudication are also quasi-judicial with requirements of notice, evidence, fairness, et cetera. Unlike rulemaking, the adjudication process only affects the single case being adjudicated. Other persons that have committed similar violations must each be given the benefits of the adjudication process. Adjudication is generally preferred by regulated industries not only because it is slow and has additional procedures, but because it permits the industry to present its own case at length with frequent appeals to courts of law.

The Food and Drug Administration's (FDA) action against the drug Panalba demonstrates the adjudication process.[9] Panalba, a combination of two antibiotics, was manufactured by Upjohn Company. Experiments conducted by drug researchers concluded that Panalba was not more effective than either drug used alone and that Panalba was hazardous to users. Based on the experiments, the FDA banned the drug. Pressure to overturn the FDA decision in Congress was defeated by members of Congress supporting vigorous drug regulation. As with all adjudicatory decisions, the FDA decision applied only to Panalba and Upjohn, but a similar decision could be expected in future cases if conditions were similar.

Law Enforcement. Policymaking through law enforcement means simply the selective application of laws; certain laws are enforced vigorously while others are virtually ignored. Some laws may be enforced against certain classes of people while other groups of people are unaffected. Examples of the federal government bureaucracy making policy through selective law enforcement are difficult to discern. Agencies with law enforcement powers such as the FBI, the Immigration and Naturalization Service, the Drug Enforcement Administration, and the Bureau of Alcohol, Tobacco, and Firearms, while sometimes visible to the general public, are rarely subjected to the scrutiny of scholars. The extent of federal policymaking via law enforcement, therefore, is somewhat of a mystery.

At the state and local level, however, countless examples of selective law enforcement are available. Police in the city of Houston, Texas, after a series of unfavorable court rulings in 1975, decided to ignore city pornography laws. As a result of this policy, the number of pornography establishments increased dramatically. The increase stimulated organized and vocal citizen opposition to the pornography policy. Not only did the Houston City Council respond with new ordinances but the Houston Police began to enforce existing ordinances in an effort to reduce the growth in this particular industry.

The Structure of Regulatory Agencies

Regulatory agencies come in three types: the independent regulatory commission, the department regulatory agency, and the department law enforcement agency. Since department law enforcement agencies such as the Federal Bureau of Investigation perform a special type of regulatory function, the normal policy decision when a regulatory agency is established is between creating an independent regulatory commission and a departmental regulatory agency. The Interstate Commerce Commission, the first major federal regulatory agency, was the first independent regulatory commission and set the pattern for other regulatory agencies.

Independent regulatory commissions are headed by a multimember commission composed of an odd number of bipartisan commissioners who establish agency policy in regard to regulation. The independent regulatory agency is literally independent; it is not housed within one of the major executive departments of government but rather reports directly to Congress. The department regulatory agency is headed by a single administrator and lodged within an executive department. The Agricultural Marketing Service (AMS), the Packers and Stockyards Administration (PSA), and the Animal and Plant Health Inspection Service (APHIS) within the Department of Agriculture are good examples of department regulatory agencies. Although some regulatory agencies are independent regulatory agencies as is the Environmental Protection Agency or department regulatory commissions as is the new Federal Energy Regulatory Commission in the Department of Energy, the independent regulatory commission and the department regulatory agency are by far the most common forms. The congressional bias for these two forms is illustrated by the changes in the Commodity Exchange Authority (CEA), an agency within the Department of Agriculture that regulated commodity exchanges.[10] In response to criticism of CEA's regulation of commodity transactions, especially those prior to the 1973 Soviet grain purchases, Congress moved CEA out of the Department of Agriculture and then transformed the agency into the Commodity Futures Trading Commission, an independent regulatory commission. In general, then, regulatory bodies within executive departments are agencies headed by a single administrator while regulatory bodies located outside the executive departments are usually headed by a commission.

The form of regulatory bodies is not without reason. Independent regulatory commissions are made independent because members of Congress recognize the ties between executive departments and organized interest groups.[11] The Department of Agriculture has strong ties to the major farm and commodity interest groups; the Department of Commerce considers big business its major clientele; the Department of Labor is tied directly to organized labor. Creating an independent agency is an attempt to free the new agency from traditional clientele ties. For example, the National Labor Relations Board was conceived as an independent commission to arbitrate labor relations; therefore, Congress established it as an independent board to avoid the pressures of either the Department of Labor or the Department of Commerce.

Department regulatory agencies, on the other hand, are usually established to aid the regulated. The Agricultural Marketing Service regulates agricultural markets with the goal of assisting farmers. Such agencies are placed within departments so that they will be responsive to the regulated interest. Evidence from interest group testimony at House appropriations hearings supports this explanation. Nine department regulatory agencies had an average of seventeen clientele each testifying for them over a three-year period while the independent regulatory commissions averaged less than two supporters each over the same period.[12] Since the department regulatory agencies are encouraged to be more responsive to the needs of the regulated, their greater clientele support is an expected result.

The structure of a regulatory body also reveals something about the agency's method of policymaking. Regulatory commissions are designed to operate as little legislatures with bipartisan members, an odd number of voters, and group deliberations. As a result, commissions should focus on the quasi-legislative process, rulemaking. Independent regulatory commissions, however, generally lack political support since only the regulated interest is concerned with this body and the interest is often hostile.[13] This environment means that independent regulatory commissions are careful not to offend the regulated interest because the regulated may well appeal to Congress to reverse the commission's decision. These agencies prefer adjudication to rulemaking, then, because adjudication provides greater opportunities for the regulated to object. The need for caution is exacerbated by procedural slowness caused by the commission's plural executive. Department regulatory agencies, on the other hand, can act much quicker and are usually not charged with functions hostile to their regulated clientele. As a result, department regulatory agencies are able to issue twice as many rules (an average of 1400 pages per agency) as independent regulatory commissions (638 pages), despite the legislativelike structure of the independent regulatory commissions.

The Environment of Regulatory Agencies

The environment of regulatory agencies is significantly different from those of other agencies with the result that regulatory agencies also differ from other agencies in terms of clientele support, possession of knowledge, cohesion, and leadership. Since regulatory agencies do not deliver benefits to the regulated, with the exception of licenses or routes, they generally have weak clientele support. Regulatory agencies have little to offer on a *quid pro quo* basis for the support of either the consumer or the regulated industry. This lack of distributive benefits is illustrated by regulatory agencies' budget to personnel ratios; the average regulatory agency has a budget of only $49,000 per employee, barely enough to cover employee salaries and administrative costs. Regulatory agencies do not have the resources to provide distributive benefits. Table 4–1 demonstrates the resulting weak clientele support for regulatory agencies; the average regulatory agency has fewer clientele supporting it than any other type of agency (see tables 4–2, 4–3, and 4–5). Regulatory agencies enjoying a fair amount of positive clientele support (for example, the Environmental Protection Agency and the Federal Aviation Administration) also provide distributive benefits, such as construction grants, to their clientele. Clientele support, therefore, is not of great assistance in building a regulatory agency's power base. Not only are the clientele of most regulatory agencies small, but in many instances the agencies were created with the intent of regulating rather than serving the clientele.

Regulatory agencies do not gain political power as a function of knowledge either. According to Clarence Davies and Barbara Davies, regulatory agencies generally lack research units to counter industry claims about regulations' impact on the industry.[14] Although many agencies without in-house research capabilities have the authority to contract with outside institutions for needed research, regulatory agencies rarely have this power.

A good indicator of a federal agency's technical expertise is the number of computers it uses to conduct its operations. Federal regulatory

TABLE 4-1   *A Statistical Summary of the Average Regulatory Agency*

Number of Personnel	5,800
Size of 1977 Budget	$241,200,000
Number of Clientele	7.1
Number of Computers	5.9
Pages of Rules Issued	765
Pages of Relevant Laws	67
Budget to Personnel Ratio	$49,400
Rules to Laws Ratio	17.0

N = 32 Federal Ruglatory Agencies and Bureaus

agencies own less than 3 percent of the federal government's computers, an average of less than six per agency. If the Federal Aviation Administration's massive computer system used for aircraft controlling is deleted from the total, regulatory agencies have less than one computer per agency with nearly half of the agencies lacking access to computer facilities. Therefore, regulatory agencies with a few exceptions (the Environmental Protection Agency, the Federal Aviation Administration, the Federal Reserve Board) cannot use expert knowledge as a source of agency power.

Lack of leadership and cohesion are also factors that weaken the regulatory agency in policymaking. Leadership is difficult to develop in agencies where a plural executive governs because any one person can easily be countered by the others. Such strong leaders as Kenneth Landis and Nicholas Johnson of the FCC were greatly restricted by the restraints of the commission form.[15] Occasionally department regulatory agencies develop strong leaders, as the Federal Aviation Administration did under its first head, General Elwood Quesada, but most regulatory agencies do not because they are restricted by their lack of clientele and expertise.[16]

Since the functions of a regulatory agency are rarely exciting, regulatory agencies usually lack cohesion. The devotion of environmentalists to their cause is rarely if ever matched by a similar devotion among people who regulate freight rates, airline routes, and utility prices. Regulatory agencies must generally do without vitality and cohesion.[17]

Since regulatory agencies usually lack strong clientele, technical knowledge, leadership, and cohesion, understanding why few regulatory agencies become powerful bureaus is not difficult. Regulatory agencies are often denied resources since their function is neither in high demand nor exciting, and Congress limits agency autonomy with careful oversight. The impact of regulatory agencies on public policy, therefore, is only in narrow specialized areas and then only with the acquiescence of the relevant congressional committees and interest groups. Those regulatory agencies with influence in the policymaking process (the Environmental Protection Agency, the Federal Aviation Administration, the Federal Reserve Board, and possibly a few of the Department of Agriculture bureaus) either have functions other than regulation that permit the development of a more permanent power base or they have developed expertise that cannot be easily challenged. Most regulatory agencies, however, are dominated by their environment rather than dominating their portion of the policy-making process.

ᴄ∾ Redistributive Policy ᴄ∾

Redistributive policy in Theodore Lowi's typology applies immediate coercion to the citizens but does it through the environment. Taxing one group of persons to provide benefits for another group is the essence of redistributive policy; such taxing is also the reason why redistributive policies are among the most controversial in American politics. Redistributive issues such as National Health Insurance, Social Security, and Welfare Reform are major legislative issues that divide the public along party lines.

Although some American policies are redistributive according to Lowi's definition, few American policies are redistributive in the classical sense of taxing the wealthy to provide benefits for the poor. The social security system, for example, raises revenue through a regressive tax system where the middle income people pay a larger proportion of their income than do wealthy persons, and the benefits are tied to income before retirement. Medicare is a redistributive benefit available to all over the age of sixty-five with some exceptions, but middle class persons who have developed a history of reliance on medical care are the heaviest users. National housing policies, in general, also favor the middle class home-owner with only small efforts to provide lower class housing.[18] This difference between redistributive policies as defined in this section and classical redistributive policies is important to note to avoid confusion with the word "redistributive."

The Scope of
Redistributive Policy

Because redistributive policy proposals are so controversial, few policy areas are characterized by redistributive policymaking in the United States. Only five major areas of public policy can be classified as redistributive policy—income stabilization, welfare, health care, housing, and income distribution.

Income stabilization policies are policies designed to smooth out major fluctuations in a person's income resulting from unemployment or retirement. Two major agencies, the Social Security Administration (SSA) and the Employment and Training Administration (ETA) in the Department of Labor (plus some retirement agencies such as the Railroad Retirement Board and the Soldiers' and Airmens' Home), operate the bulk of the income stabilization programs. The Social Security Administration, located in the Department of Health, Education and Welfare (HEW), administers not only the nation's social security program but also the supplemental income program that guarantees a minimum income to all persons over sixty-five and the cash portions of the federal welfare effort (primarily Aid to Families with Dependent Children). The Employment and Training Administration's contribution to income security is in the area of training and jobs. The largest portion of ETA's budget is the federal contribution to unemployment insurance, a program designed to stabilize the incomes of the temporarily unemployed. For longer term unemployment, ETA operates the nation's public jobs programs, the apprenticeship and training programs, and the United States Employment Service.

Although welfare policy is an area dominated by state and local governments, some federal bureaus operate in these areas. The monetary welfare programs, those providing cash directly to the recipient, are housed in the Social Security Administration while the service programs are lodged in HEW's Office of Human Development. Human Development administers a series of programs delivering services to the aged, children (Headstart), and the disabled. Generally, the office provides funds and guidelines that permit other public agencies to operate such programs.

The health care area completes those programs generally perceived as social welfare programs. The Health Care Financing Administration created in 1977 by HEW Secretary Joseph Califano operates both medicare (health insurance for the aged) and medicaid (health insurance for the indigent). The 1977 reorganization joined these similar programs that were located in two different agencies. The reorganization was perceived by observers as the first administrative step toward a full scale National Health Insurance.[19]

Federal redistributive housing programs are located in two executive departments, Housing and Urban Development (HUD) and Agriculture. Within HUD a group of agencies—the Federal Housing Administration, the Government National Mortgage Administration, and the Office of Fair Housing and Equal Opportunity—operate programs affecting the quantity and quality of housing by influencing mortgage rates and selling practices. The Farm Home Administration (FmHA) in the Department of Agriculture is a much broader agency. FmHA provides credit to rural areas not only for home purchases but for farm ownership, farm operation, farm equipment and other functions.

The income distribution aspects of redistributive policy are housed in two agencies, the Internal Revenue Service (IRS) and the Bureau of Public Debt. The IRS, of course, administers the nation's tax system with the exception of that portion administered by the Bureau of Alcohol, Tobacco and Firearms in the Department of Treasury.[20] The myriad of tax programs, running some 1200 pages in the *U.S. Code* and supplemented by 6,500 pages of IRS rules, is far too complex to be discussed here in any comprehensive fashion. The Bureau of Public Debt handles the administrative matters related to financing the nation's seven hundred billion dollar public debt. The bureau's functions are generally administrative with little policy activity although decisions made by the bureau do affect individual bondholders.

The Structure of Redistributive Bureaus

Unlike regulatory policy, redistributive policies form a common pattern, and this commonality affects the type of bureaucracy needed to administer the policy. American redistributive policies at the federal level rarely provide services directly; they provide money either to an individual to procure services or to a public or private agency, which in turn provides the services. Redistributive federal bureaus, therefore, are large (they average 14,000 people) transfer payment agencies; they are excellent examples of government by checkwriting. As transfer payments agencies, they are resource intensive despite their large size. Although only 7 percent of federal employees work in redistributive bureaus, these employees handle over half the federal budget. Stating this relationship another way, federal redistributive agencies spend $1.9 million for every person they employ, by far the highest ratio in the federal government (see table 4–2).

Redistributive agencies may also be considered cybernetic. A cybernetic agency is an agency operating under legislation that anticipates environmental changes and adjusts agency actions to the changing conditions.[21] For example, the unemployment insurance program is tied to local conditions. If local unemployment is severe for a long period of time, benefits can be extended. Social security benefits also respond to the environment by increasing as the cost of living increases. Cybernetic agencies, in short, have enabling legislation that automatically adjusts the agency's programs to environmental changes, thus depriving the agency of discretion normally found in other agencies.

TABLE 4–2   *A Statistical Summary of the Average Redistributive Agency*

Number of Personnel	13,600
Size of 1977 Budget	$13.8 billion
Number of Clientele	14.7
Number of Computers	10.3
Pages of Rules Issued	271
Pages of Relevant Laws	51
Budget to Personnel Ratio	$1,906,900
Rules to Laws Ratio	6.8

N = 10

Redistributive Bureau Policymaking

Despite attempts by Congress and the president to restrict redistributive bureau activities through detailed laws, redistributive bureaus do influence public policy. Redistributive agencies influence policy in four ways—adjudication, program operations, policy initiations, and proposals for policy change. Policymaking via law enforcement or rulemaking is not generally part of a redistributive agency's activities.[22]

Adjudication.   Adjudication as practiced by redistributive agencies is somewhat different from adjudication in regulatory agencies. Redistributive agencies do not adjudicate cases under vague public interest standards. Since redistributive policy provides benefits to classes of people, adjudications determine whether or not individual X is a member of class Y. In many cases determining whether X is a member of Y is simple because the law states unambiguous standards. Is X over sixty-five and, therefore, eligible for social security? Is X unemployed under certain conditions and, therefore, eligible for unemployment compensation? Although most redistributive agency adjudications concern such simple matters, some cases are more difficult. The Social Security Administration administers a disability insurance program. Certifying a person as disabled is more difficult than determining if a person is over sixty-five. In these more difficult cases agency discretion permits some limited policymaking. Federal agency discretion even in these areas is limited; however, because a great many federal redistributive programs are actually administered by state agencies. Federal programs on unemployment and welfare (Aid to Families with Dependent Children, for example) are administered and adjudicated by state agencies, thus, blunting the impact of the federal bureaucracy.

Program Operations.   In areas where legislative standards are not as precise as social security, federal bureaus can influence public policy via program operations. Implementing a program reveals countless instances where discretion must be exercised, since even in redistributive policies Congress cannot anticipate all possible circumstances. The Federal Housing Administration's (FHA) implementation of housing standards noted in chapter 1 is an excellent example of policymaking through program operations.[23] Designed to upgrade housing standards by providing guaranteed mortgage money for homes meeting FHA standards, the agency applied conservative economic standards to transform the program. The practice of redlining poor areas (not guaranteeing mortgages in those areas) resulted in an efficient FHA program that provided greater access to middle-income and suburban-area homes through lower mortgage rates, but it also contributed to a general housing decline in poorer neighborhoods because only more traditional, and more expensive, mortgages were available there.

Policy Initiation.   Policy initiation, the process of proposing new policies and under certain conditions implementing them, is a long accepted method of bureaucratic policymaking. Redistributive bureaus can affect public policy either by implementing their own policy proposals or by commenting on the policy proposals of the president, Congress, interest groups, or others. A good example of policy initiation by a redistributive bureau is an action taken by the Department of Health, Education, and Welfare (HEW) in early 1976. Motivated by high costs in the Aid to Families with Dependent Children (AFDC) program, HEW initiated a new pilot program to counter one of the abuses. In many cases divorced fathers who were ordered by a court to support their children, refused to make support payments and moved without leaving a forwarding address. If the mother could not support the children alone, the children often became AFDC recipients. If fathers could be found and court orders enforced, AFDC costs would decline. Another HEW agency, the Social Security Administration, had information on the location of all workers since social security earnings are reported to the agency. Health, Education, and Welfare established a pilot program whereby it provided information from social security files that permitted AFDC recipients to find non-supporting fathers and take legal action to enforce payment orders. Using social security accounts for non–social security purposes was a major, and potentially dangerous, policy innovation by the bureaucracy.[24]

Policy Proposals. Federal redistributive bureaus also affect public policy by assisting the president and Congress either by writing new legislation for them or by commenting on new legislative proposals that others are considering. This legislative clearance function is more important for redistributive bureaus than for other bureaus because redistributive legislation contains more specific policy directives than does legislation in other areas. President Carter's 1977 proposals for welfare reform based on a negative income tax plus work incentives is a good example of such an instance. The specific reform proposals were written by civil servants in the Departments of Labor and Health, Education and Welfare and reflect the biases of those agencies.[25] HEW's reputed position was that only a negative-income-tax-based welfare reform would work; this position is a function of the perceived weaknesses of the state agencies currently administering welfare programs and the expertise of HEW in cash transfer programs. Bureaus such as the Department of HEW play an important role in the policy formulation stage of policymaking because a bureau's opposition can be fatal to a program if the bureau possesses expertise sufficient to convince Congress that a program will not work.[26]

The Environment of Redistributive Agencies

The environment of federal redistributive agencies is intensely political, reflecting the major divisions between the Democratic and Republican parties. This partisan atmosphere creates a unique environment that affects the clientele support, knowledge, leadership, and cohesion of redistributive bureaus. Congress responds to the partisan atmosphere with policies that restrict agency opportunities to cultivate clientele; Congress perceives redistributive issues as so important that they should be resolved in the legislative branch rather than by the bureaus in consort with their clientele. The appropriations testimony figures demonstrate the resulting lack of agency clientele support (table 4–2). The average redistributive agency has fifteen groups supporting it over a three-year period. A closer examination reveals that this figure is inflated by a few strong clientele agencies; four agencies—the Farmers Home Administration, the Federal Housing Administration, the Employment and Training Administration, and the now defunct Social and Rehabilitation Service—have 78 percent of all redistributive clientele. Deleting these four bureaus from the figure in table 4–2 would demonstrate that redistributive bureaus rival regulatory agencies for weak clientele. Even those redistributive bureaus with strong clientele support lack many advantages of clientele support because the salience of redistributive bureaus virtually insures that one of the major political parties will oppose the clientele's position.

Knowledge is a valuable asset to redistributive bureaus because US redistributive programs are massive. Despite the average redistributive agency's access to ten computers, computer expertise for these bureaus is related to processing huge workloads not to research as it is in other agencies. As a result, redistributive agency knowledge relies heavily on social science knowledge, a much weaker variety of professional knowledge than that based on physical science and technology.

The benefits of strong leadership and organizational cohesion can be developed in some redistributive agencies. The influential position of Wilbur Cohen in Social Security reform and of Sargeant Shriver in the early poverty program demonstrates the role leadership can play in redistributive policymaking. In general, redistributive bureaus also have political functions that excite people and motivate agency employees. Health care, providing for the nation's aged, and caring for the poor are functions that attract highly committed people. At the federal level, however, congressional policies prevent federal bureaus from being action agencies. Federal bureaus must be content to fund state and local projects. As a result of these restrictions, the potential vitality and cohesion of federal redistributive agencies are lost in routine administrative procedures.

Although redistributive agencies fare better on the dimensions of political power than do regulatory agencies, they are not among the most powerful federal bureaus. Occasionally an Internal Revenue Service (IRS) or a Social Security Administration may greatly influence policy because they possess policy knowledge and leadership, but generally these agencies are subject to strong congressional control. To be sure, redistributive agencies have access to great amounts of resources; over half the federal budget is spent by redistributive bureaus. Unfortunately for these bureaus, however, the resources are usually transferred directly to the citizen. Agency discretion, and therefore autonomy, is generally low. Although a bureau may occasionally develop autonomy as strong as the IRS did in 1973 when it was able to refuse John Dean's request for audits of President Nixon's "enemies," a redistributive agency rarely concentrates sufficient leadership and expertise to refuse a presidential request.[27]

ᕙ Distributive Policy ᕗ

Distributive policymaking is the most common form of federal action to solve public problems. According to Theodore Lowi distributive policy relies on remote coercion with application to individual conduct.[28] In less abstract terms government distributive policies use general tax revenue or other nonuser taxes to provide benefits directly to individuals. National parks, health research, federal crop insurance, federal law enforcement grants are all examples of federal distributive policymaking.

The Scope of Distributive Policy

A full listing of all federal government distributive programs is impossible; there are simply too many. Federal distributive policies may, however, be classified into five main types—the distribution of subsidies, government sponsored research, the collection and dissemination of information, the creation of distributive public goods, and the use of the federal government's resources to provide insurance.

Distribution of Subsidies. The distribution of grants and subsidies is a well accepted method of federal public policymaking. The nation's agricultural system, for example, is at times plagued with large surpluses. Rather than bear the consequences of lost production resulting from surplus induced low prices, the government pays subsidies to farmers who voluntarily limit production when farm commodities are in oversupply. The federal government does not directly force farmers to limit production but rather grants them some benefits (subsidies, for example) if they agree to reduce production. The lure of federal money is also used to stimulate state and local governments to take specified actions. Law Enforcement Assistance Administration (LEAA) grants, mass transit grants, and education grants all attempt to influence the actions of state and local government by providing federal grants as incentives. In 1975 some $42.7 billion in grants, exclusive of revenue sharing, was distributed to state and local government by the federal government.[29] These distributive benefits are usually cash grants either with or without restrictions; rarely does the federal government provide services directly to state and local government.[30]

Government Sponsored Research. Distributive policy also includes government acting as the research arm for American industry. Government supported research can be justified by the argument that many industries are too small and too fragmented to support the research necessary for improving productivity. Government, on the other hand, with its great resources can easily bear the costs of such research and distribute the results to industry with the public benefiting from an improvement in goods and services. Although the public, or more cynically industry, is normally perceived as the recipient of government research benefits, the most direct beneficiary is the researcher who could not support large-scale research without federal funds. Federal research efforts occur in numerous agencies, but most distributive research is located in six general areas.[31] The federal government's major contributions in the research area are in agriculture (the Agricultural Research Service, the Cooperative State Research Service), environmental matters (the National Oceanic and Atmospheric Administration and the Environmental Protection Agency), health (the National Institutes of Health), education (the National Institute of Education and the Office of Education), energy (the Department of Energy), and general science (the National Science Foundation).

Collection and Dissemination of Information.   A distributive benefit related to government sponsored research is government collection and distribution of information. Individuals and organizations at times need to know the results of government and academic research or trends in the US economy or demography. Although some private organizations are able to earn a profit by distributing such information, in many areas only government disseminates this information. The agricultural research results of the Agricultural Research Service and the Cooperative State Research Service are transmitted to local farmers through the Agricultural Extension Service. The US Geological Survey collects and distributes information on possible mineral deposits collected in its geological studies. The US government does not restrict itself to distributing information to producer organizations; the United States Travel Service, for example, disseminates information about the United States to prospective tourists, thus benefiting the travel industry by distributing information to other persons.

Creation of Distributive Public Goods.   All governments create public goods that can be enjoyed by their citizens. In some cases, such as national defense, these public goods are collective so that a citizen cannot choose whether or not to use them. All persons receive the benefits of public collective goods whether or not they desire them. Distributive public goods, on the other hand, are provided by government, but an individual citizen decides if he or she will use the public good. National parks and recreation projects, federal highways, and conservation projects are all examples of government creating distributive public goods. Government can also create a distributive public good by permitting an individual to exploit a government protected monopoly. Granting a patent, for example, rewards inventors by granting them monopoly use of their inventions.

Creating a distributive public good always implies regulating public access to that good. Just as broadcasting frequencies can be destroyed by too many broadcasters, overuse and abuse of highways, parks, and patents also denegrates these public goods. As a result, distributive agencies that create distributive public goods must also perform some regulatory functions.

Government Insurance. The final area of distributive policy is the provision of insurance benefits. In areas where private insurance is not feasible, the resources of government are sometimes used to provide the distributive benefit of insurance. Federal crop insurance and federal flood insurance are areas where private industry needs assistance in providing insurance protection. Such insurance is a distributive benefit because it provides the benefits of disaster protection that would not be available without the actions of government.

The Structure of Distributive Bureaus

Similar to redistributive policy, the political environment of distributive policy affects the type of bureau that administers distributive policy. Distributive bureaus are small with an average size of 9,100 persons (see table 4–3); this size would be expected of an agency that distributes benefits to only a small portion of the American people. The nature of distributive policy generates large amounts of resources for a bureau rather than large numbers of personnel. Since many distributive bureaus provide cash sub-

TABLE 4–3   *A Statistical Summary of the Average Distributive Agency*

Number of Personnel	9,100
Size of 1977 Budget	$1,272 million
Number of Clientele	58.1
Number of Computers	47.3
Pages of Rules Issued	205
Pages of Relevant Laws	49
Budget to Personnel Ratio	$843,300
Rules to Laws Ratio	7.2

N = 52

sidies or grants rather than services, the large budget to personnel ratio
($850,000 per employee) is not surprising. Only redistributive agencies
process a larger amount of resources per employee.

The administration of distributive benefits usually entails a great
deal of discretion. This discretion is reflected in two ways. First, the enabling legislation of distributive programs is brief (less than 50 pages in
the *U.S. Code*), permitting the agency some flexibility in meeting its
clientele's needs. The National Institutes of Health, for example, operate
a $2.4 billion budget under a law that runs less than twenty pages in the
U.S. Code. Second, discretion is increased by the decentralized nature of
distributive bureaus; most distributive agency employees are located in the
field delivering services or monitoring programs rather than in Washington.
For example, the Departments of Agriculture and Interior, two departments with many distributive bureaus, have less than one employee in
seven stationed in the Washington metropolitan area. As the distance
from Washington increases, discretion becomes a necessity.

Distributive bureaus are also one of the key elements in an iron
triangle of bureau, congressional committee, and interest-group subsystems.
Subsystem government (see chapter 3) is nowhere as prevalent as in distributive policymaking. Since distributive bureaus provide benefits to
small portions of the American population, only small segments of Congress have any interest in the bureau; these members of Congress are
usually on the subcommittee that oversees the bureau.[32] Any group strong
enough to pressure Congress into granting it a portion of government benefits is likely to be highly organized; the environment of distributive bureaus,
therefore, usually contains a large number of strong interest groups.

Distributive Bureau
Policymaking

The policymaking influence of distributive bureaus equals or exceeds that
of most other federal government bureaus. Although implementation is a
distributive bureau's major means of affecting public policy, some bureaus
have an impact through policy initiation and, occasionally, law enforcement. Adjudication and rulemaking, two major forms of policymaking for
other bureaus, are not major elements in distributive policymaking. Since
distributive bureaus are encouraged to deliver goods and services and since
adjudication is the usual means of determining eligibility for these benefits, distributive bureaus downplay their adjudicatory powers in preference
for maximum benefit distribution.[33] Rulemaking varies greatly among
distributive bureaus. Some agencies, such as the Maritime Administration,

the Office of Education, and the Veterans Administration, issue extension rules; but most distributive agencies eschew rulemaking.

Given the vague enabling legislation of most distributive bureaus, program implementation or operations provide numerous opportunities for agencies to guide the direction of public policy. Every law must be translated into specific programs, and this translation is at the discretion of the agency. The agricultural research establishment provides a good example of policymaking through implementation. The agricultural research establishment composed of the Agricultural Research Service (the Department of Agriculture's in-house research organization) and the Cooperative State Research Service with its affiliated college experiment stations has a simple mission. Its "basic mission is to provide the necessary knowledge and technology so that farmers can produce efficiently, conserve the environment, and meet the food and fiber needs of the American people." [34] By any standard the agricultural research establishment is remarkably successful in meetings its goals of providing for the food and fiber needs of the American people.[35] The research establishment has been criticized, however, for its implementation of these goals.[36] According to critics, the research establishment has concentrated on high-technology processes that produce great surpluses of nutritionally questionable food through extensive use of pesticides and fertilizers. According to James Hightower, implementation of this policy is driving small farmers from the land because they cannot afford the capital investment to compete in this high-technology agriculture system. A second-order consequence of this policy is the aggravation of existing problems by contributing to the flow of people to urban areas.[37] From a more empirical perspective, the actions of the agricultural research establishment can easily be explained; they simply implemented congressional legislation by meeting the needs of the Department of Agriculture's prime clientele, the large technologically advanced farmer.[38] The resulting policy is greatly different than it would be if the agricultural research establishment implemented programs with the intent of benefiting small farmers or more labor intensive farmers.

Distributive bureaus and their clientele can become so powerful that they not only dominate policy implementation but also control the policy initiation stage. In 1964 after wheat farmers rejected a major portion of President John Kennedy's farm program, President Lyndon Johnson called together leaders of the major agriculture interest groups and asked them to formulate a farm program.[39] The Wheat-Cotton Bill of 1964 was a product of the Department of Agriculture and the major farm interest groups. Congress accepted the Wheat-Cotton Bill, thus writing into law many of the bureaus' and interest groups' proposals. Until recently, agricultural policy proposals without the support of bureaus in the Department of Agriculture and their clientele had little chance of passage. The continued decline of rural representation in Congress along with the rise of food as an issue after the 1973 Soviet grain sales has weakened the bureaus' influence.[40]

Although distributive agencies are rarely law enforcement agencies, occasionally they can influence policy either by not enforcing a law or by selective law enforcement. The Federal Reclamation Act of 1902 attempts to support the small farmer by limiting any one farmer to 160 acres of land irrigated by federal reclamation projects. The Bureau of Land Management in the Department of Interior, the agency that administered the law, never enforced the 160 acre provision permitting some landowners to accumulate several thousand acres of reclamation irrigated land. As a result of nonenforcement, a government policy designed to benefit small farmers was transformed into a policy not incongruent with the Department of Agriculture's preference for large farmers.[41]

The Environment of
Distributive Agencies

Distributive agencies have the most favorable political environment of all federal bureaus. No type of agencies fits the powerful bureaus described in chapter 3 as well as distributive agencies because their environment is so conducive to strong clientele, knowledge, leadership and cohesion. Not only is a distributive bureau's environment full of strong clientele groups, but the agency is also encouraged by Congress to meet clientele needs. For the most part, distributive agencies were created in response to organized groups' needs; therefore, little conflict exists between Congressional intent and clientele needs. Table 4–4 shows the top ten clientele agencies of the US government ranked according to the number of interest groups that testified for them at appropriations hearings. All ten bureaus from the Army Corps of Engineers to the National Endowment for the Arts and Humanities are distributive policy bureaus. Large clientele support is characteristic of most distributive bureaus as reflected in the average of fifty-eight supporting clientele groups per bureau (see table 4–3). This average is over four times the number of supporters for any other type of bureau. Distributive politics is clearly clientele politics.

Where strong clientele support for distributive bureaus can be combined with expert knowledge, bureaus are in enviable positions of power. Agencies with research functions (National Institutes of Health, the Agricultural Research Service, the National Aeronautics and Space Administration) have a built-in advantage on the knowledge dimension.

TABLE 4-4   *Top Ten Clientele Agencies of the Federal Government,* 1974-1976

Agency	Number of Groups *
1. Army Corps of Engineers (Defense)	1028
2. Bureau of Reclamation (Interior)	326
3. Forest Service (Agriculture)	275
4. National Institutes of Health (HEW)	223
5. Office of Education (HEW)	156
6. Bureau of Indian Affairs (Interior)	153
7. National Parks Service (Interior)	96
8. Agricultural Research Service (USDA)	90
9. Soil Conservation Service (USDA)	85
10. National Endowment for the Arts and Humanities	79

* Number of groups supporting the agency before the appropriate Subcommittee of the House Appropriations Committee.

Although distributive agencies use two of every five federal government computers, the distribution of the computers, similar to the distribution of expert knowledge, is uneven. The bulk of distributive policy computers are located in these research agencies, especially the Department of Energy and the National Aeronautics and Space Administration. Most other distributive agencies must rely on expertise generated by their familiarity with programs and clientele rather than technologically based expertise. Expert knowledge, therefore, is an asset only some distributive bureaus have.

Strong leadership in distributive bureaus is usually related to clientele support. Where bureau chiefs have strong clientele support and good congressional ties, agencies can be relatively autonomous *vis-à-vis* the president. Although in some cases, such as Earl Butz and Robert Bergland, department heads and bureau chiefs are recruited from the agency's clientele, the normal bureau chief-clientele ties are less obvious. Bureau chiefs develop strong clientele ties through long-term working arrangements with the bureau's clientele. The normal bureau chief may spend thirty or more years in the agency before assuming the top position. Much of this time is spent delivering services to the agency's clientele. During this time any rational future bureau chief realizes his agency's future is tied to clientele support; therefore, he cultivates clientele ties.

Since distributive agencies are charged with improving people's lives and since they are action agencies unlike redistributive bureaus, they can develop into cohesive organizations. The Forest Service uses personnel rotation plus heavy doses of socialization to instill organizational loyalty in its personnel.[42] The dedication of NASA employees in the early years of the space program was legendary. In some agencies cohesion is a function of professional commitment to scientific goals. Other agencies consciously develop techniques to strengthen their employees' commitment to the organization's ends.

Despite the advantages of distributive agencies in regard to clientele support, expert knowledge, leadership and cohesion, these agencies are still influenced by other portions of their environment. When a distributive agency's environment is quiescent, the political subsystem functions to protect the bureau and its clientele. Under these conditions distributive bureaus are among the most powerful in government. When the political environment is turbulent or politicized (that is, others are concerned about the policy in the subsystem area), distributive bureaus may be overwhelmed by their environment.[43] For example, in 1973 agricultural bureaus were overwhelmed by the public's reaction to high food prices forcing the bureaus to accept many policy changes they opposed.[44] Only the strongest agencies can weather an all-out attack by the president, the Congress, and other interest groups.

In normal political times distributive agencies do well in aggrandizing resources. Without severe fiscal constraints, as might be imposed by recession or war, distributive agencies get average or better increases in resources every year. Although distributive agencies are not among the fastest-growing agencies, their budget growth is stable.[45] In tight fiscal times, however, such as the 1970s, when inflation easily outruns agency budgets, distributive agencies take a backseat to uncontrollable programs. Programs that have benefits written into law and tied to inflation rates or unemployment rates (for example, social security or employment programs) have first claim on most resources when revenues are scarce. Distributive agencies fare less well in these situations.

Distributive agencies are also highly autonomous when the scope of their actions is relatively narrow. When agency actions only affect the bureau's clientele directly, the bureau can usually operate without the intervention of the president or Congress as long as no portion of the subsystem is unsatisfied. When issues outside the normal subsystems are concerned or when the environment is politicized, distributive bureaus become only one actor among many.

⟪ Constituent Policy ⟫

Constituent policy, according to Theodore Lowi, uses remote coercion applied through an environment of conduct.[46] Although constituent policy when expressed in Lowi's terms is a logical fourth type of public policy, it is really a residual category that includes all the remaining types of public policy. Since many constituent policies such as reapportionment or setting up a new bureau are legislative policies, many constituent policies are not administered by government bureaus.[47] Bureaus administer constituent policy only when agencies are established to deliver services directly to the nation as a whole or its government. In national defense, foreign affairs, or selling government bonds the constituency of constituent policy is the government.

The Scope of Constituent Policy

Constituent policy bureaus are divisible into two types. National security-foreign affairs bureaus serve the nation by providing it with mechanisms for defense, diplomacy, intelligence, and propaganda. The Department of Defense and its major operating units—the Army, Navy, and Air Force—along with the auxiliary agencies (for example, the Defense Mapping Agency) provide one core of bureaus in the national security area. Attached to this core are the Selective Service System, now in mothballs, the intelligence community, and parts of the Coast Guard with defense-related functions. The second core of the national security bureaus are the diplomacy agencies with the Department of State at the core. A variety of agencies from other departments assist the State Department in its functions—the Foreign Agricultural Service, the US Information Agency, the international business divisions of the Department of Commerce, et cetera.

The government service bureaus—the second type of constituent bureau—perform a somewhat different role by providing services to government rather than to the nation. The Office of Personnel Management, for example, supplies government with its personnel system. The General Services Administration operates the physical resources of government, the supplies, the buildings, and other such needs of government. Several bureaus in the Treasury Department coin the nation's money and supervise the physical aspects of the government's money system. The Secret Service provides security for government officials as well as performing some regulatory functions.

Structure of
Constituent Policy

Since constituent policy bureaus contain two divergent types of institutions, any generalizations about the structure of constituent bureaus must be qualified. Constituent policy bureaus, especially the national security bureaus, are massive government bureaucracies. The average constituent policy bureau is five times the size of the average redistributive policy bureau, the next largest type of bureaucracy (see table 4–5). Fully 65 percent of federal civilian employees are members of constituent policy bureaus. The large size and massive functions make constituent bureaus people intensive despite the large capital needs of the armed forces. The average constituent bureau spends $121,000 per employee, a figure that exceeds only the ratio for regulatory bureaus. Unlike distributive or redistributive bureaus, then, constituent bureaus deliver services rather than money to procure services.

As bureaus with the nation as their primary clientele, constituent policy bureaus are open to the environmental influences of government and politics. According to Scott A. Harris' study of US China policy, the key variable in such circumstances is issue politicization—the degree to which the issue under consideration is subject to partisan debate.[48] If an issue is

TABLE 4–5   *A Statistical Summary of the Average Constituent Agency*

Number of Personnel	73,000
Size of 1977 Budget	$4.04 billion
Number of Clientele	8.3
Number of Computers	172.0
Pages of Rules Issued	363
Pages of Relevant Laws	79
Budget to Personnel Ratio	$121,000
Rules to Laws Ratio	4.2

N = 25

not politicized (for example, US-Columbia relations), decisions are made by the bureau at low levels. If issues are politicized as the issue of relations with China was during the 1950s and 1960s, then decisional authority moves upward with politicians resolving issues and imposing uniform behavior on bureaucracy.[49] In short, as issues become politicized, the bureaus lose influence in the policy process to the politicians.

Constituent Bureau Policymaking

Constituent policy bureaus influence governmental policy within their sphere of activities in a variety of ways. Implementation, policy initiation, and bureaucratic routines are the major methods of policy impact although rulemaking is important in some instances. Unlike other agencies, especially regulatory agencies, adjudication is not a major means of policymaking. To be sure, the Merit Systems Protection Board does adjudicate federal employee grievances, and the Selective Service System at one time adjudicated draft deferments, but in general constituent policy bureaus have few opportunities for adjudication.

Implementation. Constituent policy bureaus affect public policy through implementation in processes similar to those of other federal bureaus. Since legislation or executive orders establishing policy are normally vague, bureaus must specify policy as they implement it. A good example of policymaking through implementation is the Civil Service Commission's (now the Office of Personnel Management) implementation of equal employment laws for federal government employment.[50] Before May 11, 1971, government policy on minority employment was one of nondiscrimination; government would not discriminate in hiring on the basis of race, color, religion, sex, or national origin. The Commission's decision to alter this policy was forced by certain environmental events. First, the nondiscrimination policy was not successfully placing minorities in high-level positions in the federal bureaucracy; most minorities were located in low-level bureau positions. Second, the Commission was perceived as ineffective by other policymakers.[51] Two bills were introduced in Congress to remove the equal-employment functions from the Civil Service Commission and place them in the Equal Employment Opportunity Commission. To forestall this threat and gain back clientele support from minorities, the Civil Service Commission announced a new policy: federal agencies were to use goals for minority hiring and timetables for reaching those goals. Many observers believed that this change in policy marked the first use of quotas in federal government hiring policy.[52] The Commission's change from a policy of nondiscrimination to a policy of goals and time-tables was accomplished administratively without altering the basic legislation covering the civil service.

Policymaking by implementation is also a major activity in national security bureaus. Chapter 1 provided several examples of national security agencies implementing policy during the Cuban missile crisis. In fact, the implementation decision of the US Air Force not to remove missiles from Turkey was a major factor in the Soviet decision to place missiles in Cuba.

Policy Initiation.   Constituent bureaus may also alter and formulate policy through the process of policy initiation, by creating new policies and proposals to replace current policy. Although United States' policy toward China in an area where the president has been the dominant force in recent years, the State Department was not without influence.[53] Bureaucratic tactics focused on demonstrating that the seamless web position, which held that American actions should not tolerate *any* interaction with China, no longer dominated the perspectives of US elites. Bureaucrats pursued alternative policies in the 1970s by isolating small components of China policy such as easing the trade embargo and encouraging the exchange of scholars and journalists. These incremental bureaucratic changes had a profound impact on US China policy by demonstrating the general ideological reaction to China was weakening, thus, permitting additional steps toward normalization of relations.[54]

Policymaking through policy initiation is also widespread in other constituent policy agencies. The Defense Department is usually the main initiator of policy on new weapons systems with assistance from the defense industry. Other policymakers can usually just respond to Defense Department initiatives. In the government service area the US Civil Service Commission provided a good example of policy initiation when its Chairman Alan K. Campbell proposed the modification of veteran preference in federal government hiring.[55]

Bureaucratic Routines.   Constituent policy bureaus can also influence policy through bureaucratic routines—the standard operating procedures and organizational biases that most agencies possess. Since constituent policy bureaus are generally large organizations, they tend to be more bureaucratized than other federal bureaus with set methods of handling problems that occur. Routines affect policy when a bureau must act in a manner that violates the bureau's perception of how the activity ought to be done. According to Adam Yarmolinsky, the US Army in the early 1960s perceived its functions as fighting large massed land battles.[56] When President Kennedy attempted to create a more flexible army through counterinsurgency training with the famed Green Berets, the innovation was strongly resisted by the regular army. The Green Berets soon were perceived as an unwanted assignment and were shunned by many of the Army's best officers, thus, weakening the nation's counterinsurgency ability. The rigidities of constituent policy bureaus' routines, therefore, can affect policy decisions that others make either by preventing the selection of one policy or by handicapping the policy if the "wrong" alternative is selected.

Rulemaking. Although most constituent policy bureaus use rulemaking as a strictly administrative function concerned with contract specifications and similar functions, some constituent bureaus establish public policy through the rulemaking procedure. The Office of Personnel Management, for example, has issued over four hundred pages of rules and regulations covering federal employment practices. The defense agencies issue a variety of rules on military procedure and practices, some with policy impact. In general though, constituent policy agencies, as illustrated by their low rules to laws ratio (see table 4–5), are not rulemaking agencies.

The Environment of Constituent Policy Bureaus

The political environment of constituent bureaus conditions their ability to use clientele support, expert knowledge, leadership, and cohesion to strengthen the power base of the bureau. Despite the well stablished belief in the military-industrial complex, constituent bureaus are not strong clientele agencies. Since the prime recipient of a constituent bureau's services is government, few opportunities exist to develop potential clientele. Clientele support for constituent bureaus is, in fact, no stronger than is clientele support for regulatory agencies (see table 4–5). Although Defense Department operating bureaus average twice as many clientele as nondefense constituent bureaus do, they cannot rival the clientele powers of bureaus in distributive agencies.[57] This lack of clientele means that constituent policy agencies are sensitive to their environment. When issues are highly politicized as Harris notes, constituent bureaus are not strong policymaking actors.[58] Constituent agencies unlike distributive bureaus lack specific clientele support to withstand the pressure of unfavorable diffuse support. As a result constituent bureaus must bend to the winds in their political environment. When issues are not politicized, however, bureaus have more influence because they are favored with expert knowledge, leadership, and cohesion.

A major factor permitting bureaus to exercise policymaking power is a bureau's expert knowledge. Constituent bureaus are complex, technical agencies administering massive programs. Of the three major types of constituent policy agencies only foreign policy agencies do not claim technical expertise. The intelligence bureaus, the defense bureaus, and the treasury bureaus all develop expert knowledge to accomplish their tasks. Cryptographers, linguists, physicists, and economists are only a few of the technical specialists in constituent bureaus. One good indicator of the technical capacity of these bureaus is that 56 percent of the US government's computers are used in constituent policy agencies, an average of 172 per agency. With such expertise the absence of clientele support may be an advantage. In areas of "national interest" policy, clientele support may well be inappropriate since it indicates ties to special, nonnational interests. Bureaus can argue that their lack of clientele support makes them neutral, technical experts when evaluating policy. Although other policymakers are less inclined to accept that argument than they were in the past, it is a more tenable position for constituent bureaus than it is for distributive bureaus with their strong clientele ties.[59]

Leadership as a source of bureau power in constituent bureaus resembles leadership everywhere else; potential leadership exists. Unlike regulatory agencies headed by commissions, constituent bureaus are structured to permit leadership. Given the importance of most constituent policy, agency heads are usually either recruited from the outside with a reputation for leadership (Defense Secretary, Robert McNamara; Civil Service Chairman, Alan K. Campbell) or develop expertise and leadership ability inside the agency (former Admiral Elmo Zumwalt; Chairman of the Joint Chiefs of Staff George Marshall).

Organizational cohesion is also especially easy to develop in some constituent bureaus. The importance of these bureaus' functions supplemented by extensive socialization make the defense and the intelligence bureaus among the most cohesive in the federal government.[60] The ability of intelligence agencies to operate in secrecy so long is a testimony to their organizational cohesion. Where bureau tasks are less vital, organizational cohesion is weaker. Foreign policy bureaus are at times marked by strong internal squabbles. Government service bureaus appear to lack the exciting missions necessary to develop strong cohesive organizations.

The ability of constituent bureaus to aggrandize resources and develop autonomy is a function of the above environment. Where the environment is politicized, bureaus must yield to the pressures of the environment. Where the environment is not politicized, the bureaus can dominate portions of their environment if they possess expert knowledge, leadership and cohesion. Although constituent bureaus, especially defense bureaus, receive a large share of the government resources, they are currently suffering a relative decline in resources compared to other government bureaus. Since constituent policy is an area where expenditures are controllable, they are the first to be sacrificed to the needs of uncontrollable programs. In the last ten years constituent agencies have had difficulty in competing against redistributive bureaus for a portion of the inflation diminished budget.

Constituent policy bureaus, especially the defense and intelligence bureaus, also have suffered a decline in policymaking autonomy. In the politicized environment of the Vietnam War, many people were quite willing to evaluate the performance of these bureaus and to evaluate them negatively. Where the results were not positive, as they were not in Vietnam or in Chile or in other areas for intelligence policy, bureau autonomy was gradually restricted.

Although these statements on constituent bureaus' resource and autonomy weaknesses apply mostly to defense and intelligence bureaus, other constituent bureaus are much weaker. Treasury bureaus, government service bureaus, and foreign affairs bureaus lack the vital missions of defense and intelligence agencies. Although some of these constituent bureaus under given circumstances can develop into powerful bureaus, most must be satisfied with lower objectives.

⟋⟍ Summary ⟋⟍

This chapter traced the policymaking process in federal government bureaus. Because the myriad of public policies differ more than they are similar, the US policy process was divided into four types—regulatory policy, redistributive policy, distributive policy, and constituent policy. The impact of government bureaucracy in each of these areas was examined. Bureaus have their greatest influence in distributive and constituent policies. In distributive policy, the area with the greatest bureaucratic impact, bureau policy influence is a function of strong clientele support and good leadership with an occasional assist from expert knowledge in the research agencies. Bureau influence in constituent policy is a function of knowledge, leadership and organizational cohesion. Although both types of bureaus cannot resist the pressures of a hostile, mobilized political environment, distributive bureaus have more success because their strong specific clientele support can counter diffuse opposition. While distributive bureaus can influence policy more often, this power is limited by the narrower functions that distributive agencies perform. Regulatory agencies and redistributive agencies have a much weaker influence on public policy. Such bureaus become powerful policymakers only in special circumstances where they develop expert knowledge or are permitted to cultivate clientele support.

Bureau activities in the policymaking process also vary by policy area. Government bureaus influence public policy through rulemaking, adjudication, law enforcement, program implementation, policy initiation, comments on proposed policy changes, and bureaucratic routines. Bureaus in different policy areas engage in different policymaking activities with varying effectiveness. Not all government bureaus are power brokers in the policy process, and not all bureaus influence the process in the same manner.

✑ Notes ✑

1. James E. Anderson, *Public Policy-Making* (New York: Praeger, 1975); See Charles O. Jones, *An Introduction to the Study of Public Policy* (North Scituate, Mass.: Duxbury Press, 1977) for a good discussion of definitions.

2. Theodore J. Lowi, "Four Systems of Policy, Politics, and Choice," *Public Administration Review* 32 (July/August, 1972), pp. 298–310, at p. 299.

3. Ibid., p. 300.

4. Dean Mann, "Political Incentives in U.S. Water Policy," in *What Government Does*, eds. Matthew Holden, Jr. and Dennis L. Dresang, (Beverly Hills: Sage Publications, 1975), pp. 94–123.

5. Paul Sabatier, "Social Movements and Regulatory Agencies," *Policy Sciences* 6 (1976), pp. 301–342.

6. The direct cost of regulation does not include such costs as higher prices for consumer goods that result because worker safety regulations increase production costs. These indirect costs are generally invisible to consumers. The direct cost entails only the operating expenses of the agencies.

7. The case study is taken from A. Lee Fritschler, *Smoking and Politics* (Englewood Cliffs: Prentice Hall, 1975).

8. Robert Fellmeth, *The Interstate Commerce Commission* (New York: Grossman, 1970); Kenneth C. Davis, *Discretionary Justice* (Urbana: University of Illinois Press, 1971).

9. Mark Nadel, *The Politics of Consumer Protection* (Indianapolis: Bobbs-Merrill, 1971).

10. "Ford Signs Bill to Regulate Commodity Futures," *Congressional Quarterly Almanac* 30 (1974), pp. 215–220.

11. The argument presented here is similar to that of Harold Seidman, *Politics, Position and Power* (New York: Oxford University Press, 1975). Seidman does not limit his discussion to just regulatory agencies as this chapter does.

12. The clientele measures were developed from a content analysis of all House Appropriations Committee Subcommittee hearings for the years

1974–1976. For a complete description of these measures see Kenneth J. Meier, "Building Bureaucratic Coalitions," in *The Politics of Food*, ed. Don F. Hadwiger et al. (Lexington, Mass.: D. C. Heath, 1978).

13.   Anthony Downs, *Inside Bureaucracy* (Boston: Little, Brown, 1967); Marver Bernstein, *Regulating Business Through Independent Commission* (Princeton: Princeton University Press, 1955).

14.   J. Clarence Davies and Barbara S. Davies, *The Politics of Pollution* (Indianapolis: Bobbs-Merrill, 1975).

15.   Louis Kohlmeier, *The Regulators* (New York: Harper and Row, 1970).

16.   Robert Burkhardt, *The Federal Aviation Administration* (New York: Praeger, 1967), especially pp. 41–49.

17.   A reason why regulatory agencies lack cohesion may be the bipartisan requirement for commissioners. This insures that partisan cleavages are always possible at high levels. At the professional level the oft-noticed conflict between economists and lawyers may handicap agency cohesion.

18.   See the extended presentation in chapter 1. See also Harold Wolman, *The Politics of Federal Housing* (New York: Dodd, Mead, 1971); and Brian D. Boyer, *Cities Destroyed for Cash* (Chicago: Follett Publishing Co., 1973).

19.   "Califano Reorganizes HEW, Predicts Eventual Savings of $2 Billion A Year," *Congressional Quarterly Weekly Report* 35 (March 12, 1977), p. 446.

20.   The classification of the IRS as a redistributive agency is open to question. Since the IRS enforces the nation's tax laws, it could easily be classified as a regulatory agency.

21.   Allen Schick, "Toward the Cybernetic State," in Dwight Waldo, *Public Administration in a Time of Turbulence* (Scranton: Chandler Publishing Co., 1971), pp. 214–233.

22.   On this dimension the IRS is definitely more like a regulatory agency than a redistributive agency. The impact of the IRS on the nation's tax policy is through rulemaking and law enforcement as well as on proposals for tax reform.

23.   See Wolman, *The Politics of Federal Housing;* and Boyer, *Cities Destroyed for Cash.*

24.   The program was given a major push when one of the national network news programs presented a program on the HEW policy and provided information to mothers on how to use the pilot program to find fathers.

25.   *National Journal,* August 27, 1977, p. 1928.

26.   Note that in the welfare reform instance the structure of re-distributive agencies affected the policy proposal. HEW supports negative-income-tax-based proposals probably because it could not with current resources handle a national welfare program that was service oriented. With the expertise of the Social Security Administration, however, a negative income tax would be feasible. The 1977 HEW reorganization, in fact, moved the cash welfare programs of the national government from the now defunct Social and Re-habilitation Service to the Social Security Administration. This move probably reflects the department's preference for welfare reform in the form of transfer payments.

27.   Another reason for the resistence of the IRS to the overtures of Mr. Dean may well have been the partisan orientation of the IRS. The IRS, as are most federal agencies, is staffed primarily with Democrats. The presidential tapes from the Watergate era reveal that Mr. Dean blamed some of the un-responsiveness of the IRS on its partisan composition. See Joel Aberbach and Bert Rockman, "Clashing Beliefs Within the Executive Branch," *American Political Science Review* 70 (June, 1976), pp. 456–468.

28.   Lowi, "Four Systems of Policy," p. 300.

29.   David B. Walker, "The Changing Pattern of Federal Assistance to State and Local Governments," in *Public Administration and Public Policy*, ed. H. George Frederickson and Charles R. Wise (Lexington, Mass.: D. C. Heath, 1977), pp. 81–98.

30.   The range of subsidy programs operated by the federal govern-ment covers a great many areas. Subsidies or grants are provided in agriculture, law enforcement, Indian affairs, disease control, maritime shipping, mass transit, railroads, health care services and resources, education, veterans affairs, small business, and fine arts and humanities.

31.   Distributive research has research results that directly benefit industry. Nondistributive research is a major federal activity. Research on weapons systems or treasury policies are intended to directly benefit government rather than industry although industries do benefit by applying defense research to nondefense areas (for example, application of military aircraft research to provide aircraft development).

32.   J. Leiper Freeman, *The Political Process* (New York: Random House, 1965).

33.   The Veterans Administration (VA) is an example of an agency that does use adjudicatory processes to determine if individuals are eligible for VA benefits. Unfortunately little is known about the impact of this agency's adjudications on veterans' policy.

34.   *U.S. Government Manual* (Washington, D.C.: U.S. Govern-ment Printing Office, 1976), p. 121.

35. Ernest Moore, *The Agricultural Research Service* (New York: Praeger, 1967).

36. James Hightower, *Hard Tomatoes, Hard Times* (Washington: Agribusiness Accountability Project, 1972).

37. Ibid.

38. Ibid. Sidney Baldwin, *Poverty and Politics* (Chapel Hill: University of North Carolina Press, 1968).

39. Theodore Lowi, *The End of Liberalism* (New York: Norton, 1969), pp. 102–103.

40. Weldon V. Barton, "Coalition-Building in the United States House of Representatives: Agriculture Legislation in 1973," in *Cases in Public Policymaking*, ed. James E. Anderson (New York: Praeger, 1976), pp. 141–161; Garth Youngberg, "U.S. Agriculture in the 1970s," in *Economic Regulatory Policies*, ed. James E. Anderson (Lexington, Mass.: D. C. Heath, 1976), pp. 51–68.

41. *Time*, October 17, 1977, p. 20. This nonenforcement came to light as a result of a law suit that demanded that the law be enforced. The decision of the court touched off a series of demonstrations by California farms protesting the law.

42. Herbert Kaufman, *The Forest Ranger* (Baltimore: The Johns Hopkins University Press, 1960).

43. Scott A. Harris, "Issue Politicization and Policy Change," paper presented at the Eighteenth Annual Meeting of the International Studies Association, St. Louis, Missouri, March 16–20, 1977.

44. Youngberg, "U.S. Agriculture"; Barton, "Coalition-Building."

45. The fastest growing federal agencies are newly created agencies or agencies whose function has recently increased in importance. Among the fastest growing agencies in the federal government in the early 1970s was the Environmental Protection Agency benefiting both from newness and concern about the environment. Energy related agencies are likely to be the fastest growing agencies in the near future if inflation declines enough so that the federal government's revenues are not outstripped by uncontrollable expenditures.

46. Lowi, "Four Systems of Policy."

47. Ibid., p. 300.

48. Harris, "Issue Politicization."

49. Ibid.

50. David H. Rosenbloom, "The Civil Service Commission's Decision to Authorize the Use of Goals and Timetables in the Federal Equal Em-

ployment Opportunity Program," *Western Political Quarterly* 26 (June, 1973), pp. 236–251.

51.   Ibid., p. 239.

52.   Ibid., p. 236.

53.   Harris, "Issue Politicization."

54.   Ibid.

55.   Joel Havemann, "Will the Players Accept Carter's Rules for the Federal Personnel Game?" *National Journal* 9 (October 29, 1977), pp. 1676–1682, at 1681.

56.   Adam Yarmolinsky, *The Military Establishment* (New York: Harper and Row, 1971).

57.   Defense bureaus may well receive no benefits from their clientele. With the exception of some veterans organizations and some ex-officers associations, most defense clientele are defense contractors. Since much of defense contracting is competitive at its early stages, most defense policies will have groups on both sides of the issue. Clientele support for specific weapons systems may be difficult to translate into more diffuse support for the agency.

58.   Harris, "Issue Politicization."

59.   Don K. Price, *The Scientific Estate* (Cambridge: Harvard University Press, 1965).

60.   Morris Janowitz, *The Professional Soldier* (New York: The Free Press of Glencoe, 1960); Phillip Agee, *Inside the Company* (London: Allen Lane, 1975); Patrick J. McGarvey, *CIA: The Myth and the Madness* (New York: Saturday Review Press, 1972).

CHAPTER FIVE

Administrative power is cause for concern because the exercise of administrative power differs little from the exercise of political power except that political power is often more open and subject to public view. Past scandals such as Teapot Dome and Watergate indicate that the people who occupy positions of power in American government are susceptible to corruption. We would be irrational to assume that the nation's bureaucrats are exempt from the same pressures that cause politicians to abuse the public trust. Our expectations of bureaucrats are not low; we expect effectiveness, efficiency, loyalty, innovation, responsiveness and countless other things from them; and the temptations to abuse our trust are high because bureaucracy exercises a great deal of discretion over the allocation of scarce societal resources. The prospect that administrative power can be abused must be considered.

ᕫ Two Standards for Bureaucracy ᕬ

In general the scholars seeking means to control bureaucracy set two standards for bureaucracy: responsiveness to public needs and competence in the performance of tasks.[1] Responsiveness as a criterion of administrative behavior raises many additional questions; the most basic is to whom should the bureaucracy be responsive? Bureaucracy can be responsive to the general public, to organized groups with an interest in the bureau, to the public affected by the bureau's administration, to political institutions and to the law. The first step in determining if a given bureaucratic action is responsive is defining the reference group.

Bureaucracy and the

Responsive administrative behavior can also be either passive or active. A bureau can be characterized as responsive if it responds to the demands of its environment; that is passive responsiveness. Many times, however, waiting for environmental pressures, especially where the environment is not organized, is counterproductive. In these cases responsiveness requires active anticipation of public problems and innovative, creative solutions even before demands have materialized.

Competence involves the bureau doing the best job that is technically feasible within the constraints placed on the organization (for instance, the Postal Service must deliver all mail, not just the mail easiest to deliver). Competence also involves active and passive elements. We expect that a bureau will not only use the best possible knowledge available when presented with problems (passive), but that it will also use its expertise and knowledge to forecast problems and develop the technology to deal with them while they are still small enough to be managed (active).

The expectations of competence and responsiveness may be jointly exhaustive, but they are not mutually exclusive. In practice, as opposed to the abstract, the values of competence and responsiveness often conflict. The current problems facing the US Postal Service concisely illustrate this conflict. We, as citizens and policymakers, expect that the Postal Service should be responsive to the wants and needs of those it services, the American public. Judging from the frequency of headlines devoted to rate increases and subsidies, the Postal Service is also assessed on the competence dimension, which, for simplicity, we will refer to in this instance

Public's Expectations

as delivering mail as cheaply or efficiently as possible. If efficiency were the only value that the Postal Service should maximize, nothing would be more efficient than if all marginal post offices were closed or consolidated with large regional centers. In addition, efficiency could be enhanced by eliminating door-to-door delivery, substituting instead delivery to a central location in a neighborhood and having the residents pick up their own mail at these centrally located boxes. Such ruthless efficiency would clearly conflict with the public's responsiveness and service desires (even if the price of postage could be halved). Responsiveness supports not only small nearby post offices but also door-to-door delivery six days a week.

Although competence and responsiveness are often conflicting values, we expect the bureaucracy to meet both values. This conflict of expectations may well lead to the perception of abuse of administrative power because the bureaucracy is expected to maximize values that are not always internally consistent. In short, much of what people cite as abuse of administrative power and much of what we will cite may well be the result of well-intentioned bureaucrats attempting to maximize a dearly held public value through actions that conflict with other expectations of bureaucracy.

This chapter attempts to specify with some precision what the American population and students of bureaucratic politics expect from administrative agencies. The goals of competence and responsiveness will be set within a variety of contexts to illustrate the variety of often conflicting demands made on the civil servant. Since our concern is with the exercise of administrative power in pursuit of these goals (competence and responsiveness), this chapter will also note by example the various ways that administrative power can be abused.

ᏋᎦ Dimensions of Bureaucratic Behavior ᎶᏋ

The first dimension of administrative behavior that is related to public expectations about bureaucracy is the generality of impact. Administrative behavior can establish general rules, as it does, for instance, when it deals with such questions as what constitutes an integrated school or what criteria should be used to determine if a television station is granted a license. When the impact of the behavior is on the general environment rather than on a single individual, the behavior is referred to as *policy-making*. Administrative behavior also consists of applying general policy to specific cases. Does Johnny Jones get bussed to River Oaks? Will WSYR continue to serve upstate New York for the next three years? When the impact of the administrative behavior is on a single individual (corporations may be treated as individuals), the behavior is referred to as *administration*.

Despite the division of bureau activities into policy and administration, this division does not mean to imply that one of these functions authoritatively allocates societal values and the other does not. Both policy and administration are political functions in that each entails discretion and each applies the coercive forces of government against the individual. At one time students of government believed that only Congress performed policy functions and only the bureaucracy performed administrative functions.[2] As Chapter 4 demonstrated, bureaus perform both policymaking and administrative activities. In practice, determining whether a given act of administrative behavior is policy or administration may be difficult since the two behaviors are extremes on a continuum. Making the distinction, however, will increase our understanding of the exercise of administrative power and the abuse of that power because public expectations differ depending on whether the behavior in question is policymaking or administration.

The second contextual dimension related to the public demand that bureaucracies pursue responsiveness and competence is the generality of the administrative behavior. The generality of administrative behavior is defined as the degree to which the behavior can be attributed to the bureau. Is the action accepted by most members of the bureau as the action of the bureau? If the behavior is accepted by most members of the bureau as bureau policy, then the behavior is the *bureau's behavior*. On the other hand, if the administrative behavior may be viewed solely as one person's action, the behavior is a *bureaucrat's behavior*. Some ambiguity exists on this dimension because bureaus do not act; only bureaucrats act; but the distinction is between whether the individual acts within the normal operating procedures of the bureau or whether the individual's actions are out of the ordinary. The generality of administrative behavior is important because our expectations for bureaus differ from our expectations for individual bureaucrats.

The two standards (responsiveness and competence) and the two dimensions can be combined into an eight-cell matrix. The remainder of this chapter will examine each cell of the matrix (see figure 5-1), noting within each cell the expectation concerning administrative action and the possible abuses of the standard proposed by that cell.

Responsiveness: Bureaus and Policy

When making policy with the goal of responsiveness in mind, bureaus should act as an open system, that is they should be sensitive to the environment and the demands that the environment places on the organization. Immediately the question is raised, to whom should the bureau be

RESPONSIVENESS   Generality of Impact

Generality of Behavior	Policy	Administration
Bureau	Sensitivity to Political Institutions and Public Demands, Rule of Law	Flexibility Openness to criticism
Bureaucrats	Responsiveness to Standards of Administrative Behavior—No Misconduct Ethics	Impartiality Fairness

COMPETENCE   Generality of Impact

Generality of Behavior	Policy	Administration
Bureau	Effectiveness	Timeliness
Bureaucrats	Efficiency	Reliability: Knowledgeable Consistency Predictability

FIGURE 5–1   Expectations of Bureau Behavior

sensitive when making policy? That question is difficult to resolve. First, and least controversial, bureaus should be sensitive to other political institutions when actively making policy. Sensitivity to other political institutions requires that the bureau respect the role other political institutions play in the policy process. Responsiveness to the president requires that a bureau recognize the president's position as formal head of the bureaucracy. As the legitimate leader of the bureaucracy, presidential intentions should be treated as orders rather than as obstacles to subvert. Responsiveness to Congress entails respect for the congressional role as policymaker. Since modern technology has required Congress to concentrate on general policy, responsiveness to Congress requires that a bureau comply with the intent of Congress rather than seeking loopholes. Given the closeness of contact between Congress and the bureaucracy, congressional intent is not difficult to discern. Finally, responsiveness to other political institutions includes recognition of the doctrine of supremacy of law. The behavior of civil servants is subject to legal restraints. A public office does not bestow on its occupant any special status in regard to overriding the law. In fact, the possession of an office of public trust requires that bureau actions should never violate criminal laws no matter what the reason for the action. Essentially, responsiveness to other political institutions requires that bureaucrats realize that bureaucracy was created as a subordinate institution designed to help political institutions perform their functions more adequately.

Journalists frequently report a bureau's failure to respect the role of other political institutions. Byron Pepitone vocally criticized then-President Ford's decision to turn his Selective Service System into a skeleton operation.[3] Pepitone's criticism came despite the president's role in setting national priorities and eliminating wasteful programs. The US Army recently reported juggling its books and failing to return to the US Treasury $150 million in savings that resulted from the withdrawal of troops from Vietnam. The army spent this money for other purposes without approval of Congress (in effect, reprogrammed the money, a function of Congress).[4] Recent reports of FBI activities in the early 1960s demonstrate a failure to respect law. The FBI not only engaged in wiretapping the conversations and sexual activities of civil rights leader Martin Luther King, Jr., but also sent a note to Dr. King implying that his only hope to retain respect was suicide.[5] In other activities the FBI attempted to provoke warfare between the Communist party of the United States and the Mafia, exceeding by great lengths any reasonable definition of the legal bounds of the agency.

Examples exist of agencies being too sensitive to occupants of political offices rather than to the more general rule of laws. For example, the IRS has often been charged with being too responsive to the man who occupies the presidency, by providing him with tax returns and audits, rather than being sensitive to the laws protecting an individual's right to privacy.[6] Responsiveness to political institutions and law means that the bureau should recognize that it is not the primary representative institution, that it was created to be subservient to both the president and the Congress, and that it should be responsive more to those institutions as institutions and to the Constitution and the law, rather than to the temporary occupants of the presidency and the Congress.[7]

Bureau policymaking behavior should also be responsive to the needs and demands of the general public. Assuming for a moment that the demands of the public with regard to administrative behavior could be unambiguously defined, the degree of responsiveness and the focus of the responsiveness is controversial. Ideally the administrative behavior ought to be responsive to the entire general public, but *the public* is an amorphous mass that never speaks with one voice and rarely makes unambiguous demands on the bureaucracy. In fact, two prominent political scientists feel that bureaus should not be responsive solely to the needs of interested parties, but should contrast those interests which are always present with the needs of all the people who are not represented in the administrative policy process.[8] Lester Salamon and Gary Walmsley argue that bureaus are without exception responsive but are responsive to narrow interests.[9] According to these scholars the Department of Agriculture is responsive only to the prosperous farmer; the Federal Communications Commission responds only to broadcasters; the Interstate Commerce Commission listens only to a portion of the transportation industry. This over-responsiveness to narrow interests allows the bureau and the represented interest to set policy without regard for the needs and preferences of the great majority.

Administrative agencies, therefore, may abuse power both by being unresponsive to the needs of the public affected by the agency or by being too responsive to a narrow range of interests. Recently both industry and labor unions charged that the Equal Employment Opportunity Commission was too responsive to the demands of minorities and not responsive enough to the counterdemands of industry and nonminority workers.[10] Then-President Gerald Ford argued that the Civil Aeronautics Board had ceased listening to broader public interests and responded only to the needs of the airlines, and as a result limited access to air routes, restricted competition, and artificially inflated prices, costing the public millions of dollars.[11] Scarcely a month goes by without some businessman reporting a horror story about the forms, red tape, and regulations of the Occupational Safety and Health Administration. Critics charge the agency with being unresponsive to the needs of small business and their need to compete in the market place.

To end on a more positive note, the past year has seen the Federal Trade Commission become more aggressive in pursuing the interests of the consumer versus egg producers, funeral directors, lawyers and doctors. This action has not occurred without strong protests from those industries. Therein lies a dilemma for public bureaucracy, responsiveness to any one interest will likely bring the protests of others. Given the conflicting demands placed on any public bureaucracy, the bureaucracy can never be responsive to all demands.

Responsiveness: Bureaucrats and Policy

The public also expects individual bureaucracies to be responsive when making public policy. Since the entire bureau is expected to be sensitive to the demands of the public and the affected interests, responsiveness on the individual level means responsiveness to acceptable standards of administrative behavior. In both behavior and appearance bureaucrats are expected to avoid misconduct; misconduct is defined as failing to obey all restrictions of law in public actions. Since a position of public trust includes expectations far greater than the norms of behavior expected of private sector bureaucracies, the public bureaucrat must abstain not only from actual misconduct but from the appearance of misconduct. Arthur Miller has argued that political alienation and cynicism have increased dramatically in the contemporary United States and that the increase is directly related to the activities of government.[12] If the nation's public servants are perceived as criminal or dishonest, whether or not they are, the public's distrust of government can only increase. The position of former President Richard Nixon that occasionally the president may act outside the law if the action is in the public interest has no place in the administrative service. The standards of personal behavior for the administrative elite can never be set too high.

Examples of unlawful behavior by federal civil servants are difficult to find perhaps because they are rarely reported, or more likely, as Robert Fried argues, the United States federal service is fairly incorruptible.[13] Some instances, however, do occur. In 1976 the Department of Justice charged that former Export-Import Bank head Henry Kearns sold stock worth less than $175,000 to a Japanese firm for $500,000. The firm conducted a great deal of business with the Export-Import Bank, and Kearns made 37 different decisions on the company's proposals. Although the Justice Department did not seek an indictment against Kearns, the appearance of bribery caused faith in the bank to waiver.[14] In a more clear cut case Charles R. McDonald, deputy director of the Federal Bureau of Drug Abuse Control for Baltimore, was convicted of conspiracy and distribution of heroin while a federal employee.[15] Finally, in 1972 agents of the federal Drug Enforcement Agency were charged with illegally breaking into homes without warrants (into the wrong homes for that matter), harrassing the occupants, and destroying property.[16]

Despite the greater and greater detail of state and federal codes, the law is far from an unambiguous thing. The responsiveness of individual administrative policy behavior to law includes a prohibition of actions that, while not strictly illegal, are of questionable propriety (unethical behavior, for instance). The most prominent example of such an action is when an official makes a decision that he or she stands to benefit from personally, or appears to benefit personally. In the mid-1970s 22 Department of Defense officials who oversaw defense contracting were officially reprimanded for allowing Northrop Corporation, a large defense contractor, to entertain them at a Delaware hunting lodge. The 22 officials made decisions that affected the future profits of Northrop though they themselves had nothing to gain.[17] In another instance Clarence D. Palmby, Assistant Secretary of Agriculture for International Affairs and Commodity Programs, in 1972 negotiated the generous credit terms that permitted the Soviets to purchase large quantities of grain from the United States. Three weeks later Palmby resigned to work for Continental Grain Company, a major grain exporter to the Soviets.[18] Although Palmby did nothing illegal, his actions created the appearance that he placed the interests of Continental above those of the nation.

Bureaucrats can behave unethically not only for personal gain but also to build the power base of an agency and, thus, make the bureaucrat's position more secure. J. Edgar Hoover gathered files on the sex and drinking habits of congressmen and their families. Hoover would then let the member of Congress know he held the information and would expect favorable treatment for the FBI. At his peak Hoover did not need to reveal he possessed any information; the thought that he might was sufficient for the FBI to benefit.[19]

The standards for individual behavior in the policymaking process while general and often vague are clearly high. As citizens we believe as did Thomas More that public officials were not placed in their positions for their own benefit but rather for our benefit. The decisions they make must, therefore, be responsive to legal rules and unwritten standards of conduct.

Responsiveness: Bureaus and Administration

When bureaus implement policy, responsiveness requires that the bureau be open to environmental pressures, but pressures much different from those in the policymaking process. In the implementation process bureaus must be flexible in dealing with problems. If the facts of a situation do not fit previously defined categories or if the citizen is an exception to normal rules, then the bureau should be flexible and make exceptions rather than rigidly, and possibly incorrectly, applying rules that are not appropriate. Another aspect of responsiveness in policy administration is openness to criticism directed at the agency. The ideal agency admits its mistakes willingly and alters the questioned behavior.[20] Whether the source of criticism is other political elites, the public that interacts with the agency, or the agency's own employees, the criticism and possible changes should be considered.

The 1975 Voting Rights Act and the Federal Trade Commission provide two examples, one negative and one positive, of bureau flexibility. Under the Voting Rights Act of 1975 the Civil Rights Division of the Department of Justice required that in any locality where a minority made up at least 5 percent of the voting-age population, the election ballot in that region must be printed in both English and the minority language. Since the law is the law and must be enforced, Elko County Nevada was required to print its election ballots in Paiute and Shoshone. Unfortunately for the state of Nevada neither of these languages has a written alphabet. The Justice Department later relented, permitting oral voting in this county. In another example of flexibility, the Federal Trade Commission, which requires that every garment sold contain a label with washing instructions, was persuaded by the arguments of Stardust Inc., manufacturers of string bikini panties, that the label which would be nearly as large as the garment itself would destroy the value of the product. The FTC granted Stardust an exception.[21]

Although agencies are normally responsive to clientele criticism because an unhappy clientele is a dangerous clientele, they are not as responsive to criticism by their own employees. A. Ernest Fitzgerald, a Department of Defense Cost analyst, repeatedly reported cost overruns on the Air Force C5A cargo plane and offered corrective recommendations. When internal warnings proved to no avail, Fitzgerald testified at a congressional hearing. Fitzgerald was rewarded for his criticism with a transfer to a bowling alley in Thailand and later dismissal from the agency.[22] Only strong congressional pressure forced his reinstatement. Another example concerns William C. Bush of NASA's Marshall Space Flight Center. After complaining publicly that he was underworked by the agency and could do more, Bush was demoted from GS14 to GS12 with a $10,000 cut in salary.[23]

The reaction of the Veterans Administration (VA) to the Vietnam veteran provides an example of both inflexibility and the failure to consider criticism. When Vietnam veterans returned to the United States, the VA was faced with drug and rehabilitation problems of a magnitude never encountered before. The problems did not respond to traditional treatment. When veterans' groups began openly and massively criticizing the agency, the VA responded by contending that no problems existed. Only after criticism became more vocal and some senators intervened did the VA leadership change; with the change the demands of the Vietnam veteran received more consideration.

Although the expectations concerning responsiveness of bureau administration appear simple, they may be the most difficult ones to meet. Asking that a bureau be flexible is asking that the bureau take a public chance rather than playing it safe behind standard operating procedures. Asking a bureau to be open to criticism is asking the bureau to occasionally admit it has failed. Admission of failure, rightly or wrongly, is perceived as a fundamental weakening of the bureau's power position.

Responsiveness: Bureaucrats and Administration

The responsiveness demands on bureaucrats' behavior when administering policy can be summed up in two words, impartiality and fairness. Bureaucrat-public interactions on administrative matters should be characterized by responsiveness to the American values of equity and procedural fairness. Bureaucrats should not show favoritism to any individual regardless of his or her political affiliation, political influence, wealth, friends, or relatives. All people appearing before the bureaucracy should receive equal treatment. This equal treatment, however, does not mean equally abusive treatment but rather treatment in accord with due process. Due process in administrative law requires at a minimum that an individual be given notice of a proceeding affecting him or her, the right to be heard in front of the agency, the right to hear and challenge any evidence against the individual, the right to a decision by an impartial arbitrator, and some limited right of appeal.[24]

If in the best of all possible worlds the bureaucracy treated all citizens in a spirit of equality and procedural fairness, criticism of bureaucrats' behavior by citizens would not cease. As Peter Blau and Marshall Meyer so effectively argue, people do not necessarily like impartial, albeit fair, treatment.[25] Blau and Meyer contend that much of what is derogatorily referred to as red tape is, in fact, procedural safeguards and impartial treatment. On the other hand, simply because a bureaucracy should be impartial does not mean it cannot be humane. Bureaus should facilitate public interaction by correcting petitioners' mistakes and guiding the person through the maze of procedures.

Since procedural fairness and equality are often confused with red tape, clear examples of bureaucrats abusing administrative power by being unfair or partial are scarce. In 1975 the US Civil Service Commission charged the Small Business Administration (SBA) with partiality in their personnel policies. SBA was charged with using political qualifications rather than merit in selecting at least four district managers. The SBA aggressively replaced civil servants with Republican politicians.[26] In a more substantive policy area, the *Washington Post* revealed that the Internal Revenue Service's tax audits varied a great deal in detail and severity. Among the more easily treated persons were Congressman Al Ullman, Chairman of the Ways and Means Committee which oversees the IRS. The *Post's* implication was that Representative Ullman received favorable treatment as a result of his position.[27] For examples of administrative agencies violating procedural safeguards in administering policy one need go no further than the loyalty and security cases of the 1950s. In a political climate fostered by Joe McCarthy's attacks on communism, many federal employees were charged with disloyalty and fired. These persons were often discharged without hearing the evidence against them, being able to confront their accuser, or being granted any other procedural safeguards.[28]

The problem with attempting to determine how well the American federal bureaucracy treats individuals is that one never knows if the reported cases are the full extent of the violations, the extent of the newsworthy cases, or the extent to which the bureaucracy is open to the news media.[29] Before progressing, a caveat is in order. If American bureaucracy were totally impartial and procedurally fair, this would not solve any of the other problems of responsiveness. Kenneth Davis, the foremost authority on administrative law, has frequently warned us that procedural fairness and substantive merit are totally independent dimensions.[30] For example, bureaucrats may set airplane fares to a city too low to permit airlines to operate at a profit. This decision could be reached even after granting the public and the airlines full procedural rights in a hearing. Even though a procedure is in full compliance with due process, a policy may be detrimental. The substantive value of a bureaucratic action must be assessed on its own merit.

Competence: Bureaus and Policy

Our expectations regarding the competence of a bureau's policymaking can be summed up in one word, effectiveness. Does the bureau achieve the policy objectives stated for it by other political decisionmakers? [31] The concern is with the stated objectives of other political elites, preferably those objectives stated in law not the manifest or latent objectives of the bureau. We are not concerned if the Interstate Commerce Commission is able to survive (the ICC's goal) but if it has promoted policies that achieve a healthy and competitive interstate commerce. We are concerned not with the Department of Energy's ability to expand the range of its functions but rather the extent to which it makes US energy policy more rational. The concept of effectiveness, when examined, requires not only performance but also innovation, both in the formulation of goals and in the methods used to achieve those goals. An agency cannot be considered effective if it efficiently pursues a goal no longer considered necessary. Agencies must adapt their goals to changing environments.

Ineffective administrative programs are usually considered major news stories. As part of former President Nixon's war on drug abuse, the Drug Enforcement Administration (DEA) was created to combat the drug problem. Two years later in 1975 White House sources privately admitted that DEA had failed.[32] In an attempt to dry up the supply of heroin, the DEA purchased the entire Turkish opium crop, but other areas in the world quickly supplied the demand. In the United States the agency's tactic of concentrating on arrests of small dealers failed to reveal major suppliers, the program's objective.

Since many federal programs involve several agencies, lack of interagency cooperation often hinders program effectiveness. Senator William Proxmire in 1976 publicly blamed the Comptroller of the Currency, the Federal Deposit Insurance Corporation and the Federal Reserve Board with failing to prevent bank failures. Proxmire attributed this failure to the lack of cooperation among the three agencies.[33] In a case dealing with the fundamental goal of an agency, a study of the US Marine Corps by the Brookings Institution argued that the USMC's traditional role of amphibious attack was no longer a needed function in America's defense arsenal. The Marine Corps, in short, failed to innovate and change its goals with the changing needs of the nation's defense.[34]

To prevent the reader from becoming overly skeptical about the effectiveness of bureaucracy, some favorable instances should be cited.[35] Although some effective performances are major news such as NASA landing a person on the moon, most examples of agency effectiveness are conspicuous by their lack of newsworthiness. The Social Security Administration, for example, successfully processes billions of checks every year; by implementing new safety procedures, the Federal Aviation Administration has virtually eliminated skyjacking in the United States.

Competence: Bureaucrats and Policy

When bureaucrats engage in policymaking, competence demands that their actions be efficient. Efficiency should not be confused with effectiveness since effectiveness concerns meeting goals and efficiency concerns the costs of programs. A program is efficient if it has the lowest cost/benefit ratio of all the feasible programs. Efficiency without regard for effectiveness, however, is a false economy. An efficient program that is not effective is still a waste of money. The objective is to achieve stated goals at the least possible cost. Since agencies must advocate their positions, the temptation not to consider efficiency is great. The Army Corps of Engineers has frequently been accused of authorizing special projects with low cost/benefit ratios (or adjusting the ratios) because those projects would have a great deal of local political support.[36]

Since administrative efficiency is a widely studied phenomenon, the wealth of examples comes as no surprise. First, in the Department of Defense, the home of cost/benefit analysis, and the air force, Congressman Aspin has noted several problems with the B1-bomber program. The air force required that the B1, the plane designed to replace the aging B52, be able to fly at supersonic speeds, which increased the cost of the plane by $6.4 billion. To perform its intended mission, bombing the Soviet Union, the B1 must fly low to avoid radar; but supersonic speeds are not possible at so low an altitude without destroying the plane. Excess specifications, therefore, added 30 percent to the cost of the B1.[37]

Second, as the result of inefficient procedures, some 43,000 ineligible families with incomes of $18,000 or more received USDA food stamps in 1975. Two months after this Treasury Report was revealed, the Department of Agriculture reported that it could not locate an additional $6.7 million in the food stamp program.[38] Third, the new Consumer Product Safety Commission sent 4 federal employees from Washington, D.C. to Hutchinson, Kansas, to inspect a mattress factory which employed two people and produced only 100 mattresses a year.[39] Clearly one inspector would have been sufficient. Finally, neither rain, nor snow, nor gloom of night prevents the US Postal Service from occasionally acting inefficiently. The service has run up greater and greater debts despite postal rate increases and consistently compares unfavorably with private competitors in terms of cost, speed, and breakage.[40] Recently the Postal Service revealed that it auctions all the debris left from packages that the parcel post people destroy. Unfortunately, the costs of storing the debris and conducting the auction exceeded the income from the auction.

Competence: Bureaus and Administration

When administering a policy, a bureau is expected to be timely in the disposition of cases; that is, it should act with all reasonable speed. One of the advantages of bureaucracy is that through specialization and routinization, it can deal with thousands of cases fairly quickly. In addition to the citizen's desire for speed, the bureau is well advised to process its cases quickly since timely action can contribute to the bureau's power base both by gaining pleased clientele support and by adding to its reputation for effectiveness.

A classic case of bureaucratic delay involves the Immigration and Naturalization Service (INS). Soviet Jews immigrating to the United States can be admitted under a "parole system" decision which takes five to six weeks. In 1974, however, the INS used a "conditional entry permit" system which took an average of seven months. The problem was that the costs of feeding and housing these refugees were paid for by the US Department of State at an additional cost of $1,700 per person.[41]

Because they handle large caseloads, few service agencies are immune from charges of delay. The Social Security Administration, normally an extremely well-run agency, hears disability cases for those persons who believe they qualify for disability pensions. Recent studies revealed that the agency took between 150 to 300 days to settle the average case and had a backlog of 105,000 cases. The problem was severe enough to motivate Congress to take action.[42] The Veterans Administration, as a result of using outdated equipment, admitted in February of 1976 that some 647,000 veterans' checks would be delayed. Although the delay would only be for a few days, with advance planning the delay might have been avoided.[43]

Competence: Bureaucrats and Administration

Competence when bureaucrats administer policy requires that the bureaucrats be reliable; reliability includes three specific criteria that bureaucratic behavior should meet. First, we expect that the bureaucrats should be knowledgeable, that they should know what they are doing. Second, the civil servant should act consistently from case to case and from time to time on the same case. Neither should a civil servant advise a citizen something will result if a given action is taken and then react differently when the action is taken. Third, bureaucratic behavior ought to be predictable. The petitioner of a bureau should know in advance that the case will be decided a specified way if certain standards are met.

Since each component of reliability is somewhat distinct, the ways each may be abused will be discussed separately. Regarding knowledge, the Internal Revenue Service provides assistance to taxpayers in filling out their tax returns. Since IRS agents are trained specifically for this function, knowledge is not an extraordinary expectation. An IRS internal audit of its agents, however, revealed that agents made mistakes on 24 percent of the cases where they gave advice. Two studies using cases with difficult and technical questions found errors in 55 percent and 80 percent of the cases.[44] This lack of knowledge by IRS agents would not be problematic if the IRS was bound by agents' advice, but unfortunately the individual taxpayer is liable for any mistakes made with IRS assistance.

The lack of confidence a citizen should have in an IRS agent's advice brings up the questions of consistency. In a real case that was finally decided against the agency by the Supreme Court (*FCIC* v. *Merrill* 332 U.S. 380), an Idaho farmer asked the Federal Crop Insurance Corporation if 400 acres of spring wheat reseeded on winter wheat could be insured by the corporation. The corporation agreed it could and insured the crop. When drought destroyed the crop, the farmer filed a claim. Checking its records, the corporation found that the crop had been reseeded; and since corporation regulations prevented recovery on reseeded crops, the claim was denied. The Supreme Court eventually reversed the agency's decision by denying the agency's claim that the farmer should have read the *Fed-*

eral Register which contained the regulations, but the court has upheld agency inconsistency in other cases (or refused to grant estoppel in legal terms, see *Moser* v. *United States* 341 U.S. 41).

Predictability of agency actions is important when people must make decisions now based on future agency decisions. Kenneth Culp Davis presents a hypothetical example based on several real cases concerning the Immigration and Naturalization Service.[45] An alien woman enters the United States and is later engaged to an American professional. INS regulations require two years' foreign residence by the American citizen before they will admit the spouse to immigrate to the United States, although they waive this if it provides a hardship. Since the couple must plan their marriage, they must consider the possibility that the woman will not be granted immigrant status. The question is, will two years' residence in a foreign country with the loss of income it entails be a "hardship" permitting an exception to be made in this case? The INS, according to Davis, refuses to give out information on the way they will decide this case or have decided similar cases in the past; they advise the couple to apply and take their chances. The lack of predictability offers the couple little certainty.

⟱ Summary ⟱

Our expectations concerning the performance of American bureaucracy are not modest. No political institution in the world, and the US federal bureaucracy is no exception, can meet all the expectations outlined in this chapter. In a small nation with strong political institutions, a well trained civil service, and few governmental functions, the bureaucracy might be able to attain most of these goals; but in the United States where the bureaucracy must deal with thousands of problems daily each somewhat unique, the bureaucracy is doomed to occasionally fail.

One reason why the US bureaucracy cannot meet all our expectations is that the expectations often conflict. Effectiveness sometimes conflicts with responsiveness to political institutions. The US Army in Vietnam, for example, could have effectively "ended" the conflict in Vietnam if all restrictions on the use of weapons and manpower were removed. Through a massive invasion of the North along with nuclear weapons, the Army could have destroyed North Vietnam. This tactic, however, would have generated some political costs that the US public and its elected representatives did not wish to bear. In this situation responsiveness took precedence over one definition of effectiveness.

Bureaucratic procedure can also be consistent and predictable but not fair. The Immigration and Naturalization Service's procedures on resident aliens who leave the country and wish to return are consistent and predictable but sometimes not fair to the individuals involved. If a resident alien voluntarily leaves the United States, the INS can prevent the individual on his or her return from entering the United States. INS can deny entry without a hearing or informing the alien why entry is denied. The procedures are consistent, predictable and well within the law; but occasionally an individual who has resided peacefully in the United States for several years will be refused reentry without an opportunity to discover why.[46]

Public administrators often feel the conflict between the goals of flexibility and timeliness. In the Social Security Administration's disability program, Congress publicly favors quick response to disability claims. Unfortunately, the disability claimants also want SSA to be flexible and to consider individual circumstances. If SSA set up rigid uniform procedures for judging disabilities, decisions would be more timely but only at the cost of decreased flexibility.

Efficiency may also conflict with openness to criticism. Efficient treatment in Veterans Administration hospitals might require the hospitals to adopt certain procedures that treat the patients as units to be processed rather than as individual patients. Such a system would be more efficient if it were not open to criticism. If a patient processing system responded to criticism, its efficiency would suffer. As agencies respond to criticism, they must often take time away from their normal functions. If the criticisms do not indicate how to make agency procedures more efficient, then responsiveness to criticism will lead to decreased efficiency.

The above are only four of the possible conflicts in the expectations of bureaucracy. Clearly all eight cells in the responsiveness-competence matrix (figure 5–1) can conflict with each other under certain circumstances. In fact, some of the individual cells contain items that are not always internally consistent. The examples presented only scratch the surface of the possible conflicts among the different expectations of bureaucracy.

Given the conflict in expectations, an interesting question is how agencies resolve the conflicting demands. Although studies of bureaucracy have not addressed this question, we can hypothesize about the ways bureaus would resolve this conflict if we accept the assumption that bureaus are rational power-seeking organizations. Such a bureau would resolve the conflicting expectations by responding in a manner that would have the greatest impact on the bureau's power base. For example, the Army Corps of Engineers is more than willing to sacrifice efficiency to congressional responsiveness. The Army Corps' major source of influence is its close congressional ties, which have developed as a result of its projects in members' districts. Since the Army Corps' power base would be improved by building more dams and other projects rather than less, it would rationally emphasize responsiveness to political institutions over efficiency, even if this strategy entailed building a few dams that were not justified on a cost/benefit basis.

Another agency might choose efficiency rather than responsiveness. The Bureau of Public Debt in the Treasury Department, for example, could be more responsive to banks and other financial institutions by borrowing money at interest rates higher than necessary. This tactic would be less than rational for the Bureau of Public Debt, however, since its influence is based on its reputation for efficient program operations. The Bureau of Public Debt in this situation would likely maximize efficiency at the expense of responsiveness.

Knowing the power base of a bureau, then, will increase our ability to predict how a bureau will resolve conflicting expectations. From a systemic perspective, however, bureaus should not be permitted to respond to some expectations and not to others, especially if the bureau can decide which expectations are important. The nation needs a bureaucracy, particularly a bureaucracy exercising political power, to meet as many expectations as possible. To achieve such a bureaucracy, a system of checks and balances must be designed to generate the greatest possible responsiveness and competence. The following two chapters lay the foundation for such a system by analyzing the various means available to control bureaucracy.

⤜ Notes ⤛

1.   In general, the "public expectations" discussed in this chapter are those noted by scholars not by public opinion instruments. The responsiveness/competence distinction was first made to my knowledge by Carl Friedrich when he argued that bureaucracy ought to be subject to public opinion and the best scientific knowledge available to the bureaucrat. Other scholars suggest other values. Francis Rourke proposes openness and effectiveness as the key criteria; Robert Fried suggests liberalism, effectiveness, and responsiveness. The present distinction especially when fit within the framework of figure 5–1 should cover all the suggestions of the other authors (Gilbert, for example, suggests twelve values we expect bureaucracy to maximize). The concept of law which is Fried's definition of liberty should be noted since it seems not to fit within the typologies presented here. Law underlies most of the other values we wish bureaucracy to maximize because law is a series of constraints on the actions of bureaucracy. We expect a bureaucracy, therefore, to be responsive within the restraints of law and expect it to be efficient also within those restraints.

2.   The argument that all government could be divided into two functions was first presented by Woodrow Wilson in 1887. Wilson's ideals were expanded by Frank Goodnow in his classic *Politics and Administration*

(New York: MacMillan, 1900). The argument presented here follows that of Martin Landau, "Political Science and Public Administration," in Martin Landau, *Political Theory and Political Science* (New York: MacMillan, 1972), pp. 177–210. If the definitions of policy and administration are too narrow for the reader, they should be interpreted as stipulative definitions rather than as descriptions of policy and administration.

      3.   "Draft Head Hits Funds Cut," *Houston Post* (January 22, 1976).

      4.   "Army Admits Spending Money without OK," *Houston Post* (October 23, 1975).

      5.   See "The Crusade to Topple King," *Newsweek* (December 1, 1975), pp. 11–12.

      6.   Carl T. Rowan, "IRS Needs to be Abuse Proof," *Houston Post* (October 8, 1975), p. 2c.

      7.   The reader will note that none of these prescriptions is easy to meet. Resisting the influence of the president is at times a blessing and at other times an abuse of power. A bureau without strong clientele support will have great difficulty resisting presidential and congressional requests that require unethical actions.

      8.   Avery Leiserson and Fritz Morstein Marx, "The Formulation of Administrative Policy," in *Elements of Public Administration*, ed. Fritz Morstein Marx (New York: Harper and Row, 1959), pp. 337–351.

      9.   Lester M. Salamon and Gary L. Walmsley, "The Federal Bureaucracy—Responsive to Whom?" (Paper presented at the 1975 annual meeting of the Midwest Political Science Association, Chicago, May 1–3, 1975).

      10.   Jim Asker, "Federal Attempts to Halt Job Discrimination Have Failed, EEOC Chief Says," *Houston Post* (December 19, 1975), p. 6b.

      11.   "Ford Asks Greater Airline Competition," *Houston Post* (October 9, 1975).

      12.   Arthur H. Miller, "Political Issues and Trust in Government," *American Political Science Review* 58 (September, 1974), pp. 951–972.

      13.   Robert Fried, *Performance in American Bureaucracy* (Boston: Little, Brown, 1976); see also Arnold Heidonheimer, *Political Corruption* (New York: Holt, Reinhart, and Winston, 1970).

      14.   "Profit in Office Claimed Made by Nixon Official," *Houston Post* (October 15, 1975).

      15.   "Ex-U.S. Drug Official Indicted," *Houston Post* (December 4, 1975).

      16.   The Bureau of Drug Abuse Control and the Drug Enforcement Administration are the same agency. Often as Harold Seidman, *Politics, Position*

and Power (New York: Oxford University Press, 1976) points out, the names of bureaus are changed to give the impression that the bureau has changed and is pursuing new policy. The drug control programs of the Department of Justice underwent a series of name changes in an unsuccessful effort to combat the nation's drug problems.

17. "22 Defense Employees Admonished," *Houston Post* (November 12, 1975), p. 12a.

18. William J. Lanovette, "The Revolving Door—It's Tricky to Try to Stop It," *National Journal* 9 (November 19, 1977), p. 1799.

19. Peter Goldman and Anthony Marro, "J. Edgar Hoover's Secret Files," *Newsweek* (March 10, 1975), p. 16.

20. An agency will not necessarily admit mistakes out of altruism but as a rational process. Observation indicates often that admission of failure often does more to quiet criticism and does less to harm the agency than denying the accusation which is later revealed to be correct. The rational agency will often attempt to cut its losses and regain support by admitting mistakes.

21. "FTC Strings Along Garment," *Houston Post* (November 27, 1975).

22. The Fitzgerald case is discussed in detail in Ralph Nader et al., *Whistle Blowing* (New York: Grossman, 1972), pp. 39–54.

23. "Underworked for Less," *Houston Post* (November 28, 1975).

24. The due process required varies with the type of agency. Where the agency deals in denials of liberty, property, or life, the procedural rights should be all encompassing. When the question of general policy is considered that affects the individual only indirectly, the procedural limitations are substantially less.

25. Peter M. Blau and Marshall W. Meyer, *Bureaucracy in Modern Society* (New York: Random House, 1971).

26. Douglas Watson, "SBA Found Violating No Politics Regulation," *Washington Post* (April 13, 1975), p. A9.

27. "Tax Favoritism for Rep. Ullman Denied by IRS," *Houston Post* (February 3, 1976).

28. See Kenneth Culp Davis, *Administrative Law* (St. Paul: West Publishing Co., 1965).

29. Robert Fried, *Performance in American Bureaucracy* (Boston: Little, Brown, 1976).

30. Davis, *Administrative Law.*

31. Unfortunately the policy objectives of other decisionmakers may not be clear. Programs may not have clear objectives because members of Congress cannot agree on objectives but do agree on the need for a program.

32.   Nicholas M. Horrock, "Drug Agency Has Failed to Stop Drugs," *New York Times* (May 26, 1975), p. 3.

33.   "Proxmire Blames Agencies for Possible Bank Failures," *Houston Post* (January 15, 1976).

34.   "Institute Says Marines Out of Step with Times," *Houston Post* (February 2, 1976), p. 19a.

35.   Again we have little evidence as to the effectiveness of American bureaucracy in general. The media present enough unfavorable instances to not accord bureaucracy a perfect rating. On the other hand, effective performance on a continuing basis is rarely publicized.

36.   Louis Kohlmeier, *The Regulators* (New York: Harper and Row, 1969).

37.   "U.S. Wasted Money on B1 Says Aspin," *Houston Post* (January 4, 1976).

38.   "Some Got Food Stamps Despite Pay Over $18,000," *Houston Post* (October 25, 1975).

39.   "Federal Travel Curbs Planned," *Houston Post* (December 4, 1975).

40.   David Boorstin, "Postal Re-evaluation," *Houston Post* (December 13, 1975), p. 2c.

41.   Susan Jacoby, "Long Wait, High Costs," *Washington Post* (March 2, 1975), p. B4.

42.   "Social Security Speed Bill Pushed," *Houston Post* (November 19, 1975), p. 14a.

43.   "Veteran Checks Delayed," *Houston Post* (February 7, 1976).

44.   "IRS Taxpayer Help Admitted Failure," *Houston Post* (December 16, 1975).

45.   Kenneth Culp Davis, *Administrative Law* (St. Paul: West Publishing Co., 1965).

46.   Ibid.

CHAPTER SIX

The exercise of administrative power is a growing problem for American democracy. The full force of legitimate government power is being exercised by a group of nonelected bureaucrats who, for the most part, are hidden from public view. Administrative power has increased concomitant with the increased intervention of government into people's personal lives. The questions remain—can bureaucracy be controlled by the people it is meant to serve? Can bureaucracy be made responsive to public demands and desires? [1] This chapter and the next will examine the various methods proposed to control bureau power and evaluate each method's likelihood of success.

ᕫᔓ Overhead Democracy ᕫᔓ

The most frequently proposed method of controlling bureaucracy is making bureaucracy subordinate to the will of elected public officials; a series of mechanisms described by Emmette Redford as overhead democracy.[2] Overhead democracy was originally presented as a means of controlling bureaucracy by Woodrow Wilson twenty-five years before his election as President.[3] Wilson and many later followers believed that government could be divided into politics and administration. Politics concerned establishing

Controlling

External Checks by

public policy, and administration dealt only with implementing public policy decisions. Because the political branch of government (in Wilson's view Congress) was in charge of politics and policymaking, the bureaucracy should limit its concerns to administration. The dichotomy between politics and administration quite naturally led to the prescription that the bureaucracy should be subordinate to the will of the politicians. Although most students of bureaucracy now reject the politics-administration dichotomy as a false description of reality, overhead democracy as a control on bureaucracy has widespread support.[4]

Overhead democracy as a control mechanism is divisible into two distinct stages. The first stage requires popular control over elected officials through the sanction of elections. Voters must rationally select candidates who support the same policies that they do and must punish retroactively candidates who fail to fulfill their desires or who do not act consistently with their campaign promises. The second stage, which is the main concern of this chapter, requires that elected officials control bureaucrats through one of the many means they have at their disposal. Some people feel the most effective means of control is hierarchical control by the president; others favor congressional control over bureaucracy via budgets, oversight and casework. Many people believe that supremacy of law and

Bureaucracy:
Political Institutions

the right of disaffected persons to appeal administrative wrongs to the courts for redress is the major check on bureaucracy. Still others place little faith in current institutions and advocate the independent office of the ombudsman to prevent administrative abuse of power.

Popular Control of Elected Officials

The first step in the overhead democracy model is popular control over public officials. Clearly this step is the *sine qua non* of overhead democracy's controls on administration. How well politicians can exact compliance from the bureaucracy is an academic question if citizens are not able to first control the politicians. In this post-Watergate era we can imagine the danger if politicians controlled the bureaucracy and the people did not control their elected officials.[5]

Early studies of voting behavior attempted to determine if Americans were rational voters capable of controlling the actions of elected officials. To control public officials, most students of voting agree that voters, at a minimum, need to have some policy issues that concern them, know the candidates' positions on these issues, and vote for the candidate whose positions resemble their own. In 1948 a group of sociologists from Columbia University in a classic study of Elmira, New York, found the average voter had little knowledge of the electoral process and usually rationalized his perceptions of the political process to coincide with his candidate preference.[6] Berelson, Lazarsfeld, and McPhee concluded that the average voter was sadly lacking the qualities necessary to control elected officials.

In a major study of the 1952 and 1956 elections, Angus Campbell and others found a similar average voter with "sheer ignorance of the existence of major social and economic problems."[7] If the voter did not know the important issues in the election, he could hardly be expected to rationally select candidates, and without rational selection the process of control breaks down. Other members of the same research team studying the 1968 election admitted that some voters actually responded on the basis of issues but that these responses were far fewer than nonpolicy responses to politics.

Since the above findings dominated the study of electoral politics until the 1970s, many scholars quite logically concluded that overhead democracy lacked the initial control mechanism and, therefore, would be ineffective in insuring administrative responsiveness. This conclusion is premature especially in light of more recent evidence on voting behavior. The Campbell and Berelson studies were both conducted during the post-

New Deal era when politics was candidate-image oriented. Candidates campaigned on such "issues" as "I Like Ike" and "I Adore Adlai," hardly the type of issue demanded of a political process where elections worked as a control device. When issue positions are not presented by the candidates during the campaign, voters have difficulty reaching a rational control-oriented decision.

Beginning with the 1964 Johnson-Goldwater election, American presidential politics became more issue centered. Studies conducted since 1964 qualified some of the early findings and dispelled even more. In a study of the 1964 presidential election in Hawaii, Michael Shapiro was able to relate 85 percent of the voters' choices to issues they felt were important in the campaign.[8] Redefining the question somewhat, two other political scientists argued that issue voting was fairly common but only on the one or two issues that the respondent cared about.[9] When voter information and rationality were assessed on *issues that voters felt were salient,* voters were well informed and selected candidates according to their own political preferences.[10]

To explain the discrepancy in these findings, Gerald Pomper examined all the presidential elections from 1952 to 1968. He found that issues were more important in 1964 and 1968 than they were in the earlier elections. More important for our purposes Pomper found that during campaigns that presented issue positions, citizens became more aware of issues and acted on the basis of those issues to select candidates. Although the 1972 election was not covered by Pomper's study, it also was an election with one candidate raising several issues including amnesty, defense spending, new approaches to foreign policy, welfare reform, and countless others.

A series of articles by a Syracuse University research team addressing the question of issue voting in the 1972 election supported the Pomper findings.[11] They found that voters were well informed on eleven issues presented by the candidates via the mass media. The voters were able to accurately perceive differences between George McGovern and Richard Nixon; both candidates' policy positions were clear to the voters. On those issues the voters felt were important, they selected the candidate with positions similar to their own. The most important finding of this research is that the voters actually held their own issue positions before they selected their vote choice. The relationship between issues and the vote was clearly not one of *post hoc* rationalizing by changing one's issue positions to conform to the selected candidate's position.

The evidence regarding the voter's ability to rationally select a candidate and, thus, control the policy preferences of elected officials is clear. Electoral politics has changed significantly in the past thirty years. Despite the flurry of books denouncing media politics, image-oriented politics has declined with the increase in appeals to voters on the basis of issues.[12] As a result the voters are better able to judge the actions a candidate will take after the election. The increased ability to judge translates into an increased ability to control elected officials with the ballot. Some evidence now exists that the issue campaigns of the sixties and seventies have conditioned voters to demand that candidates run on issues. Jimmy Carter initially captured the Democratic nomination for president on an image and style campaign. In response to pressure from other candidates and polls showing that people believed he was fuzzy on the issues, Carter began to present position papers and stress some traditionally Democratic issues. At the present time at the presidential level, studies of voting behavior indicate voters have the ability to rationally choose between candidates.

Do Politicians Act on Their Promises?

The second linkage in the overhead democracy model concerns the ability of politicians once elected to fulfill their commitments. Many students of bureaucracy believe that the elected officials are restrained in the implementation of electoral promises because policy problems change after the election or because the elected official cannot induce other politicians and bureaucrats to accept the official's position.[13] The scholars, however, needlessly confuse the issue by addressing the wrong question. The initial question is not do electoral promises become public policy because this implies politicians can control bureau policymaking, but whether or not elected officials act consistently with their electoral pledges.

Even the most casual observer of American politics can cite examples of a politician changing his policy positions after being elected. President Lyndon Johnson was criticized for running as the peace candidate in 1964 and then proceeding to implement much of Senator Goldwater's Vietnam position. President Richard Nixon made several promises during the 1972 election campaign to root out corruption in his administration wherever he found it and later was implicated in the Watergate coverup. One problem with citing examples to demonstrate whether or not elected officials try to redeem their campaign promises is that the analyst is never sure if the cases are exceptions or the rule. For example, in 1964 President Johnson also pledged his effort to enact health insurance for the aged, and he was instrumental in the passage of medicare. In 1972 President Nixon vowed that he would not grant amnesty to draft evaders and deserters from the Vietnam War, after the election Nixon upheld this promise. Expecting an elected official to be bound by *all* campaign statements in the face of changing circumstances and information is needlessly handicapping elected officials. The electorate would be more secure if the politician upheld most of his campaign promises and adapted others to changing circumstances than if the politician pursued ill-conceived alternatives merely because they were campaign pledges.

Several studies have systematically examined campaign promises; these studies indicate that an elected official will attempt to redeem campaign promises. John Sullivan and Robert O'Connor examined the election promises made by congressional candidates concerning the Vietnam War and other issues in 1966.[14] Where highly salient issues such as the war were involved, people elected to Congress generally behaved consistent with their preelection statements. Sullivan and O'Connor argued the linkage between the public and the politicians was fairly strong.

In two separate examinations of national party platforms, one by John Bradley on social security issues and one by Gerald Pomper on all campaign promises, presidential candidates acted on 85 percent of the promises listed in the platform.[15] This percentage is especially impressive because platforms are often used as campaign devices to attract support and may or may not be supported by the party nominee. The empirical evidence, then, indicates that politicians do attempt to implement campaign promises after taking office. Promise and performance may differ because circumstances dictate different policy or because other political actors prevent implementation, but we are not so cynical as to believe that campaign statements are mere rhetoric. In fact, judging from the intensity of platform disputes, politicians must consider platform statements as real policy commitments.

Based on the evidence presented thus far, we can assume that under the conditions where candidates run on issues people have a mechanism to control the actions of elected officials. We can also assume that politicians act consistently with the promises they make to gain office. We must now examine the resources elected officials have to control the actions of bureaucrats to make them responsive to public demands. The remainder of this chapter will examine control of bureaucratic power by four institutions: the legislature, the judiciary, the executive, and the ombudsman.

⤴ Legislative Controls on Bureaucratic Power ⤴

Congressional control of bureaucracy was one of the first proposals for checking bureaucratic abuse of power. Since Congress was created as the nation's representative institution, congressional controls were a means to insure that the bureaucracy was responsive to the American people. The role of Congress in controlling bureaucracy also followed logically from

Woodrow Wilson's dichotomy of politics and administration and his designation of Congress as *the* political branch of government. Political supremacy in Wilson's view meant congressional supremacy.

V. O. Key outlines five ways the legislature can serve as a check on administration actions.[16] First, the legislature can pass legislation determining the extent of governmental activities, setting limits on bureau actions, describing procedures, establishing limits of authority and delimiting tasks and responsibility.[17] Second, Congress has control over fiscal and personnel resources through the appropriations process. Although an agency can spend less than is appropriated, the agency will find it difficult to operate without resources if Congress decides to deny them. Congress in some instances has gone so far as to deny all funds to an agency, thus eliminating the agency. The Subversive Activities Control Board and the Area Redevelopment Administration are two recent examples of agencies terminated because Congress refused to fund them.[18] Third, Congress can use the legislative veto to control administrative action. Under the legislative veto, Congress will authorize an agency to set policy in a given area. All regulations issued or decisions made must then be submitted to Congress for approval, by either one house, both houses, or a single committee.

The first three methods of controlling bureaucracy all contain sanctions that can be invoked against the bureaucracy. The final two methods are used to gather information, but they are always backed up by the possibility of the other three congressional sanctions. The fourth way the legislature serves as a check on bureaucracy is through its oversight functions. Congress can review bureaucratic actions, uncovering in the process information useful to the lawmaking or appropriations process.[19] Finally, informal means exist that allow a legislator to exert some influence on the bureaucracy. Constituents request congressional assistance in dealing with the bureaucracy; this casework is the prime way a legislator informally intervenes in the administrative process in an effort to alter the outcome.

Legislation

The use of legislation to control administrative action has received much theoretical attention but very little empirical analysis on its effectiveness as a check on bureaucracy. To be sure many, though by no means all, agencies have their origin in legislation and their duties delimited by law.[20] Congressional legislation forms broad boundaries beyond which bureaus cannot go. According to one observer Congress must receive the credit for establishing Social Security disability insurance, pension reform, air pollution controls, food programs for the poor, and many other program initiations.[21] Although bureaus can influence the size and direction of these programs, the decision whether or not to have such a program rests with Congress.

Legislation also has been used to reverse administration policy and organizational decisions. For example, when pressured by tobacco producing interests, Congress prevented the Federal Trade Commission from requiring a health warning on cigarette packages and from prohibiting cigarette advertising.[22] Later Congress relented on both issues. Congress' interest in bureaus' organizational activities is highlighted by the Manpower Administration's reorganization of 1965.[23] The Manpower Administration attempted to decentralize its operations and grant field installation more autonomy. Congress noted its displeasure with the reorganization during hearings and did not need to go as far as legislation to reverse the decision.[24]

Not all legislative attempts to control the bureaucracy via legislation are successful, however. Joseph Harris provides a case study of Congress' attempt to limit the number of permanent employees during the Korean War to prevent bureaucratic expansion.[25] The Whitten Amendment set personnel ceilings and allowed promotions only after a person had spent at least one year in grade. Bureaus affected by the amendment appealed to their friends in Congress to exempt them from the requirement. Agencies that were denied exemptions demonstrated a great deal of ingenuity in their ability to follow the letter but not the spirit of the law. Harris concludes that the Whitten Amendment did not prevent bureaucratic expansion. Even if the amendment were successful, Harris contends that administration would have been hampered by limiting agency flexibility and thus preventing the agency from attracting qualified personnel.

Although the case studies demonstrate both instances of success and instances of failure for legislation as a control on bureaucracy, legislation has some inherent limitations preventing it from being an effective check on bureaucratic power. First, legislation by definition is general and devoid of detail. Even the *United States Tax Code*, possibly the most detailed law the nation has filling eleven hundred pages, is so vague that the Internal Revenue Service must issue an additional six thousand pages of regulations interpreting the law.[26] Second, laws are often blunt instruments. While Congress would like more influence in the administrative process, it does not wish to unnecessarily hamper effective administration. According to M. W. Kirst Congress relies on nonstatutory means of control such as suggesting changes during hearings, putting congressional recommendations in committee reports, and urging action in conference reports.[27] Third, legislation is often more effective in preventing action than in initiating a policy. Positive actions provide more opportunities for bureaus to influence the policy because they usually require nonspecific, discretionary changes in agency behavior. Prohibitions, on the other hand, can often name the specific behavior that is prohibited. Finally, a problem related to all three previous limitations is the size of Congress. Congress is too small and too unspecialized to effectively control the bureaucracy through the legislative process. Although Congress has bureaucraticized by adding personnel and specialized staff, the other political duties of members of Congress mean they cannot always be watching the bureaucracy.[28] For example, Congress has perhaps forty staff members specializing in agriculture divided among four committees. Forty people, usually trained as lawyers, are simply no match for the hundreds of experts the Department of Agriculture can marshall on most issues.

Budgeting

An objective scholar interested in maintaining political control over administration would probably design a process similar to the appropriations process. In the appropriations process the elected officials have a clear sanction to apply against administrators who disregard congressional intent; they can withdraw the resources that the administrator needs to conduct programs. Budgeting's advantage over legislation is that it has periodicity; Congress is required to annually scrutinize administrative budgets and programs. The decision to use the sanction, therefore, occurs at frequent intervals and is an accepted means of exercising control.

Empirical analyses of budgeting, however, have revealed that the budget is not as potent a weapon as it appears to be. Most studies of congressional budgeting find that the budgetary process does not examine policy issues but proceeds incrementally.[29] Past budget decisions are considered final. An agency, therefore, asks for a given percentage more than it received last year, and the appropriations committee examines only the difference between this year's budget and last year's budget. Although some agencies raise congressional ire and find their entire budget reevaluated, most can assume that last year's base is safe.[30]

Incremental budgeting usually means that budgets are concerned with percentages rather than programs. Arnold Kanter, in a study of the Defense Department appropriations, found an exception.[31] Rather than being concerned with personnel or funding increments, the defense subcommittees centered their decision time on either research and development projects or on procurement. In this manner the committee could affect defense policy. Unfortunately for any control mechanisms, the committees were more concerned with rewarding the individual services and penalizing the office of the secretary of defense than in carefully examining programs.[32]

With the executive budget and the flow of political power from the Congress to the president, congressional budgeting has become even less influential. The congressional Budget and Impoundment Control Act of 1974 was a rather frank admission that Congress had lost much of its budget powers to the president. The solutions in the legislation, however, actually strengthen the bureaucracy because presidential powers (impoundment) not bureaucratic powers were the target. Congress has become increasingly bold in recent years using its budget powers to check the president (by cutting off funds to bomb Cambodia and cutting off military aid to Turkey). In this struggle Congress often sees the bureaus as willing allies in their war with the president. Congress always provides a sympathetic ear to the National Institutes of Health, the Rural Development Service and other agencies whose funds the president cuts. The congressional budget process, as a result, is in danger of becoming an appeals process whereby Congress acts to restore presidential budget cuts rather than examining the budget programmatically. In short, while the budget process appears to have potential to check the expansion of bureau power, the evidence indicates that it is not being used.

Legislative Veto

Congress has increased its use of the legislative veto in an attempt to regain some influence over the bureaucracy. Under the procedures of the legislative veto, Congress authorizes a bureau to take certain actions (such as allocating oil supplies). When the bureau exercises its authority under the legislative grant it must inform Congress and send the proposed action to Congress. Congress, then, within a specified period of time can veto the administrative action.[33] Recently the use of the legislative veto has increased with veto provisions in the War Powers Act, the Campaign Reform Act, the impoundment sections of the Budget Reform Act, as well as in minor legislation, such as HEW sex discrimination regulations and GSA regulations concerning presidential papers. The Congressional Research Service revealed in 1976 that the veto was in 196 different pieces of legislation, 89 of which were passed since 1970.[34]

The increased use of the legislative veto by Congress may well be an admission of Congress' own failure to maintain control of the policymaking process. First, the veto relegates Congress to a negative role in checking administrative policymaking. Congress in a sense admits that it cannot positively command action through legislation, so it must command others to initiate and respond to the initiatives. A negative role reduces the options Congress has to control bureau policymaking since it is restricted to the options the bureaucracy proposes.

Second, increased use of the legislative veto sanctions the decay of the legislative process. Theodore Lowi argues that legislation has ceased to be legislation and has become instead grants of authority to administrators.[35] With the legislative veto Congress can be even more vague, assured that it can meddle in administrative matters at its leisure. Increased use of the veto causes congressional policy to lose its coherence because vetoes narrow the perspective of Congress to the single question involved rather than broader questions of policy. As a result congressional vetoes may well hinder effective policymaking as they did for the first Federal Elections Commission.

Third, the number of items submitted to Congress under veto provisions may exceed its capacities. If veto provisions are in 196 pieces of legislation, then 196 sets of actions will be presented to Congress to consider. Because Congress can consider only a limited amount of legislation every year, the increased use of the veto may overload the capacities of Congress and reduce the performance of Congress in other areas.

Oversight

Investigation/oversight is a congressional information-gathering function. The Legislative Reorganization Act of 1946 requires that the House and Senate Government Operations Committees oversee all government activities, reorganizations, and intergovernmental relationships. Other congressional committees also perform oversight during legislative or appropriations hearings. The potential volume of congressional oversight, as a result, is massive.

The oversight process is fairly simple; a congressional committee investigates a bureau or policy by holding hearings, conducting staff evaluations, or requesting audits by the General Accounting Office or other staff units. The General Accounting Office is especially active in conducting oversight studies, completing between fifty and one hundred studies a month.

Although oversight itself may be a sanction because administrators seek to avoid painful congressional hearings, usually oversight is the initial step in invoking one of the other three sanctions of Congress. Most oversight, as a result, blends into legislation, budgeting, or the veto process so that it cannot easily be distinguished as oversight.

The oversight function of Congress has been documented in three excellent case studies of the process.[36] In the early 1950s a Republican Congress, dissatisfied with the prolabor performance of the National Labor Relations Board (NLRB), held a series of hearings detailing areas where they felt the NLRB had failed to be neutral.[37] The hearings created pressure on then-President Eisenhower to appoint more conservative and business oriented members to the NLRB. The resulting changes in labor regulation were more congruent with the sentiments of the Republican members of Congress and the interests they represented.

In his study of the congressional elimination of State Department public opinion polls, MacAlister Brown found another example of successful oversight.[38] During hearings the Department of State revealed that it commissioned several public opinion polls on American attitudes toward foreign aid. The department later used the same polls as justification in requesting increased funds for foreign aid. Because these actions were viewed by Congress as an attempt to unfairly influence congressional decisions, Congress forbade future polls.

Third, a case study of the NASA decision to use liquid rather than solid fuel rockets illustrates an oversight failure.[39] Despite continued congressional pressure on NASA to consider solid fuel the agency successfully resisted with arguments based on expertise.[40] When the scientific arguments failed, NASA conducted token analyses to placate the committee but did not change its policies.

Although no one has empirically analyzed the impact of congressional oversight, most students of the area believe that the NASA instance is more common than the successful NLRB case.[41] Several logical reasons support this view. First, oversight is less than universally successful because the oversight function does not fall within most congressmen's perceptions as to the role of Congress. The function of Congress is legislation, and through legislation members of Congress establish their institutional reputations. The rewards of legislation and casework far exceed those in oversight.[42] To be sure some members of Congress, such as Congressman Aspin (with DoD) or Senator Proxmire (with NSF), concentrate on oversight, but these are exceptional cases.

Second, staffing problems also limit the quantity and quality of oversight given the massive task of overseeing the entire federal bureaucracy. Oversight is essentially an extra function, peripheral to budgeting and legislation. The time pressures to complete these tasks often drive out the opportunities for oversight. Because Congress, until the 1974 budget reforms, consistently failed to pass a budget by the start of the new fiscal year, little time was left for oversight. Congress is not staffed well enough to legislate, appropriate, and also effectively oversee bureau operations.

A third and perhaps more important reason why oversight does not occur more frequently is that members of Congress lack the motivation for oversight. Oversight places the member of Congress and the bureau in adversarial positions. A congressman who expects his constituents to benefit a great deal from agency programs may jeopardize those benefits with overzealous oversight. Because oversight does not help a member's standing either in Congress or with his constituency, few members will spend much time in oversight.

Oversight much like budgeting and legislation is potentially an effective way to control bureaucracy. Unfortunately most students of oversight agree that it is not being used because Congress lacks the resources to effectively oversee bureaucracy.

Informal Contacts

The final legislative mechanism available to control administrative agencies is the legislator's informal contacts with administrative officials. These contacts can be used to advise on policy or to point out errors that the bureau might have made. The major reason why a member of Congress contacts a bureaucrat is because one of the member's constituents requested some assistance. William Gwyn estimates that Congress receives over 200,000 requests a year from constituents for assistance with the bureaucracy.[43]

Although no one has systematically examined congressional mail, Dean Mann did a detailed study of three California legislators' casework.[44] Mann found the informal contact process is used fairly infrequently; the three legislators handled 81 cases in a 3-month period, an average of 9 each per month. The cases came generally from middle class constituents.[45] The cases constantly dealt with minor matters with the most frequent request concerning automobile registration. Not once, in all the cases, according to Mann, did an agency change its policy in response to a legislative contact.[46]

Complaints registered with legislators are not only minor, they usually request special favors that the administrative process will not permit.[47] Congressional pressure on administrators means special treatment for the few with access to a member of Congress, not more effective policy action.[48] Legislative casework, therefore, is unlikely to be an effective means of countering administrative power. Rather casework introduces an element of political bias that administration was originally designed to eliminate.

If the sole function of Congress was to control the bureaucracy, Congress would not be credited with a good performance. Because Congress has directed its attention to major policymaking issues and presidential activities, bureaucracy receives relatively less scrutiny. Still if the process worked as designed, budgeting, oversight, legislation, and the legislative veto in combination could provide the tools necessary to check administrative power. Casework would counter the benefits of the other mechanisms. In practice, however, the strongest tools of legislative control are not being used. Although sometimes Congress cannot use these control mechanisms because it lacks the necessary information and resources, in many cases Congress does not want to restrict the bureaucracy. During the Nixon administration when the president was viewed as the enemy of the Congress, the bureaucracy was often perceived as a friend. In such circumstances, control of the bureaucracy is not a high congressional priority.

❧ Judicial Controls on Bureaucratic Power ❧

The courts have a few simple mechanisms designed to limit administrative discretion. Under the separation of powers the judiciary's role is interpreting laws and declaring executive/bureaucratic action *ultra vires*. For example, a state highway department began constructing a four lane highway through a midwestern university creating safety hazards for students. The university students appealed to the federal courts to prevent construction because the highway department failed to file an environmental impact statement. The federal district court agreed and enjoined the highway construction.[49] The courts are, thus, an aid to Congress insuring that administrators do not overstep the bounds of legislative intent.

Courts can limit administrative actions either prior to any damages with declaratory judgments and injunctions or after the fact through damage suits against the bureaucracy. The administrative actions that courts are designed to prevent, however, are limited. Courts are more concerned with procedural fairness than with substantive issues of responsiveness. Courts wish to know if the correct procedures were followed not if the policy is responsive or beneficial. Despite these limits many students of bureaucratic power believe, as William Robson does, that "the strongest safeguard against maladministration in the US appears to the Courts of Law." [50]

Despite such bright prospects judicial controls on administration have not met Robson's expectations. The problems with courts as a check on bureaucratic power are numerous. First, Kenneth Culp Davis, the nation's foremost expert on administrative law, argues that relying on judicial controls has judicialized the administrative process, a current deficiency of American regulatory policy. Since regulatory agencies are concerned that their decisions will be reversed by the courts, these agencies have established elaborate procedural safeguards. Regulatory agencies ceased using their more general rulemaking powers relying instead on case by case ajudication procedures similar to courtroom procedures. Adjudication requires that each case be tried on its merits after the fact rather than applying a general principle to all cases. The reliance on adjudication means that the public lacks clear guidelines about how a regulatory agency will act before it rules on a specific case, that regulatory agencies will be slow, and that often a regulatory agency will ignore policy for procedure.[51]

Second, Theodore Lowi argues that despite their vigilance courts have been ineffective in controlling administrative action.[52] According to Lowi, the courts have been an active partner in permitting the legislative branch of government to delegate its political power to bureaucratic agencies without legislative guidelines for its use. Not since the first New Deal measures were voided in the *Panama* and *Schecter* decisions have the courts prevented Congress from granting vague powers to an agency. Courts of law in the United States, Lowi concludes, have willingly sanctioned the congressional abdication of power to the bureaucracy.

Third, suing an agency in court does not guarantee a citizen any success. Bradley Cannon and Micheal Giles, studying regulatory agency cases before the US Supreme Court, found that the Court rarely reverses administrative actions; the Federal Power Commission and the Federal Trade Commission win 91 percent of the cases they argue in front of the Supreme Court. The National Labor Relations Board wins 75 percent, and the Internal Revenue Service 73 percent; only the arbitrary Immigration and Naturalization Service has a mediocre record of 56 percent.[53] An agency loss in court, however, does not necessarily mean a citizen victory. Kenneth Davis contends that when an agency loses a case, the case is often remanded to the same agency for a new decision. Using the reasoning provided by the court, the agency normally decides the initial decision was correct *especially in light of the recent court decision.*[54]

A fourth reason why judicial controls on bureaucracy are ineffective is the high cost of litigation. Samuel Krislov notes that the average race relations case cost the NAACP between $50,000 and $100,000 to take to the Supreme Court; the classic Brown school desegregation case cost $200,000 in the preinflation 1950s.[55] With lawyers' fees of $50 per hour plus expenses in most metropolitan areas (more for a good lawyer versed in administrative law), an injunction in federal court that requires any research at all will cost about $1,000. With the costs of research, briefs, transcripts, and lawyer's time, judicial appeals are beyond the financial means of most citizens.

A fifth criticism of the courts as a check on bureaucratic power is the excessive delay involved in adjudicating issues. Crowded court dockets mean that several months are necessary before a case can be heard in federal district court. Samuel Krislov estimates that traveling the road to the Supreme Court requires from 2 to 5 years.[56] An extreme example, the classic Ohio Bell Telephone case, was before the courts for 17 years before it was finally resolved. Unless the citizen can demonstrate a pressing emergency, judicial remedies are available only long after the deleterious action has occurred.

A sixth and final criticism of judicial controls is that the agencies can use the judicial process for their own ends. Agencies can coerce citizens by withholding benefits and pointing to the courts as a remedy if they are wrong. The IRS, for example, can disallow tax exemptions, forcing the taxpayer to sue the IRS to regain the tax payments. In effect the agency forces such people to undertake a long, costly court fight if they decide to challenge the agency.

The courts provide one of many checks on the bureaucracy in the American political system. As the sole or even major control on bureaucracy, the courts have fundamental weaknesses that prevent them from adequately checking bureaucratic power. For those with the resources and the patience to work the system, results will be forthcoming. For the normal citizen the courts, in most cases, are not a viable option.

☞ Presidential Controls on Bureaucratic Power ☜

The American contribution to the control of bureaucracy is the elected chief executive. Early scholars of administration, such as Woodrow Wilson and Frank Goodnow, treated the president and the bureaucracy as one, a situation that today is inconsistent with reality. The bureaucracy owes little loyalty to the president and may see the president more as an outsider than as a fellow bureaucrat. The president knows or should know that he does not control the bureaucracy even though the president is hierarchically superior to the bureaucracy.[57]

The president cannot be ignored as a possible control over administrative power. The president, no less than a member of Congress, is a politician responsible to the people for actions taken while in office. In fact, since the president is more visible to the public than is Congress,[58] the probability of popular control through the president is greater.[59] The Constitution underscores the importance of the presidency by granting it "executive power," the powers of commander-in-chief, and the charge that the laws be faithfully executed.[60] These provide a Constitutional imperative that the president attempt to control the bureaucracy.

The president's relationships with bureaucracy, however, are not so clear-cut as the Constitution presents them. Modern presidents are handicapped by being strangers to bureaucracy. Recent presidents (for example, Nixon, Kennedy, Johnson, Truman, Ford) were trained in Congress where contact with the bureaucracy is more cooperative than hierarchical. This problem was never more evident than when President Richard Nixon, a former vice-president, expressed surprise during his first term that many of his policy initiatives were delayed by the bureaucracy.[61]

Despite the presidential-bureaucratic estrangement, many students of bureaucracy see presidential control as potentially the most effective. Given congressional ties to more specialized interests, Powell and Parker argue for a bureaucracy responsible to the president rather than one responsible to the Congress.[62] Arthur Maass and Lawrence Radway contend that the bureaucracy should be directly responsible only to the president and that all other means of controlling the bureaucracy should be exercised through the president.[63]

Presidents have numerous tools at their disposal for controlling bureaucratic behavior. Presidential powers may be divided into organizational powers, budgetary powers, powers of command, and powers of motivation and tone. Although these powers are more effective in making bureaucracy responsive than in insuring competence, they can have impacts in both areas. Each of the presidential powers will be examined separately.

Organizational Powers

Organizational powers of the president include the president's appointment of line officials, his ability to use staff personnel, and his power to reorganize the federal government. The president appoints all cabinet officers and most bureau chiefs in the federal government. Although this power once extended even to minor clerical posts, the growth of the merit system has restricted presidential appointments to about twenty-five hundred. Of these some six hundred are policymaking positions—cabinet posts, subcabinet positions, and bureau chiefs. Another twelve hundred are subordinate positions (schedule C appointments) meant to provide the president with a source of patronage and a source of information within the bureaucracy. Another five hundred are professional and technical positions the president may fill but usually go by default to career civil servants.

Presidents can influence bureau behavior by appointing an administrator in tune with the president's political philosophy and by granting the administrator ample presidential support in any and all disputes. A classic example of this process is President Kennedy's appointment of Robert McNamara as secretary of defense. Secretary McNamara had experience with managing large bureaucracies (Ford Motor Company) and a mind capable of bringing great quantities of information to bear on national problems. McNamara introduced his Planning, Programming, Budgeting System (PPBS), which combined budgeting and managerial control to make decisions on military strategy and hardware. To provide himself with sufficient information on technical defense decisions, the secretary, by adding computers and systems analysis, increased the monitoring capacities of the office of the secretary. Despite the size of the Defense Department, McNamara received better information than most other secretaries and exerted more control over the military than any secretary before or after his tenure.

McNamara was able to increase civilian control over the military services and make them more responsive to the president for three reasons. First, McNamara's actions had the full support of the president. Second, Congress in general accepted the secretary's decisions; where they did not, the impoundment powers were used to reverse the decision. Third, the Department of Defense is a hierarchical organization, one designed to follow orders. Once the decisions were made and accepted by the initial layers of the military, implementation was not difficult.

Although the circumstances favored strong presidential control, the Department of Defense is not merely an exception. David Stanley analyzed six agencies in depth during the Kennedy transition and found that if the political appointee had clear goals regarding the agency's programs and took immediate action (sometimes before taking office), bureaucratic activities could be affected.[64] Joseph Zentner's study of presidential transitions found bureaucrats will respond to political pressures only if the pressures are strong and enduring and if they feel the pressures have presidential support.[65]

Creative staffing is another presidential approach to controlling bureaucracy. One problem that concerns many presidents is the tendency of political appointees to go native; they yield to the pressure from other members of their bureau to advocate the interests of the bureau. The president's person who was sent out to control a bureau ends up being coopted by the bureau. One solution to this problem used by President Eisenhower and Nixon was to vest control over programs in the White House staff, people with loyalties to no one other than the President.[66] Nixon attempted to not only control the bureaucracy but to coordinate domestic policy by creating the Domestic Council under John Erlichman. The Domestic Council was to be a domestic National Security Council that monitored all aspects of domestic policy. Unfortunately for any evaluation of the Domestic Council, Watergate distracted President Nixon from his goal of controlling bureau policymaking.

The staffing approach to control has limitations not present in the line administrators' approach. Because the federal bureaucracy is so large and diverse, controlling bureaucracy via staffing requires a large White House staff. Under this approach the cure for bureaucracy becomes more bureaucracy. In addition, because bureaus are perceived as biased, the White House staff often rejects all bureau-generated information, denying themselves their most important sources of information and making their task difficult if not impossible. The White House staff must then establish duplicate information sources. Finally, presidential staffers who act in the name of the president often develop power bases independent of the president. Since the president cannot monitor all staff activities, responsive bureaus may well become responsive to a staff member rather than to the president.

Former Budget Bureau official Harold Seidman believes that reorganization can be an effective tool to check bureaucratic power.[67] A major theme of Chapter 3 was that bureaus are influenced by their environment; reorganization can be used to shape the environment of an agency by creating a climate either hostile or receptive to organizational programs. The president, who has the power to reorganize the federal government subject to legislative veto, can stress a program by granting an agency organizational autonomy. For example, to emphasize President Nixon's commitment to cancer research, the National Cancer Institute was granted substantial independence and privileges not given to other bureaus in the National Institutes of Health. Reorganization can also handicap a program. If pesticide regulation was transferred back to the Department of Agriculture from the Environmental Protection Agency, pesticide users would have a more sympathetic ear than would environmentalists. Administrators in USDA are more sympathetic to farmer needs than environmentalist demands.

Creative placement of programs and careful reorganizations can create climates of opinion favorable to the president's policies. For example, a president hostile to the regulations of the Occupational Safety and Health Administration could place OSHA in the Department of Commerce. The probusiness biases of the Commerce Department would stifle many OSHA policies. Affecting organizational performance by manipulating the organization's environment has the advantage of not requiring constant monitoring by the president or his staff. With reorganization bureau biases can be made to work for the president.

Although reorganization can be an effective control weapon, Seidman contends that Franklin Roosevelt was the last president to have a comprehensive organizational strategy.[68] To use reorganization as a method of controlling the bureaucracy, Seidman believes that policymakers must first reject the orthodox belief that the end of reorganization is economy and efficiency. The end of reorganization is policy responsiveness to the president with bureaus organized so their environments reflect the priorities of the president.

Budget Powers

After a century and a half of experimentation with legislative budgeting, Congress, in 1921, authorized the president to prepare the budget and present it to Congress for review. The president, as a result of the executive budget and later reforms, can withhold resources from an unresponsive agency at both ends of the budget process. Initially, the Office of Management and Budget can deny an agency funds for a program, if OMB denies a request, agencies are not permitted to directly request those funds from Congress.[69] After funds are appropriated by Congress, the president can, if he deems it necessary, impound funds subject to legislative veto. Concomitant with the budget powers are the powers of legislative clearance. Any agency request for additional legislation, whether or not it requires funding, must be certified by the OMB as consistent with the president's program.

In combination, the budget and legislative clearance powers are formidable. President Johnson successfully used these powers to restrict domestic growth to free funds for the Vietnam War. President Johnson used these powers so enthusiastically that he actually submitted a balanced budget for fiscal year 1969. President Nixon also used budget powers to further policy control over the bureaucracy. At different times in his administration he requested no funds for the Office of Economic Opportunity and for the Rural Development Act. Budget powers may also be used in a supportive manner. President Kennedy used the budget to build a commitment for manned space, and President Nixon used them to fight his war on cancer.

If the president fails to restrict a bureau during the budget process, he has additional options after the budget is passed. The Budget and Impoundment Control Act of 1974 legalized the longstanding practice of impoundment whereby the president may refuse to spend funds or delay spending funds appropriated by Congress. President Kennedy used this power to prevent the armed services from building a new manned bomber. President Nixon impounded funds for policy purposes in a wide variety of programs ranging from social services to pollution grants.[70]

The use of the budget powers to control bureaucracy is enhanced by the professionalism of the Office of Management and Budget and OMB's ability to serve presidents of different political philosophies with equal enthusiasm. The budget process is a powerful tool because it creates an environment of expectations; if a bureau responds in certain sanctioned ways, it will be rewarded in the executive budget. The power is not without limits, however. The president is not the final step in the budget process; agencies can and often do appeal successfully to Congress for more funds. The budget cannot be used with maximum effectiveness as a control device because the budget is too large, detailed, and difficult to understand for any one set of actors. Even OMB usually adopts an incremental approach to the budget with an emphasis on only a few priorities, because only through an incremental approach the budget is simple enough to be passed in a single year. The president's budget powers are also restricted by uncontrollable expenditures. Certain portions of the budget are committed in advance to contractors or pledged without limit to American citizens who qualify (for example, social security, welfare, unemployment insurance). These funds are beyond the control of the president in the short run. Estimates of uncontrollable expenditures in the federal budget range from 50 percent to over 75 percent, a severe restraint on presidential power.[71]

The Powers of Commander-in-Chief

The president is given the power of commander-in-chief of the armed forces with precedent generalizing this power to all domestic policy, theoretically making all bureaus subordinate to the president. As a result of his position, the president in most cases can reverse administrative decisions as President Ford did when he revoked a HEW decision that prohibited schools from sponsoring father-son or mother-daughter events because they were sexually discriminatory.

Richard Neustadt has analyzed the powers of the president in great detail with special emphasis on three presidential decisions—Truman's removal of General MacArthur, Truman's seizure of the steel mills during the Korean War, and Eisenhower's decision to send troops to Little Rock to desegregate the schools.[72] Neustadt argues that the president can issue an order and command obedience only when five conditions are met.[73] First, the president's involvement must be unambiguous; the other actors must be certain that the president is concerned with the administrative actions. Second, the president's orders must be clear and unambiguous so that the recipient of the order knows precisely what is expected. Third, the orders must be accompanied by widespread publicity so that disobedience will attract the attention of the media and, thus, be relayed back to the oval office. Fourth, the recipient of the order must have the resources necessary to carry out the president's intent. Fifth, the actors must have no doubt that the president has the authority to direct the actions ordered.

Neustadt's detailed analysis of these three case studies convinces him that the real power of the president is the power to persuade. Instances where the president can issue a direct order and have it obeyed are few and far between. The small range of presidential command is further limited by resistance to presidential orders after they are issued. The resistance may be covert as was the air force's delay in removing offensive missiles in Turkey in 1962; or the resistance may be overt. In a classic case of overt resistance to presidential directives, 2,000 HEW executives and professionals (during 1970) petitioned HEW Secretary Finch to defend the administration's weak position on civil rights. When a spokesman for the secretary responded to criticism at a meeting, he was loudly booed.[74] Despite President Nixon's orders to ease the pressure on schools to desegregate, HEW bureaucrats vigorously pursued pre-Nixon policies.[75]

Tone and Motivation

A president attempting to control the bureaucracy must face two facts. First, the president and his staff do not have the manpower, time, or the need to control every detail of bureaucratic policymaking. Second, criticizing bureaucrats for lack of cooperation will only alienate them further and make the problem worse. If a bureaucrat is resistant to presidential direction, denouncing the official makes future cooperation impossible.

The alternative open to the president is to set the tone for his administration.[76] All presidents have general policy directions that set the tone for their administrations. Lyndon Johnson wanted his administration to be known for helping the unfortunate; Richard Nixon wanted to be known for putting a check on big federal government. To control bureaucracy the president must set and communicate a consistent tone and then motivate bureaucrats to respond.

The essence of presidential leadership is the motivation of other policymakers. Leadership requires that the president provide positive reinforcement for performance in accord with the president's program. It requires the creative use of symbols: presidential visits, promotions, and the status of the office. Presidents vary in how successfully they are able to control the bureaucracy through tone and motivation. Lyndon Johnson achieved some significant successes, but Richard Nixon met with continual frustration. The difference may be that Johnson, as an advocate of big government, was leading the bureaucracy in the direction it wanted to go. Richard Nixon worked to reduce the influence of the federal bureaucracy, and no amount of positive motivations could induce the bureaucracy to accept this reduced role. A president's ability to use tone and motivation to control bureaucracy, as a result, may be a function of the political goals of the president.

Despite the attention focused on the presidency, we know very little about the techniques that are effective in setting a tone for a presidential administration and in controlling bureaucracy through motivation.

Restraints on Presidential Controls

In addition to the limitations on presidential control noted in the individual sections, four things limit presidential controls on administration in general. First, the president's control is limited by the time he has available to devote to bureaucracy. The government currently spends several hundred billion dollars annually and is growing. Presidents also find their time dominated by the press of foreign affairs crises. As the result of size and presidential preoccupation with foreign policy, the president and his staff cannot oversee all bureaucratic behavior.

Second, the president does not have sufficient information of acceptable quality to control the bureaucracy. To be sure the president receives an excess of communications, but because the communications to the president are so massive, they cannot be analyzed to provide timely information. Public inputs in the form of letters, for example, can be a valuable guide to a bureau's performance; but the *Washington Post* estimates that the president receives as many as 300,000 letters in a single day.

Third, the control of the President over the bureaucracy is restricted by the relationship between Congress and the bureaucracy. If the bureaucracy and Congress can cooperate, they can effectively stalemate the president. Congress can supply the bureaucracy with the resources necessary to resist presidential commands. Nothing prevents Congress from appropriating more funds than the president asks, and Congress has increasingly done so. Nowhere is this ability to stalemate more pronounced than in executive reorganization. Congress has consistently resisted presidential efforts to reorganize bureaus that are congressional favorites (for example, presidents have repeatedly failed to consolidate the Army Corps of Engineers and the Department of the Interior).

Fourth, the policy preferences of the bureaucracy restrict presidential control. When presidential direction is lacking or when the presidential monitoring slackens, a bureau will generally make decisions consistent with its own biases. In general the bureaucracy is liberal, Democratic, and strongly in favor of advocating the bureau's position in policymaking.[77] This means that control of bureaucracy will probably work only where the direction of the control is consistent with the bureau's own objectives.

The Ombudsman

Since controlling bureaucracy by other political institutions does not guarantee beneficient administration, some students of bureaucracy have shown increased interest in foreign and domestic applications of the ombudsman. The ombudsman is a Scandanavian invention designed to check administrative abuse of power. An aggrieved citizen complains directly to the ombudsman, usually a public official with high public recognition and esteem. The ombudsman investigates the circumstances and tries to work out an agreement between the aggrieved and the bureaucrat. If the ombudsman fails to resolve the problem, his only sanction is to publicize poor administrative behavior and pressure the administrator to change his or her ways.

Unlike many other institutions the function of the ombudsman is controlling small bureaucratic abuses similar to the courts; it does not concern itself with broad questions of policy and public control. American analyses of the ombudsman are usually glittering reviews of the institution's effectiveness in other political systems.[78] This evaluation addresses two issues, the extent of the ombudsman's coverage and the ombudsman's limitations.

The number of complaints received by the ombudsman is generally very small. In Finland, Donald Rowat found the ombudsman received 1,200 complaints annually with about five percent requiring remedial action.[79] The Swedish ombudsman received about 1,400 complaints annually and took remedial action on fifteen to twenty. In the first year of the New Zealand ombudsman the ombudsman received 799 complaints and acted on 56. In the United States, Buffalo, New York, has experimented with two ombudsmen in the past. A newspaper ombudsman service received 313 complaints in a year with the majority concerning road and street repairs, vacant buildings, traffic control, and trees.[80] Buffalo also experimented with an actual ombudsman funded by the federal poverty program for 71 weeks; 1,224 complaints were processed, most concerning social services, public housing, and demolition.[81]

Considering the foreign examples first, ombudsmen receive very few complaints and actually seek redress on only a minute portion of those received. Clearly the ombudsman cannot be a comprehensive control over administrative action if 15 complaints a year are corrected in a nation the size of Sweden. Second, the American experience reveals that the problems considered are not of earth-shaking importance. In most cases they concern services the citizen wants, not some administrative abuse he has suffered.

Larry Hill's survey of American ombudsmen in several American cities and states reveals that American governments have adapted the institution to make it more effective.[82] The major change is the movement away from the classical independent ombudsman to the executive ombudsman who is under the hierarchical authority of the chief executive. American ombudsmen have been successful in generating a large response, over half the executive ombudsmen in the United States process more than 2,000 complaints a year. These numbers probably reflect the outreach programs of the ombudsman. Twenty percent have branch offices, almost all have toll free phone lines, and almost all receive most of their complaints over the telephone. Although most complaints remain in the category of inefficient or absent services, a fair percentage concern complaints about administration. Perhaps because the American ombudsmen are receptive to nonadministrative abuse complaints, they find a much higher percentage of complaints are valid than do the ombudsmen of other nations.

Despite the adaptation of the American ombudsman, three inherent limitations hamper the ombudsman. First, the ombudsman only handles minor matters. Angus and Kaplan caution against permitting the ombudsman to degenerate into a complaint bureau, but the American experience reveals it is primarily a place to register complaints about services denied.[83] Second, although no studies have addressed this aspect, the ombudsman's clientele are those who probably need little additional help in dealing with the bureaucracy, that is, the middle class citizen with experience in dealing with bureaucracy (the exception is the Buffalo program where field offices were specifically placed in the ghettos). Third, the ombudsman has never been implemented in a government the size of the United States federal government. Although most ombudsmen have very small staffs, they also serve small governments. A United States ombudsman would likely require a bureaucracy as large as many bureaus it would investigate. Unfortunately, as a means of controlling bureaucratic power, the ombudsman will not cure all the problems.

ᘿᕽ Summary ᕽᘿ

Overhead democracy is the traditional method of controlling bureaucracy. The method contains two separate linkages, one linking the public to elected or appointed officials and the other linking these public officials to the bureaucracy. This chapter discusses how the first linkage was met. Generally the American public is capable of rational, issue-oriented electoral choices if candidates present issues in their campaigns. Although some exceptions exist, elected officials also try to redeem the campaign pledges they make. When two conditions are met, they mean the public can control elected officials.

Control linkages between elected and appointed officials and the bureaucracy are not as strong. Congress has sanctions it can apply to unresponsive bureaus through the legislative process, through the budget process, and through the legislative veto. Gathering information to support actions in these three areas is the function of oversight and informal contacts. Other than weaknesses of size and resources, Congress has some limitations in each of these areas. Legislation has become too vague to be more than a general boundary on bureaucratic action. The budgeting process tends to be incremental rather than control oriented. The legislative veto reduces Congress to responding to bureaucratic initiatives. Oversight offers too few rewards to Congress and casework introduces harmful favoritism in the administrative process.

Although many individuals favor using the courts to check administrative abuse of power, courts are likely to be less effective than Congress. Since agencies are difficult to defeat in courts of law, legal recourses offer little chance of success. Low success is coupled with high costs and long periods of time to pursue legal redress of administrative errors. Using the courts to check bureaucracy, in fact, may be harmful because the process leads to the judicialization of administrative procedures.

The president has a variety of tools at his command to control administrative action; he may use the powers of command, his ability to appoint bureau heads and reorganize bureaus, his budget powers, and his leadership abilities. Although powers of command may be nothing more than the power to pursuade, the president's organization powers may be the most effective control on bureaucracy if used correctly. Leadership, reorganization, appointments, and budgets can control administrative action if the president focuses his attention on the bureaucracy. Unfortunately, the priorities of American politics and the preferences of most presidents are such that they eschew administrative matters for foreign policy and major domestic crises.

Because the traditional institutions of American government do not offer any guaranteed method of controlling bureaucracy, many scholars support the establishment of an ombudsman. Although the ombudsman has much to recommend it, it is designed to rectify minor administrative ills in a system that is generally competent and responsive. The ombudsman has never been successfully tested in a bureaucracy the size of the American federal bureaucracy.

∾ Notes ∾

1. The previous chapter discussed in great detail the demands and desires the American people have for public bureaucracy. Exactly, what in each instance is expected from the bureaucracy will not be specified in this chapter because such a specification would be difficult. Rather we will assume that we have some objectives in a policy or procedural sense and that bureaucracy should be required to faithfully implement these desires.

2. Emmette S. Redford, *Democracy in the Administrative State* (New York: Oxford University Press, 1969).

3. Woodrow Wilson, "The Study of Administration," *Political Science Quarterly* 2 (1887): 197–222.

4. Accepting the politics-administration dichotomy is not necessary to support overhead democracy as a control on bureaucracy. In fact, most scholars argue as this chapter does that political officials are more closely tied to the will of the people through elections. Therefore, the elected officials will

likely represent the people's desires more closely than the merit appointed civil service. For this reason overhead democracy is a preferred method of control.

5. A problem that concerned the Nixon administration was its inability to subject the bureaucracy to its policy directives. The White House approached this problem a variety of ways with only limited success. The White House tapes reveal that many attempts to abuse presidential power remained attempts because the bureaucracy would not agree to presidential directives. The IRS, for example, refused to audit for political purposes for the Nixon White House; J. Edgar Hoover effectively vetoed the Houston plan for domestic surveillance.

6. Bernard Berelson, Paul F. Lazarsfeld, and William N. McPhee, *Voting* (Chicago: University of Chicago Press, 1954).

7. Angus Campbell, Philip Converse, William Miller, and Donald Stokes, *The American Voter* (New York: John Wiley & Sons, 1960).

8. Michael Shapiro, "Rational Political Man," *American Political Science Review* 63 (1969): 1106–1119.

9. Peter Natchez and Irvin C. Bupp, "Candidates, Issues, and Voters," *Public Policy* 17 (1968): 409–437.

10. This finding corresponds to a similar finding by David E. Re-Pass, "Issue Salience and Party Choice," *American Political Science Review* 65 (1971): 389–400, on the 1964 election. RePass found substantial issue voting on issues that were personally salient to the voter.

11. Thomas E. Patterson, Robert D. McClure, Kenneth J. Meier, "Issue Voting and Voter Rationality" (Paper presented at the Annual Meeting of the American Political Science Association, Chicago, 1974); Kenneth J. Meier and James Campbell, "Issue Voting" (Paper presented at the Annual Meeting of the Western Political Science Association, San Francisco, 1976).

12. Dan Nimmo, *The Political Persuaders* (Englewood Cliffs: Prentice-Hall, 1970). Joe McGinnis, *The Selling of the President 1968* (New York: Trident Press, 1969).

13. See Harold Seidman, *Politics, Position, and Power* (New York: Oxford University Press, 1975); Francis Rourke, *Bureaucracy, Politics and Public Policy* (Boston: Little, Brown, 1976).

14. John L. Sullivan and Robert E. O'Connor, "Electoral Choice and Popular Control of Public Policy," *American Political Science Review* 66 (1972): 1256–1268.

15. John P. Bradley, "Party Platforms and Party Performance Concerning Social Security," *Polity* 1 (1968): 335–358; Gerald M. Pomper, *Elections in America* (New York: Dodd, Mead, 1968).

16. V. O. Key, "Legislative Control," in *Elements of Public Ad-*

ministration, ed. Fritz Morstein Marx (Englewood Cliffs: Prentice-Hall, 1959), p. 314.

17. See also Charles Hyneman, *Bureaucracy in a Democracy* (New York: Harper and Brothers, 1950), p. 34.

18. Randall P. Ripley and Grace A. Franklin, *Congress, The Bureaucracy, and Public Policy* (Homewood, Ill.: Dorsey Press, 1976), p. 15.

19. This study uses a broad definition of oversight. Oversight occurs not only in special oversight committees but also in substantive and appropriations committees. Reviewing past agency performance is an essential aspect of appropriations and legislation.

20. Herbert Kaufman, *Are Government Organizations Immortal?* (Washington: The Brookings Institution, 1976) discovered in his analysis of agency deaths that statutory origin was less frequent now than in the past. Agencies can be created by executive order of the president or by departmental order. Congress ratifies these creations by granting funds to operate them.

21. S. Rich, "Congress Has Lead in Major Programs," *Washington Post,* (February 14, 1975), p. A2 cited in Ripley and Franklin, 1976.

22. A. Lee Fritschler, *Smoking and Politics* (Englewood Cliffs: Prentice-Hall, 1975).

23. The Manpower Administration is known for a variety of programs including the attempt to replace all single sex job titles (for example, fire*man,* chair*woman*) with nonsexist titles. As a result the *Man*power Administration also changed its own name to the Employment Training Administration.

24. Ripley and Franklin, *Congress, the Bureaucracy,* p. 55.

25. Joseph Harris, *Congressional Control of Administration* (Washington: The Brookings Institution, 1964).

26. Actually the IRS writes much of the tax code initially. In any situation where Congress feels it necessary to write detailed legislation, it must rely primarily on bureaucratic expertise to draft the legislation. This dependence dampens the impact of a law as a check.

27. M. W. Kirst, *Government Without Passing Laws* (Chapel Hill: University of North Carolina Press, 1969).

28. Direct and indirect employees of Congress now total some 30,000 people (see Chapter 2). Approximately half of these are employed as personal or committee staff members. The rest work in congressionally controlled agencies. A list of some of these agencies reveals Congress' attempt to bureaucraticize. The Office of Technology Assessment reviews the technological consequences of new laws. The Congressional Budget Office reports on economic consequences. The General Accounting Office has been transformed

into a giant monitoring agency. The Congressional Research Service is an all purpose research agency. These four agencies are only part of the more visible congressional bureaucracy.

29. See Richard Fenno, *The Power of the Purse* (Boston: Little, Brown, 1966); Aaron Wildavsky, *The Politics of the Budgetary Process* (Boston: Little, Brown, 1964); Otto Davis, M. A. H. Dempster and Aaron Wildavsky, "A Theory of the Budget Process," *American Political Science Review* 60 (September 1966): 530–546; Robert D. Thomas and Robert B. Handberg, "Congressional Budgeting for Eight Agencies," *American Journal of Political Science* 18 (1974): 179–187.

30. This pattern may become more frequent. John R. Gist, "Increment' and 'Base' in the Congressional Appropriations Process" (Paper presented at the Annual Meeting of the Midwest Political Science Association, Chicago, April 29–May 1, 1976), argues that with the rise in uncontrollable expenditures the funds required to conduct the present programs for one year often exceed the funds available. As a result agencies can expect an increment but must fight to retain their base. See also George E. Hale and Scott R. Douglass, "The Politics of Budget Execution," *Administration and Society* 9 (1977): 367–379.

31. Arnold Kanter, "Congress and the Defense Budget," *American Political Science Review* 66 (1972): 129–143.

32. See also Douglas M. Fox, "Congress and the Military Service Budgets in the Post War Period," *Midwest Journal of Political Science* 15 (1971): 382–393.

33. The legislative veto comes in a variety of forms. It may either be positive so that Congress must act to veto an action or negative so that if Congress does not act, the action is void. The time period for veto can vary substantially. Who can exercise the veto also varies, in some instances only one house can veto the action, and in special circumstances committees of either house can veto the action. See Joseph Cooper, "The Legislative Veto," *Public Policy* 7 (1956): 128–174.

34. Clark F. Norton, *Congressional Review, Deferral and Disapproval of Executive Actions* (Washington: Congressional Research Service, 1976).

35. Theodore Lowi, *The End of Liberalism* (New York: Norton, 1969).

36. The extent to which Congress engages in oversight is unclear since oversight is difficult to distinguish from several other reasons for holding hearings. This places the analyst in the uncomfortable position of relying on case studies for generalization. William Gwyn, "Transferring the Ombudsman," *Ombudsman for American Government?* ed. Stanley Anderson (Englewood Cliffs: Prentice-Hall, 1968) reported that the 83rd Congress spent approximately $7.5 million on oversight functions.

37.   Seymour Scher, "Congressional Committee Members as Independent Agency Overseers," *American Political Science Review* 54 (1960): 911–920.

38.   MacAlister Brown, "The Demise of State Department Polls," *Midwest Journal of Political Science* 5 (1961): 1–17.

39.   James Kerr, "Congress and Space: Overview or Oversight?" *Public Administration Review* 25 (1965): 185–195.

40.   Some members of Congress were concerned about solid fuel rockets because firms in their district manufactured solid fuel propellants.

41.   Ralph K. Huitt, "Congress, the Durable Partner," in *Lawmakers in a Changing World*, ed. E. Frank (Englewood Cliffs: Prentice-Hall, 1966); John F. Bibby, "Committee Characteristics and Legislative Oversight of Administration," *Midwest Journal of Political Science* 10 (February 1966): 78–98; Ripley and Franklin, *Congress, The Bureaucracy*.

42.   Ripley and Franklin, *Congress, The Bureaucracy*, p. 54.

43.   Gwyn, "Transferring the Ombudsman."

44.   Dean Mann, *The Citizen and the Bureaucracy* (Berkeley: Institute of Governmental Studies, 1968).

45.   Past researchers have revealed that any contact with public officials is likely to be unrepresentative. People who contact public officials tend to be of higher social status than the American people in general. Aage Clausen, et al., "Electoral Myth and Reality: The 1964 Election," *American Political Science Review* 59 (1965): 321–332; Sidney Verba and Norman Nie, *Participation in America* (New York: Harper and Row, 1972).

46.   Mann, *The Citizen*, p. 40.

47.   See Robert N. Winter-Berger, *The Washington Payoff* (New York: Dell Publishing Co., 1972) for one lobbyist's view of case work and who benefits from the process. Most case work deals with getting exceptions to federal regulations, special help from the bureaucracy, or, in the prevoluntary army days, draft deferments.

48.   Kenneth Culp Davis, *Administrative Law* (Minneapolis: West, 1965).

49.   See *Nolpe v. Volpe* (1971).

50.   William Robson, *The Governors and the Governed* (Baton Rouge: Louisiana State University Press, 1964), p. 31.

51.   Davis, *Administrative Law*.

52.   Lowi, *The End of Liberalism*.

53.   Bradley Cannon and Micheal Giles, "Recurring Litigants: Fed-

eral Agencies Before the Supreme Court," *Western Political Quarterly* 15 (1972): 183–191.

54.   Davis, *Administrative Law.*

55.   Samuel Krislov, *The Supreme Court in the Political Process* (New York: Macmillan, 1965).

56.   Ibid.

57.   Seidman, *Politics, Position.* Note Richard Nixon's surprise at bureau resistance to presidential initiatives.

58.   Donald Stokes and Warren Miller, "Party Government and the Salience of Congress," *Public Opinion Quarterly* 16 (1962): 531–546.

59.   Controlling bureaucracy will not achieve the desired ends of responsiveness and competence unless the mechanism is also responsive to the public. If the bureaucracy were very responsive to Congress and Congress was not visible to the public, congressional control would not translate into public control. The president's visibility as means of public control, probably through elections, is more likely.

60.   Robert Fried, *The Performance of American Bureaucracy* (Boston: Little, Brown, 1976).

61.   Seidman, *Politics, Position.*

62.   John Norman Powell and Daniel P. Parker, *Major Aspects of American Government* (New York: McGraw-Hill, 1963), p. 357.

63.   Arthur A. Maass and Lawrence I. Radway, "Gauging Administrative Responsibility," in *Ideas and Issues in Public Administration,* ed. Dwight Waldo (New York: McGraw-Hill, 1959), pp. 440–454 at 446.

64.   David T. Stanley, *Changing Administrations* (Washington: The Brookings Institution, 1965).

65.   Joseph L. Zentner, "Presidential Transition and the Perpetuation of Programs," *Western Political Quarterly* 15 (1972): 5–15.

66.   Robert Nathan, *The Plot That Failed* (New York: John Wiley & Sons, 1976).

67.   Seidman, *Politics, Position.*

68.   Ibid.

69.   A direct request means that the bureau cannot bring up the matter before a committee. If the committee asks the bureau if OMB denied it any funds that it thinks it can effectively use, then most bureaus believe they should reply honestly. Often bureaus will attempt to plant such questions with their supporters on a committee in an effort to circumvent OMB decisions.

70. Louis Fisher, *Presidential Spending Power* (Princeton: Princeton University Press, 1975).

71. Martha Derthick, *Uncontrollable Spending for Social Service Grants* (Washington: The Brookings Institution, 1976).

72. Richard Neustadt, *Presidential Power* (New York: John Wiley & Sons, 1960).

73. Ibid., p. 19.

74. Robert J. Sickels, *Presidential Transactions* (Englewood Cliffs: Prentice-Hall, 1974), p. 72.

75. Nathan Glazer, *Affirmative Discrimination* (New York: Free Press, 1976). The HEW is an exceptional case in the directness of the challenge to the president; it is not exceptional in its resistance. In the early 1970s VISTA executives angered at the agency's reception in the Nixon White House publicly advocated that the agency's strong grass roots support be used to defeat Nixon in the 1972 election (see Sickels, *Presidential Transactions*, p. 73).

76. Robert R. Sullivan, "The Role of the President in Shaping Lower Level Policymaking Processes," *Polity* 3 (1970): 201–221.

77. Joel D. Aberbach and Bert A. Rockman, "Clashing Beliefs Within the Executive Branch," *American Politicial Science Review* 70 (June 1976): 456–468. Kenneth John Meier and Lloyd G. Nigro, "Representative Bureaucracy and Policy Preferences," *Public Administration Review* 36 (1976): 458–469.

78. Stanley V. Anderson, *Ombudsman for American Government* (Englewood Cliffs: Prentice-Hall, 1968); William P. Gwyn, "The British PCA: *Ombudsman or Ombudsmouse?*," Journal of Politics (1973): 45–69.

79. Donald C. Rowat, "The Spread of the Ombudsman Idea," in *Ombudsman for American Government*, ed. Stanley V. Anderson (Englewood Cliffs: Prentice-Hall, 1968), pp. 7–36.

80. William Angus and Milton Kaplan, "The Ombudsman and Local Government," in *Ombudsman for American Government*, ed. Stanley V. Anderson (Englewood Cliffs: Prentice-Hall, 1968), p. 124.

81. Lance Tibbles and John H. Hollands, *Buffalo Citizens Administrative Service* (Berkeley: Institute of Governmental Studies, 1970).

82. Larry B. Hill, "The Citizen Participation-Representation Role of American Classical and Quasi-Ombudsmen" (Paper presented at the Annual Meeting of the American Political Science Association, Washington, D.C., September 1–4, 1977).

83. Angus and Kaplan, "The Ombudsman and Local Government."

CHAPTER SEVEN

M any students of bureaucracy believe that overhead democracy is not an effective check on administrative power. The essence of overhead democracy as a control mechanism is the accountability of the bureaucrat to another person for his or her behavior. Even with multiple checks administration always involves discretion, and discretion opens the administrator to temptations which may be contrary to the public's best interest. Where oversight fails to be constantly vigilant, abuse of administrative power becomes possible. External means of controlling administrative action can be only partially effective because they operate retroactively and then only infrequently. The initial control on a person's behavior according to Robert Dahl must be the norms the person internalizes.[1]

The problem for responsive and competent administration is how to structure the inevitable discretion of administrative action so that it is responsive to public needs and desires. Those scholars who criticize overhead democracy as a control see two different approaches to controlling bureaucratic power—establishing ethics for administrators and making sure all interested parties are represented in the administrative policy process. Between these two polar approaches at least five methods of controlling bureaucracy have been proposed. These five approaches will be analyzed: the administrative Platonist, the scientific administrator, the new public

Controlling

Ethics and

administration, representative bureaucracy, and participative administration. This chapter will determine the effectiveness of these five approaches.

❧ The Administrative Platonist ❧

The driving force behind the school of thought that believes administrators should possess high ethical standards is Paul H. Appleby, past Dean of the Maxwell School of Citizenship and Public Affairs and one-time high-level administrator for Franklin Roosevelt. Appleby has described at length the characteristics that an ethical administrator should possess.[2] The administrator must be willing to assume responsibility, be able to deal with people, have a sense of urgency, be a good listener, be effective with people, surround himself with the ablest of people, use institutional resources effectively, avoid using power for its own sake, be self-confident, welcome troublesome problems before they get out of hand, be a team worker, and be an initiator.[3] Administration, according to Appleby, has a moral quality when it conforms to the process of political freedom, leaves itself open to public modification, and responds to publicly felt needs; and the pursuit of the public interest ties it all together.[4]

Bureaucracy: Participation

Stephen K. Bailey, also a former Dean of the Maxwell School, continued the Appleby tradition through his interpretations of Appleby's writings.[5] Bailey's administrator would recognize moral ambiguity; that is, administration cases are neither black nor white only shades of gray. The administrator would perceive that contextual forces condition moral priorities in the public service so that what is moral depends on the situation. Bailey's administrator would also recognize the paradox of procedures—that procedures established to treat all people equally inevitably discriminate against those who are ill-equipped to deal with bureaucracy. In addition, Bailey believes that three moral qualities are needed—optimism, courage, and fairness tempered by charity—to be an ethical administrator. Bailey and Appleby felt that a public administrator has a moral responsibility to "the highest ethical and moral principles of the state and society in which he lives." [6]

Ethics as a check on bureaucratic power has been subject to a great deal of criticism. This approach to controlling administrative discretion has declined as the example of Paul Appleby, one who administered as he wrote, grew distant. The difficulties of using ethics as a control device are numerous.

First, the writings and the concepts used (moral ambiguity, courage, optimism, et cetera) are so ambiguous as to defy definition. Because everyone has different definitions of these terms, an administrator can never be sure whether a specific action is or is not ethical. To Daniel Elsberg releasing the *Pentagon Papers* conformed to the highest ethical principles. To his critics Elsberg put personal policy preferences over his position of public trust. Appleby's writings provide us with ambiguous answers to this and many other administrative dilemmas.

Second, the approach is open to the normative criticism that it sets up ethical guardians (hence the term administrative Platonist). If ethics rather than overhead democracy is used as a control, bureaucrats will be responsible to no one other than their own self-conception of morality. Herbert Kaufman argues that precisely this attitude caused New York City civil servants to see themselves as protectors of their clientele against the evil politicians.[7] As a result, they resisted political control and gave the city noninnovative and nonresponsive administration.

Third, neither Appleby nor Bailey are clear on how to instill ethics into administrators and why the administrator will engage in ethical behavior. Presumably ethics will result from an administrator's training, but in the United States, unlike many other countries, administrative training is not uniform. In fact, most high-level administrators in the federal government were trained as technical specialists not as administrators. Even high-level administrators trained in administration were usually trained in techniques of administration rather than ethics. At the Maxwell School, the home of the administrative Platonist, bright young MPA candidates eschew occasional "ethics and the public service" courses for budgeting, personnel, and public policy courses. Even if education for the public service did instill ethics, Anthony Downs argues that the pressures of everyday administration would force the bureaucrat to be an agency advocate rather than an Applebian statesman.[8]

Fourth, the question of training uniformity raises another question. To what exent do administrators hold the values espoused by Paul Appleby? If public bureaucrats, especially those at high levels, have personal ethics like those of Paul Appleby, then the citizen can sleep soundly knowing that bureaucratic power will rarely be abused. Unfortunately, we must plead ignorance on this question. No student of bureaucracy has ever attempted to "measure" the ethics held by the nation's public servants. Until this question is resolved, those who rely on ethics to check bureaucratic power hold a very tenuous position.

ভ্ঞ The Fellowship of Science ঞ্ভ

A second proposal for an inner check on administrative action developed from the influx of scientists and professionals into national government. Demand for sophisticated military technology, space hardware, and health care made the national government the nation's largest employer of professionals. Soon professionals were not subordinate to political masters but were actively participating in policy decisions because policy decisions could not be made without their specialized knowledge. Policy questions, such as developing a supersonic transport, determining the relative effectiveness of the cruise missile and the B1 bomber, and assessing the impact of various energy development proposals requires expertise that only scientists can provide. Not only were professionals making policy, they were making policy in terms incomprehensible to the lay politicians.

Carl J. Friedrich argued that the situation posed new problems for politicians, but that the need was not to restrict professional discretion but to motivate professionals to anticipate the needs of the public.[9] Public policy decisions, according to Friedrich, should be accountable to both public sentiment and technical knowledge. The former could be achieved by inputs from elected officials, the latter through a fellowship of science where fellow scientists interpreted and challenged the results of the scientists in government. Friedrich's solution to the problem of scientists in government was to add more scientists. These scientists, by advocating both sides of a policy issue, would give the elected official the information necessary to decide complex issues. Although Friedrich's proposal was controversial, his proposal gathered a great deal of support from other students of science and government. C. P. Snow, Don K. Price, and Frederick Mosher echoed both Friedrich's fears and his solution, emphasizing the need for both professionalized decisionmaking and competing scientists.[10] Unlike Appleby's proposals, Friedrich is concerned more about competence than responsiveness. Friedrich argues that administrative behavior must respond to public sentiment, but his major emphasis is on the improved performance of bureaucratic policymaking.

Although Friedrich's government by scientists and fellowship of science cover only a portion, albeit a growing portion, of public policymaking, the major shortcomings must be noted. We know very little about the impact of professional norms on administrative behavior. A great deal of academic training is actually a socialization process whereby young professionals accept the norms of their profession.[11] The economist, for example, is trained to perceive most policy problems as market system failures. Although not all professionals in a given speciality share the identical norms, the greater the consensus on norms, the more difficult controlling professionals will be. Friedrich's proposal requires professional conflict and competition. If these factors are absent because scientists are professionally socialized to similar values, then one group of scientists cannot serve as a check on another.

The problems of controlling scientists are not just public policy problems. Some excellent studies of scientists and the difficulties of controlling scientists concern private sector organizations.[12] Unfortunately, this literature is fairly pessimistic about the ability of generalists (which most politicians are) to direct scientists in directions that they do not wish to proceed. Using their technical superiority, scientists can limit the alternatives considered to those acceptable to the scientists. If a generalist-administrator cannot understand the scientific issues in a given area of public policy, then that administrator is at the mercy of his scientists.

Another problem is that the relationship between technical responsibility and public sentiment had not been fully explored. To what extent are these two goals incompatible? Public opinion, as expressed through the positions of elected officials, has favored more applied science to produce immediate benefits for mankind. To accomplish this end, a division of the National Science Foundation, Applied Science and Research Applications (ASRA) was established. With ASRA a great deal of scientific resistence to applied science was brought to the surface. While public policy demands applied research, the rewards within a profession are geared more to basic research that deals with theoretically important scientific issues. Thus, in some cases technical responsibility opposes public sentiment.

Another limitation of the fellowship of science approach is that competition and disagreement among scientists are not a solution to the problem. In the debate over funding the supersonic transport (SST), experts presented conflicting testimony on the environmental dangers of the SST. Science is not so exact that it consistently produces uniform advice, especially when it deals with social problems. When scientists disagree on the SST or the efficacy of a cruise missile system, politicians have no objective means of resolving the dispute. Disagreement may well be no guide to policy decisions at all.

Another limitation, according to Herman Finer, is that relying on a fellowship of science to check scientific decisionmaking may be an abdication of public power to private groups.[13] Simply because a group of people are scientists who possess technical knowledge does not mean that they do not also have policy preferences. The American Medical Association (AMA) has been a vocal opponent of government interference in health care. If the AMA were the fellowship of science on Medicare or National Health Insurance, effective public policy would be hampered. All professionals have goals including the economic security of fellow professionals. Whenever professionals advise on their own professions, the advice becomes less reliable.

⤷ The New Public Administration ⤶

In the late 1960s and early 1970s the American Society for Public Administration and practicing public administrators were rocked by a group of insurgents who became known as the new public administration.[14] Under the auspices of the Maxwell School the young turks of the discipline attempted to reformulate the "values of public administration." Members of the new public administration charged that administrators were to blame for many of the injustices of modern society. The professed neutrality of administration was not neutrality at all. The "bias-free" procedures used by modern administrators were nothing more than procedures designed to allow the white middle class to interact favorably with the bureaucracy and to shut the poor and the minorities out of the process. Procedures, such as impersonality, written forms, a long series of steps to receive some benefit, were acceptable to the middle class but were difficult for the poor.

Administrators, according to the new public administration, had long created inequities in power, influence, income and services. If administrators were responsible for these injustices, then administration must be reformed. The new public administration would actively foster conditions which furthered social equity.

Unlike other proponents of the inner check to control bureaucracy, the new public administration had policies and programs to achieve their ends. Bureaus should be decentralized and designed so that the people affected by the programs had more control over them. Through organizational development techniques administrators should be made sensitive to the needs of the people they serve. Because bureaucrats often become committed to agencies and obsolete programs, which do more harm than good, organizations should be temporary, set up to achieve a single task and disbanded after task completion. To further prevent harmful bureau loyalties, the new public administration strongly supported contracting out services, perhaps to the service recipients so that they could provide their own services. Incremental policymaking with its emphasis on the status quo should be rejected; goals must constantly be reexamined to determine if progress is being made. The new public administration even advocated confrontation as an administrative tactic; disrupting normal bureaucratic services serves to focus attention on problems that are not being solved.

Although the new public administration caught the imagination of the discipline, it was not really new at all. Much of the new public administration with its emphasis on values is similar to Paul Appleby's writings on administrative ethics with advocacy added. Fifteen years before the new public administration, Arthur Maass and Lawrence Radway argued that administrators must equalize the differences between organized and unorganized interests.[15] Such action would mean that the administrator would either advocate the interests of the disadvantaged or discount the interests of the better represented.

The new public administration is concerned with the responsiveness of both policy and administration; effectiveness is not usually a goal sought by the movement. In attaining this goal the new public administration has two major weaknesses. First, the solutions advocated by the new public administration—decentralization, confrontation, organizational development, nonincrementalism—do not logically result in greater social equity. New public administrators make a great leap of faith from the suggestions they advocate to the results they wish to achieve. The US Department of Agriculture, for example, has long used decentralized programs and participation by farmers to run their programs. The USDA techniques, however, have been condemned for leading to benefits only for the progressive farmer rather than the disadvantaged farmer.[16] In the Department of Agriculture, some critics would contend that new public administration techniques were used to foster social inequity. Confrontations, for another example, is an excellent means to focus attention on problems, but continued use of confrontation in administration becomes completely disruptive. Confrontation may well disrupt service delivery to all clients including the disadvantaged rather than reallocate benefits to the disadvantaged.

A second problem plaguing the new public administration is an ambiguity of goals. Although "social equity" is a widely held value, exactly what social equity means is difficult to discern. Usually the goal is expressed in terms of providing everyone with equal opportunities, but in many cases equality of opportunity results in outcomes much like the current state of affairs because people lack the necessary skills and education. In such cases social equity requires ameliorative or reverse discrimination. Exactly which cases require ameliorative discrimination, however, is not clear. The new public administration faces a problem similar to Appleby's administrative Platonist, the administrator is never sure when a given action is acceptable. When consensus is lacking on the goals of administration, the new public administration can also develop into ethical guardians.

Representative Bureaucracy

To meet the demands for both increased administrative discretion and more responsive bureaucratic power, Norton Long, Paul Van Riper, Donald Kingsley and others suggest making the bureaucracy more representative in the demographic sense. If policymaking bureaucrats hold attitudes similar to the attitudes and values of the general population, then the proponents of representative bureaucracy feel that policy will be more responsive to the needs of the public. They assume that when making a policy decision, the bureaucrat will attempt to maximize his or her own personal policy values. If the values of the bureaucrats and the citizens are similar, then the policy made by the bureaucracy should be responsive to the desires of the public. How might these similar attitudes be achieved? If the socialization experiences of the bureaucrats are similar to those of the people, attitudes should be similar since attitudes are a product of the socialization process. How can policymakers assure that socialization experiences are similar? If the bureaucracy is recruited from a wide range of people, then the socialization experiences of the bureaucracy and the people ought to be similar. If, therefore, the social origins of the civil service mirror the social origins of the general population, then we can be sure that socialization experiences are similar, attitudes are similar, and policy is responsive to public needs.[17]

Notwithstanding the impressive theoretical justification for representative bureaucracy as a check on bureaucratic power, some reasons suggest that a representative bureaucracy may not be a responsive bureaucracy. First, similar social origins do not necessarily lead to similar socialization experiences. To be sure the family, education, and social status do have an impact on values as the political socialization literature demonstrates, but that impact is far less than total.[18] Detailed political biographies have shown that people with such diverse backgrounds as Richard Nixon and

Herbert Hoover had similar socialization experiences.[19] The cause of a person's attitudes and values is often so idiosyncratic that social origins are only a rough indicator of a person's socialization experiences.

Second, the linkage between social origins and values is not very strong either. Socialization as a learning process continues throughout the lifetime of an individual. Continuous socialization limits the ability of a personnel officer to predict a person's values from that person's social origins in two ways. Agencies take advantage of the socialization process; they create roles for the adult bureaucrat and socialize them to advocate the agency no matter what their personal background. With the values important to the agency, agency socialization may be as important as childhood socialization. Continuous socialization means that a group of civil servants must of necessity differ from a population with the same social origins. Civil servants will not only be more in favor of agency programs, but the simple fact that they are civil servants means their experiences are different from the general public's. Also, becoming a civil servant often means an increase in social status; James A. Barber has effectively demonstrated that upward mobile people hold different values than the values of nonmobiles with the same social origins.[20] Upward mobile civil servants, therefore, would likely hold different values than their childhood counterparts especially on policy relevant beliefs.

Third, the proponents of representative bureaucracy focus on the wrong level of bureaucracy. They consistently stress the representativeness of the bureaucracy as a whole; but as earlier chapters have argued, decisions are not made at department or entire bureaucracy levels but rather at the bureau and division levels. For bureaucracy to be representative then, every bureau must be representative of the American people or decisions made at that level must be appealed to a more representative level.

These three criticisms of representative bureaucracy indicate that a representative bureaucracy may not be responsive to the desires of the American people. A more direct way to evaluate representative bureaucracy as a means of control on bureaucracy is to examine the social origins and attitudes of the higher civil service. Table 7–1 shows the social origins on selected variables of the higher civil service, the supergrades of the career service. Clearly the supergrades are unrepresentative of the American people; compared to the population they tend to be white, male, urban, highly educated professionals from upper middle-class backgrounds. As noted earlier, whether or not the entire higher civil service is representative is an academic question because the entire bureaucracy does not make any policy decisions. Decisions are made at the bureau level; for the bureaucracy to be representative each bureau must be representative. In general, studies have shown that bureaus tend to recruit from their clientele.[21] The Department of Agriculture recruits heavily from big farm interests and state

TABLE 7–1   *Social Origins of the Higher Civil Service and the American Population, 1974*

		Population	Higher Civil Service
Father's Occupation	Blue Collar	48%	27%
	Farmer	25%	18%
	Clerk/Sales	7%	7%
	Business	13%	31%
	Professional	8%	17%
Education	Less Than High School	18%	0
	Some High School	18%	0
	High School Graduate	33%	1%
	Some College	18%	3%
	College Graduate	13%	96%
Race	White	87%	96%
	Non-White	13%	4%
Sex	Male	47%	98%
	Female	53%	2%
Birthplace	Rural	49%	24%
	Urban	51%	76%
Region	South	31%	22%
	East	28%	39%
	Midwest	32%	31%
	West	8%	8%

Source: Adapted from Lloyd G. Nigro and Kenneth John Meier, "Bureaucracy and the People," *The Bureaucrat* 4 (October, 1975): 302; and Kenneth J. Meier, "Representative Bureaucracy and Administrative Responsiveness" (Ph.D. diss., Syracuse University, 1975).

universities. The Department of Housing and Urban Development recruits more from urban dwellers and minorities. No bureau is totally homogeneous in social origins, but bureaus in most cases are even less representative than the higher civil service as a whole.

Comparing the attitudes of the supergrades and of the American people shows different results. In general, the higher civil service holds attitudes that are similar to the attitudes of the population (see table 7–2). The higher civil service is slightly more liberal than is the population (see table 7–3). The reason why two groups with such diverse backgrounds can have such similar attitudes is because social origins are weak predictors of policy attitudes. What then does predict the attitudes of bureaucrats on policy issues? According to a recent study, the agency affiliation of the supergrade has three to five times more influence on policy attitudes than the supergrade's social origins do.[22] Agencies are apparently successful in

TABLE 7–2   Public Opinion and Administrative Elite Attitudes: Percent Supporting More Expenditures*

Policy Area	Civil Servants	Population
Space	13	8
Environment	54	59
Health Care	62	64
Urban Problems	55	50
Crime Control	52	67
Drug Abuse	44	60
Education	46	50
Minorities	33	31
Defense	6	17
Foreign Aid	11	3
Welfare	12	22

* The question permits the respondent to advocate more spending, less spending, or the same amount of spending.

Source: Adapted from Kenneth J. Meier, "Representative Bureaucracy and Administrative Responsiveness" (Ph.D. diss., Syracuse University, 1975).

TABLE 7–3   *The Ideology of the Higher Civil Service and the American Population, 1974*

	Very Liberal	Liberal	Middle	Conservative	Very Conservative
Civil Service	30%	27%	14%	22%	10%
Population	23%	29%	17%	15%	9%

Source: Kenneth John Meier, "Representative Bureaucracy and Administrative Responsiveness" (Ph.D. diss., Syracuse University, 1975).

socializing their personnel to agency prescribed roles. This finding also means, however, that while the entire supergrade corps may be representative in terms of attitudes, the supergrade contingent in each bureau will be very unrepresentative.

In retrospect representative bureaucracy is hardly a check on administrative power. The United States higher civil service is not representative at the bureau level in either attitudes or origins. Certainly, no other industrialized nation has a civil service as representative of its people as the American civil service is, but our civil service still has a long way to go to be representative.[23] Even if a representative bureaucracy were achieved in the United States, the pressures on administrators to advocate the mission of their agencies would likely destroy any potential responsiveness.

✑ Participative Administration ✑

Individual participation and pressure groups have been proposed as a means of making bureaucracy more responsive. Because this proposal has a solid grounding in pluralist political science, the model makes many of the same assumptions.[24] The participation model assumes that each individual is the best judge of his or her self-interest. As the best judge each individual decides the ends they wish to achieve and the means (including organizing into groups) to achieve them. The perceptions of administrative elites on these individual's interests can be discounted. The model makes several other crucial assumptions that, if true, guarantee the responsiveness of political and administrative elites to the general population.

The participation/pressure groups model assumes all interests and/or opinions are expressed. Public demands that are not expressed cannot be considered salient to either the people or to government because these demands are not important enough to motivate people to express them. The model assumes that each individual will join others holding similar interests to form a pressure group; the end of the group is to pursue the members' common interests. Since each individual has an interest in many aspects of the positive state, everyone will join a variety of groups. Each pressure group, therefore, is composed of people who hold membership in several other groups. A close analysis of pressure group theorists reveals that the proponents feel that real interests in a society number in the hundreds rather than the millions so that aggregating all interests is physically possible.[25] People who have common interests but are not organized are a latent group. Since people are assumed to be rational, the cost of organizing a latent group probably exceeds the benefits the group would gain by being organized; or the group would organize and enter the political process.

The group participation model insures responsiveness by having groups take individual interests, aggregate them, and articulate the interests to policymakers. The groups influence political and administrative elites by offering rewards (support in battles with other elites or information that facilitates job performance) or by threatening punishments (withholding support or actual expressed opposition). Interest groups, because they represent valid interests and have political resources, have access to a wide variety of administrative policymakers.[26]

If all interests concerned with an issue are represented, then all positions on a policy issue will be presented to the decisionmaker. The decisionmaker seeks to insure his or her continuation in a position of power and influence by satisfying the demands of as many groups as possible. This statement applies to a bureaucrat as well as to a politician because a bureaucrat needs support to gain legislative authority, monetary resources and other facilities. If the decisionmaker cannot satisfy the group preferences then the disaffected groups will shift their support to another bureau that, if there is a great deal of group dissatisfaction, may be able to capture control over the program. The result should be representation of all interests in policy decisions and, therefore, a general satisfaction of most public policy demands.

A major concern of this model is the linkage between the group members and the group leaders. What is to prevent the group leaders from conspiring against the group members or nonparticipants for their own benefit? First, each group is prevented from taking extreme actions that infringe on the rights of other groups because each citizen has multiple group memberships. Taking such actions would alienate some of the pressure group's membership and, therefore, weaken the group's claim to represent a large number of people; this weakened legitimacy would cause a decline in the group's power base. Second, the model also predicts that the participants in the process cannot exploit the nonparticipants because latent groups exist. A latent group, if threatened with a denial of its interests, would soon find that organizing and participating would cost less than foregoing the organizational costs and continuing to suffer the exploitation. Third, the assumption that competing elites will cater to unmet demands of the masses prevents any elite or set of elites from long ignoring the demands of any group. If one political or administrative official ignores a group, then another eager for more political resources will adapt its policy to appeal to that group.

Because the group participation check on administrative power is theoretically different from many of the others, the evaluation of this model will progress in two parts, the first dealing with the linkage between individuals and the group participants and the second considering the linkage between group members and administrative and political elites. Too often students of administrative power assume the first linkage is sound and proceed to discuss only the second. This procedure, in fact, artificially inflates the perceived effectiveness of participation as a check.

Individual-Group Linkage

Concerning the individual-group linkages, four questions must be examined. What is the extent of individual participation in groups, is it common or fairly infrequent? What type of people belong to pressure groups, and are they different from nonparticipants? Do people in fact belong to multiple groups so that individual groups are restrained in their demands? Can individual participation be substituted for group participation so that the limitations of group participation can be overcome?

The Extent of Participation.   The pressure groups check on administrative power assumes that group participation is a universal characteristic of American society. Similar to Alexis de Tocqueville's view, the pluralists see America as a nation of joiners. If the participation is not universal, the probability is good that significant interests in society are left out of the process. We cannot assume that lack of participation is an indicator of satisfaction with the status quo so that nonparticipation can be ignored. Careful studies have shown that nonparticipation is associated with alienation and cynicism about the political process rather than satisfaction.[27] A more logical inference about nonparticipation, then, is that certain policy demands are not being met. Participation must be widespread for the model to work.

The extent of American participation in the group process has been examined by Gabriel Almond and Sidney Verba in their five-nation analysis of political culture.[28] They found that only 57 percent of the United States population belong to one or more organizations remotely related to politics. Since Almond and Verba defined groups very broadly to include unions, business and professional associations, farm organizations, social groups, charitable, religious, civic, cooperative, veterans and fraternal organizations, the extent of participation in pressure groups in the United States is not staggering. Fully two of every five adults do not belong to any groups at all. The inclusion of social and fraternal organizations (the fourth and third largest categories) as groups means participation in *political pressure groups* is much smaller. Most people who belong to these organizations, in fact, belong passively; they participate in the group's social events and rarely serve in a leadership position or represent the group to outsiders.[29]

Are Participants Representative?   The lack of widespread group participation brings up the second question—how do the participants differ from the nonparticipants? If, on the one hand, the group participants are a microcosm of the nonparticipants, the possibility still exists that all interests in the nation are represented. If, on the other hand, the participants are distinctly different from the nonparticipants, the assumption of representativeness must be challenged.

Group participation has often been characterized as so unrepresentative that as E. E. Schattschneider has suggested, the flaw in the pluralist heaven is that the heavenly chorus sings with an upper middle-class accent.[30] Sidney Verba and Norman Nie found Schattschneider's colorful prose to be fairly accurate.[31] Community activists were better educated, from higher income groups, male, middle-aged, white, Protestant, and suburban or small town. The policy interests of such people are bound to be different from those of the poor, the unemployed, the rural, the old, the young and countless other groups. The nonparticipation by society's disadvantaged groups, then, is a direct challenge to the contention that pressure group politics is an effective means of making bureaucracy more responsive to all the people.

Multiple Group Memberships.   If every individual belongs to several groups, then any one group is restricted in the actions it can take by the possibility of losing the support of its membership to a myriad of other groups. If, on the other hand, the individual participants do not belong to multiple groups, then their control over group leaders is diminished; their only alternatives to nonresponsive group leaders are to withdraw or to form an alternative group. Both options are less likely to succeed than the multiple groups reaction. If a member of the teamsters union, for example, believes the union's political alliance with the Republican party contributes to policies detrimental to the rank and file, the teamster's probability of forming a successful counter group within the union is marginal at best.

Gabriel Almond and Sidney Verba's statistics reveal that multiple group memberships are restricted to 32 percent of the population.[32] Only 9 percent of the population belongs to at least 4 groups. This number by itself is hardly sufficient to insure that extreme actions taken by one group will alienate some of the group's supporters who are active in counter groups.[33] The 9 percent figure indicates that Schattschneider may be correct when he states that possibly 90 percent of the population is shut out of the pressure group process.

Individual Participation.   The fourth question the model raises is that of individual participation. Although individual participation is not as effective as group participation, individual participation to some extent can be substituted for group participation in keeping administrators responsive.[34] For example, the intent of the community action programs in the 1960s' war on poverty was to insure responsive administration by having clientele directly participate in decisions and administration.

The extent of individual participation is not, however, impressive. A comprehensive study of American political activities classifies 12 acts of political participation ranging from voting in presidential elections to membership in a political organization.[35] Even without discounting overstated reports of participation, Sidney Verba and Norman Nie find 31 percent of the population perform no political acts and an additional 22 percent usually perform only one act (usually voting for president).[36] When the acts are classified by difficulty, fully 77 percent of the population participate in one or less political activities, hardly the massive participation needed to insure responsiveness.

The studies of participation in community action programs provide some evidence more closely related to the administrative process. The community action programs were designed to fight poverty by having the poor organize themselves and participate in administering programs. When compared to the number of eligible participants, however, only a very small percentage actually participated in any part of the program.[37]

Group-Administrative Elite Linkage

The second linkage in the pressure groups/participation model is the link between the pressure group and both group leaders and administrative elites. As Emmette Redford argues, "the attainment of the democratic ideal in the world of administration depends much less on majority votes than on the inclusiveness of the representation of interests in the interaction process among decision leaders." [38] If, as Redford contends, all relevant interests are represented in the process and political or administrative elites are held responsible for meeting the demands of the interests through some type of sanction, then the policy outputs of such a process will, in general, be responsive to the American people.

The effectiveness of pressure groups or direct participation in checking administrative power is dependent on three conditions. First, the linkage between the members of the interest group and the leaders of the interest group must be fairly strong; the leadership must be cognizant of membership desires and seek to further those desires. Second, all interests must be represented in the process or the policy will reflect the consensus of the present participating interests rather than all interests. Third, relationships between elites must be characterized by competition rather than cooptation. Administrative and political elites must compete for support of the interests, and interests must compete for favorable public policies.

The Representativeness of Interest Group Leaders. The first necessary condition for interest groups to act as an effective check on administrative power is that the interest group leaders represent members' interests not their own interests. The union leader that negotiates a sweetheart contract with a manufacturer does not represent the best interests of the rank and file. Most students of interest groups assume that leaders do, in fact, represent the members effectively, assuming that if they did not the members would leave the interest group. But continued membership cannot be taken as implicit acceptance of leadership actions because people join groups for many reasons other than policy objectives. A small farmer may remain in the Farm Bureau because the bureau provides the farmer with low cost insurance. A welder retains his affiliation with his union to avoid the social stigma of being scab labor. The manufacturer continues membership in a trade association because the national conventions provide a tax deductible vacation.

If we assume leaders are not devious and they advocate the interests they perceive the members hold, the question remains, do interest group leaders perceive the world in the same way that members do? Norman Luttbeg and Harmon Zeigler in their study of the Oregon Education Association found that leaders held positions on important educational issues that were substantially different from the positions of the rank and file.[39] Although the leadership knew the member's opinions were different from their own, they actually misperceived membership positions as being more like their own than they actually were. Rensis Likert and Samuel Hayes studied the organization of World War II dairy farmers in a midwestern state. Elite organization members reported several facts about the production capacity of the state's dairy farms and farmers' attitudes toward greater production.[40] The state agency concerned surveyed dairy farmers and found that the "facts" reported were true for the wealthy farmers but not true for the bulk of dairy farmers in the state. A consistent pattern in the linkage between interest group members and leaders is that the leaders perceive members' positions on issues to be like their own. Elites consistently hold less centrist positions than do the rank and file. Herbert McClosky verified this pattern for political parties.[41] Convention delegates were more extreme on issues than were the party rank and file.

The evidence presented here seriously questions how well group leaders represent members' interests. The representation process breaks down when leaders do not accurately perceive the interests and desires of the people they are to represent.

Are All Interests Represented?   To be an effective check on administrative power, all interests must be represented in the process so that all views are presented to the policymakers. Although no one has systematically examined the American political process to determine if all interests are represented when policy decisions are made, evidence suggests that all interests are usually not present. For example, included among the groups testifying before Congress on funds for the Agricultural Research Service are: the National Woolgrowers Association, the American International Charolais Association, the American Association of Nurserymen, the American Soybean Association, the American Honey Producers Association, the National Grange, and the Rocky Mountain Dry Bean Association. Missing from the participants are: consumers who oppose crops being developed so that they are easy to harvest but lose nutritional value, representatives of farm labor who might be replaced through research, the noncash crop farmer, and environmentalists who oppose pesticide development.[42] With little additional effort a long list of interests, which are affected by the decisions of the Agricultural Research Service but are never consulted, could be made.

A pattern similar to the agricultural appropriations is found in many other areas of public policy. Samuel Huntington argues the Interstate Commerce Commission systematically excluded nonrailroad interests from the regulatory benefits of the ICC.[43] Theodore Lowi documents several instances of public policy where all interests were not represented.[44] In fact, Lowi feels that cooptation and one-agency-one-interest politics is the dominant form of politics in the United States. Harold Seidman in his analysis of bureaucratic politics also contends that important interests are excluded from the policy process. He feels the exclusion results from interest participation in subsystem politics; if participation could be limited to large agencies or to the entire Congress, the process would benefit more people.[45] Congress specifically recognized the fact that all interests were not represented in the bureaucratic process when it proposed to create an Agency for Consumer Advocacy to represent consumer interests before other administrative bodies.

Do Interest Groups Compete?   If interests are not competitive, bureaucrats are under no pressure to respond to all groups but can respond to one interest and ignore the rest. The fact that all interests are not represented lessens the need to compete for political support. Competition among interest groups is also hindered by the fragmented nature of American politics. In regulatory and distributive politics the dominant form of policymaking is subsystem politics. Interest groups, congressional committees and bureaucracies form a triumvirate to extract resources from the environment. Interest groups receive services, bureaus receive resources, and committee members receive clientele support. Subsystem politics is too narrow to generate any competition.

The absence of competition is often institutionalized through advisory groups. The bureau names an advisory group to advise it on policy questions; the group is composed of the agency's dominant clientele. Within the advisory group the interests can reach consensus on demands to be made on the agency and present it with a *fait accompli*. Norman Keiser reports that the Business Advisory Council of the Department of Commerce plays the role of a private pressure group insuring that the department takes favorable action in regard to antitrust and labor policy.[46] The official affiliation of the council with the department allows its meetings and purposes to be kept secret although the costs are paid by the government.

Several case studies have documented other instances of noncompetitive interest groups. In his study of federal regulatory agencies, Louis Kohlmeier found little competition among the regulated industries; often a regulatory agency's policy area contained only one organized interest.[47] Usually the regulated rely on the agency to prevent competition among interests by setting prices and limiting entry to the market. Kohlmeier is so confident of his conclusion that the regulatory process lacks competition, he suggests that many regulatory agencies be abolished.[48] Robert Fellmeth in his in-depth analysis of the Interstate Commerce Commission believes that many interests are concerned with the ICC.[49] The ICC, however, has been coopted by the railroad interests who attempt to restrict competition before the ICC so that the ICC ignores other interests. Finally, Philip Selznick's analysis of the Tennessee Valley Authority demonstrates the classic pattern of cooptation.[50] The TVA ran its agricultural programs from the established local agricultural schools; the conservative schools blunted the impact of a series of potentially radical programs. The TVA permitted the agriculture establishment to coopt these programs to gain political support in the Tennessee Valley so that TVA could operate a public power program without worrying about the influence of local utilities.

The above studies indicate that competition is not always present in administrative politics, that many times the relationship is one of collusion and cooptation. The extent of competition is still an empirical question, but we have enough evidence to conclude that the process is not always competitive.

If all the assumptions of the pressure groups-participation model of controlling the bureaucracy held, it might be a way that bureaucratic power could be checked. Examining the individual linkages and assumptions, however, leads one to conclude that the ideal theory in no way resembles the actual process of American politics.

Summary

This chapter evaluated five proposals to insure bureaucratic responsiveness and competence: the administrative Platonist, the scientific administrator, the new public administration, representative bureaucracy, and participative administration. The administrative Platonist position advocates instilling ethics in civil servants. Unfortunately the proponents are vague about what values they wish to instill, about how they will instill them, and about why their proposals will not create a cadre of uncontrolled ethical guardians.

The scientific administrator approach generates competent administration by recruiting scientists to government service so that scientists can check other scientists. The professional norms of the scientist that blind them to certain options, however, may be so strong that additional, competing scientists cannot overcome them. Competing scientists, in fact, offer no solution to bureaucratic power because policymakers have no means to chose rationally between competing sets of scientists. The scientific administrator approach does not offer a solid means of checking administrative power.

The new public administration takes the values of the administrative Platonist and adds advocacy so that administrators pursue social equity. The new public administration does not circumvent the problems of the administrative Platonist. The new public administration has vague values and methods that do not insure social equity.

Representative bureaucracy seeks to control bureaucratic power by recruiting a microcosm of the American population to the higher civil service. The theory assumes these individuals will hold the same values as the rest of the American public so that as they pursue their own self-interest they will further the ends of most of the American people. Unfortunately for this theory, the higher civil service is unrepresentative of the American population, and agencies socialize the values of their employees so that they differ from the general public's.

The pressure groups approach to administrative responsibility requires that representative groups press the demands of the general public. Pressure politics does not insure administrative responsibility, however, because interest group leaders are not closely linked to their members and because interest groups represent only some segments of American society and ignore others.

Although the analysis in this chapter found weaknesses with all five approaches to administrative responsibility, it did not answer the most important question—to what extent are the ethics of the civil service responsible for the responsiveness and competence of the American federal bureaucracy? We do not know. The complexities of this question are such that no study has adequately addressed it. If the analysis in chapter 6 is correct and overhead democracy is not a strong check on bureaucracy and if the American federal bureaucracy is generally responsive and competent, then the inner check—the ethics of the civil service—must be the major reason for the quality of the American federal bueaucracy.

⤳ Notes ⤳

1.   Robert Dahl, *Preface to Democratic Theory* (Chicago: University of Chicago Press, 1970).

2.   Paul H. Appleby, "Public Administration and Democracy," in *Public Administration and Democracy*, ed. Roscoe C. Martin (Syracuse: Syracuse University Press, 1965); Paul H. Appleby, *Morality and Administration in Democratic Government* (Baton Rouge: Louisiana State University Press, 1952).

3.   Appleby, *Morality and Administration*, p. 342.

4.   Ibid., p. 342.

5.   Stephen K. Bailey, "Ethics and the Public Service," in *Public Administration*, eds. Robert Golembiewski, Frank Gibson, and Geoffrey Y. Cornog (Chicago: Rand McNally, 1966), pp. 22–32, at p. 24.

6.   Norman J. Powell and Daniel P. Parker, *Major Aspects of American Government* (New York: McGraw Hill, 1963), p. 353.

7.   Herbert Kaufman, "Bureaucracy and Organized Civil Servants," in *Governing the City*, eds. Robert A. Connery and Demetrios Caraley (New York: Praeger, 1969), pp. 41–54.

8. Anthony Downs, *Inside Bureaucracy* (Boston: Little, Brown, 1967), p. 86.

9. Carl J. Friedrich, "Public Policy and the Nature of Administrative Responsibility," in *Public Policy*, vol. 1, eds. Carl J. Friedrich and Edward S. Mason (Cambridge: Harvard University Press, 1940).

10. C. P. Snow, *Science and Government* (Cambridge: Harvard University Press, 1961); Don K. Price, *The Scientific Estate* (New York: Oxford University Press, 1965); Frederick Mosher, *Democracy and the Public Service* (New York: Oxford University Press, 1968).

11. Ian L. Mitroff, *The Subjective Side of Science* (New York: Elsevier, 1974).

12. Richard H. Hall, "Some Organizational Considerations in the Professional-Organizational Relationship," *Administrative Science Quarterly* 12 (1967), pp. 461–478.

13. Herman Finer, "Administrative Responsibility in Democratic Government," *Public Administration Review* 1 (Summer, 1941), pp. 335–350.

14. See Frank Marini, *Toward the New Public Administration* (Scranton, Pa.: Chandler Publishing, 1971); Dwight Waldo, *Public Administration in a Time of Turbulence* (Scranton, Pa.: Chandler Publishing, 1971).

15. Arthur Maass and Laurence I. Radway, "Gauging Administrative Responsibility," in *Ideas and Issues in Public Administration*, ed. Dwight Waldo (New York: McGraw-Hill, 1959), pp. 440–454.

16. Sidney Baldwin, *Politics and Poverty* (Chapel Hill: University of North Carolina Press, 1968).

17. Although the idea of a representative bureaucracy was first presented in 1942, it has been recently revived to support policies of affirmative action.

18. See Jack Dennis, "Major Problems in Political Socialization Research," *Midwest Political Science Review* 12 (1968), pp. 85–114.

19. James David Barber, *The Presidential Character* (Englewood Cliffs: Prentice-Hall, 1972).

20. James A. Barber, *Social Mobility and Voting Behavior* (Chicago: Rand McNally, 1970).

21. See Kenneth J. Meier, "Representative Bureaucracy and Administrative Responsiveness" (Ph.D. diss., Syracuse University, 1975).

22. Kenneth J. Meier and Lloyd G. Nigro, "Representative Bureaucracy and Policy Preferences: A Study in the Attitudes of Federal Executives," *Public Administration Review* 36 (July/August, 1976), pp. 458–469.

23.   Kenneth J. Meier, "Representative Bureaucracy: An Empirical Analysis," *American Political Science Review* 69 (June 1975), pp. 526–542. V. Subramaniam, "Representative Bureaucracy," *American Political Science Review* 61 (December, 1967), pp. 1010–1019.

24.   The model presented here is from a variety of sources. It most closely follows that of David B. Truman, *The Governmental Process* (New York: Knopf, 1951).

25.   A. H. Birch, *Representation* (New York: Praeger, 1971).

26.   L. Harmon Zeigler and G. Wayne Peak, *Interest Groups in American Society* (Englewood Cliffs: Prentice-Hall, 1972).

27.   Arthur H. Miller, "Political Issues and Trust in Government," *American Political Science Review* 68 (September, 1974), pp. 951–972.

28.   Gabriel Almond and Sidney Verba, *The Civic Culture* (Boston: Little, Brown, 1965).

29.   The lack of participation in the United States should not blind us to the fact that participation in the US is greater than it is in most other Western democracies. See Almond and Verba, *The Civic Culture.*

30.   E. E. Schattschneider, *The Semi-Sovereign People* (New York: Holt Reinhart and Winston, 1960).

31.   Sidney Verba and Norman H. Nie, *Participation in America* (New York: Harper and Row, 1972).

32.   Almond and Verba, *The Civic Culture.*

33.   Most overlapping groups probably have consistent policy interests so that few stands would alienate members. Finding someone who belongs to such diverse groups as the American Civil Liberties Union, the National Rifle Association, Common Cause, and the John Birch Society would be difficult.

34.   We assume group participation is more effective since groups have more resources to reward or punish policymakers than do individuals. This does not mean that individuals occasionally cannot have more influence on public policy than groups, only that this is not likely.

35.   Verba and Nie, *Participation.*

36.   Ibid., p. 34.

37.   James A. Riedel, "Citizen Participation: Myths and Realities," *Public Administration Review* 32 (1972), pp. 211–217.

38.   Emmette Redford, *Democracy and the Administrative State* (New York: Oxford University Press, 1969), p. 14.

39.   Norman Luttbeg and Harmon Zeigler, "Attitude Consensus and

Conflict in an Interest Group," *American Political Science Review* 60 (1966), pp. 655–665.

40. Rensis Likert and Samuel P. Hayes, *Some Applications of Behavioral Research* (Paris, UNESCO, 1951).

41. Herbert McClosky, Paul J. Hoffman and Rosemary O'Hara, "Issue Conflict and Consensus Among Party Leaders and Followers," *American Political Science Review* 54 (1960), pp. 406–427. A similar result was found by Barry Sussman, "Party Workers Poles Apart," *Washington Post* (September 27, 1976), p. A1.

42. Jim Hightower, *Hard Tomatoes, Hard Times* (Washington: Agribusiness Accountability Project, 1972).

43. Samuel P. Huntington, "The Marasmus of the I.C.C." *Yale Law Journal* 61 (April, 1952), pp. 467–509.

44. Theodore Lowi, *The End of Liberalism* (New York: Norton, 1969).

45. Harold Seidman, *Politics, Position and Power* (New York: Oxford University Press, 1976).

46. Norman F. Keiser; "Responsibility and Federal Advisory Groups," *Western Political Quarterly* 11 (1958), pp. 251–264 .

47. Louis Kohlmeier, *The Regulators* (New York: Harper and Row, 1969).

48. Ibid., p. 298.

49. Robert Fellmeth, *The Interstate Commerce Omission* (New York: Grossman, 1970).

50. Philip Selznick, *TVA and the Grass Roots* (Berkeley: University of California Press, 1949).

CHAPTER EIGHT

T his chapter will outline several political reforms designed to produce a more competent and responsive bureaucracy. Given the difficulty in unambiguously defining both competence and responsiveness, none of these reforms will please everyone (see chapter 5). The basic underlying assumption is that the American people have both the capacity and desire to control elected officials (see chapter 6). If they do not, then any reforms must rest on the goodwill of the bureaucracy. Before discussing the proposed reforms, the major themes of this book will be reviewed to illustrate why reforms to control bureaucracy are necessary.

Bureaucracies are political institutions of the first order. The American polity and many others no longer authoritatively allocate scarce societal values only through legislative and executive processes. Bureaucracy in the United States has developed political power through access to resources and discretion in the use of those resources. Although bureaucracy may not be the dominant political institution in all aspects of public life; in regulation, in taxation, in health care, in national defense and a variety of other areas, bureaucracy is a coequal power with the legislature and chief executive.

Bureaucracy did not become a dominant political institution because a secret group of bureaucrats with evil intentions conspired to make it so. Rather, bureaucracy gained power because people demanded

Designing
a Beneficent

that the government perform certain functions and only bureaucracy could perform them. Public policy in the latter half of the twentieth century is nothing if not complex; the task demands of public policy forced policymakers to turn to bureaucracy with its fountain of expertise. The organization of government in the United States with its checks and counterchecks stalemated each of the major political institutions; where action was required bureaucracy became the logical choice. The nature of American politics with its glorification of technology and administration and its denigration of politics forced additional public policy problems into the bureaucracy. Even the intended function of bureaucracy, implementation, required discretion for policy to be successful.

Although the nation's political institutions with the acquiescence of the American public granted great discretionary powers to public bureaucracy under an assumption that administration is different from politics, the problems of bureaucratic power are no different from the problems of political power. The founding fathers correctly believed that any unchecked exercise of political power was dangerous. Watergate is a grim reminder that political officials still succumb to the temptations of power. If American politicians have weaknesses, we should bear in mind that bureaucrats are neither more or less culpable than the rest of

Bureaucracy

the nation's citizens. Chapter 4 indicates, in fact, that bureaucrats do occasionally succumb to the temptations of political power.

Despite all the attention given to bureaucratic power, no other political institution or process to date is completely effective in controlling bureaucratic power. Congress lacks the motivation and the desire to control bureaucracy. The president has neither the time nor the staff to check bureaucracy. Courts are slow and may lack the remedies necessary to contain bureaucracy. Ethical checks are of questionable efficacy. And participation lacks the essential representativeness to ride herd on a determined bureaucracy.

Given the expectations of bureaucracy, however, that traditional controls on bureaucracy are not perfectly effective is hardly surprising. The question is not can bureaucracy be controlled perfectly, but can the system be designed to work better than it does now. Total control of the bureaucracy is neither necessary nor desirable because total control would likely eliminate more positive benefits than harmful actions. This chapter proposes a series of control devices, not to replace those currently in use, but to supplement them. Some are novel and require major changes in the American political system, and some are minor and require only slight incremental modifications. Together they provide a rough blueprint for a more responsive and more competent bureaucracy.

Chapters 6 and 7 present a case-by-case examination of the controls that operate on public bureaucracy. As mentioned, the analysis reveals that the individual controls are not totally adequate. The problem with these controls, however, is more fundamental than a simple failure to operate effectively. Each control mechanism was designed to check only one of many facets of bureaucratic power. Congressional controls, for example, were designed to insure that bureaus are responsive to the public. The use of legislation, budgets, and legislative veto attempt to persuade bureaucrats that they must respond to the people and the people's institution, the Congress. Of all the congressional controls, only oversight considers competence a goal to be maximized and then only in the limited terms of legislative intent.

Presidential controls are also designed to deal with responsiveness rather than competence. Presidential checks hope to insure that bureau behavior is responsive to the public through the elected office of the presidency. Budgeting, reorganization, powers of command, motivation and tone, et cetera, all attempt to either subordinate the bureaucracy to the president's will or motivate the bureaucracy to pursue that will. Competence is only a presidential concern when competence prevents responsiveness because public policies are ineffective.

Courts have totally different standards for public bureaucracy. To be sure, courts occasionally concern themselves with whether or not an agency has exceeded its legislative authority, but their primary concern is with procedures, an area of competence. Fairness, impartiality, and consistency are the guidelines the courts use to judge a bureaucracy's competence.

The participation and ethics approaches to controlling bureaucracy also have different expectations of bureaucracy. The administrative Platonist and the scientific administrator, while both concerned with responsiveness, feel that the key issue is competence. They are concerned with skills and performance, particularly effectiveness, innovation, and knowledge.

The other ethical approaches center firmly on responsiveness. The new public administration and its followers rarely speak of competence as a goal. They reject the goals of economy and efficiency for the broader goal of social equity in administration. Bureaucracy, in a new public administration world, responds to the needs of those excluded from normal political participation. Representative bureaucracy is nothing more than a passive form of the new public administration with the same goals. Finally, the participation model concerns responsiveness only in attempting to make the administrative process as representative of the American people and their interests as possible.

The problem faced by anyone hoping to design a system that produces both competent and responsive bureaucracy is self-evident. At present in the United States federal government we have a series of checks on bureaucracy, but each monitors only a small portion of the problem and is only partially successful.

⧫ Redundancy: The Case for Duplication ⧫

To adequately control bureaucracy, a control system must be designed that is better than the sum of the individual checks on bureaucracy. Although designing a system that on the whole is more effective than any of the elements of the system sounds impossible, in actuality the process is relatively simple. Such problems are constantly addressed by people who work in the industrial area of quality control.[1] Suppose a drug company needs rigorous quality control of a certain drug, but the company lacks the money to train a group of inspectors to examine every single capsule. The company can maintain high quality control of its drugs through a process described by Herbert Simon.[2] Simon describes several examples of pharmaceutical companies training pigeons, who have much better ability to discern differences in pills than humans, to inspect the drugs. Unfortunately, pigeons, being less than human, make some mistakes, perhaps more than can be tolerated by a drug company. If a pigeon is about 90 percent accurate in its inspection and if 90 percent accuracy is far too low, the solution is to use 2 pigeons in sequence. The first pigeon is 90 percent accurate and removes 90 percent of the defective pills; the second pigeon removes 90 percent of those that the first pigeon missed. Together they can probably attain 99 percent accuracy. With three pigeons perhaps one defective pill in a thousand will not be detected. The system can be designed through redundant controls so that the accuracy of a pigeon inspection system with only moderately accurate pigeons can be well above industry standards.

The secret in designing a control system that works significantly better than the sum of its parts, therefore, is redundancy. Each inspector in the above example does the same task and in the process catches the errors of the other inspectors. The logic of redundancy is, in fact, the logic behind most control systems.

Martin Landau argues that control systems work the same way in politics.[3] The US Constitution is designed around the principle of redundancy. In the nation's original constitutional framework, any significant policy change required the approval of the president (selected by a group of local elites), the House of Representatives (elected by the voters), the Senate (representing the state legislatures), and the courts (representing older political coalitions through the appointment process). The founding fathers designed a system with independent constituencies so that if a group harboring evil intentions was strong enough to seize control of one branch of government, the other branches because they have to agree to policy changes could prevent it from taking action. Although the major institutions of American government are no longer designed to represent the same groups that the founding fathers proposed, the major institutions still operate in sequence so that policy changes are challenged at a variety of points by other political actors.

If duplication and redundancy are characteristics that provide for quality control in industry and political control in government, why cannot the same principle be applied to bureaucracy? By combining a series of semieffective checks on bureaucracy into a redundant control system, controlling bureaucracy becomes much easier. The current bureaucratic system is redundant, even though the intent of policymakers was not to design such a system.

Redundancy permits marginal improvement in the system of checks on bureaucracy. This means that the system of checks can be improved by simply adding additional checks on bureaucracy. Assume for the sake of argument that the Congress with its myriads of checks on bureaucracy is able to eliminate 60 percent of the mistakes that bureaucracy would normally make. While 60 percent is not spectacular, it may be sufficient in combination with other political institutions. If the president and the courts are similarly 60 percent effective, and the institutions overlap (as they do), then in combination the system is 93.6 percent effective.[4] If the Congress then created an ombudsman and the ombudsman were also 60 percent effective, then the percentage for the entire control system would be 97.4 percent. The addition of a single control mechanism would reduce the amount of abuse, even in a basically responsive system, by over half.

The ability to improve a system of checks by increasing redundancy depends on two crucial assumptions. First, we assumed that no institution is so ineffective (or effective) in checking the bureaucracy that its addition actually restricts bureaucratic action more than is beneficial. Because the thesis of this book is that bureaucratic power is inevitable in modern society, this assumption is only a minor concern. Second, we assumed that each institution totally overlapped the others similar to Simon's pigeons so that one institution's oversights would be caught by some other institution. In fact, each political institution is capable of preventing certain abuses better than others. This specialization, rather than being harmful to overall control, is actually helpful. Each institution operates more effectively in some areas than in others, thus providing the major checks in one area while serving as a redundancy channel in another. Congress, for example, provides a major check in the area of responsiveness and serves as a redundancy channel in competence (via GAO audits). The specialization of each institution, therefore, permits the system to benefit from the strengths of each institution.

A second important fact about redundant control systems is that marginal improvements in any single element of the system is beneficial from a systematic standpoint. Using the examples of Congress, the president and the courts each as 60 percent effective and a 93.6 percent effective system, increases the effectiveness of Congress by 10 percent and improves the performance of the entire system to 95.2 percent. An increase of 10 percent in effectiveness of one element in the system reduces the amount of errors in the system by 25 percent.

Although we cannot confidently estimate control systems parameters (that is, are the courts 60 percent effective? 40 percent effective?), the basic principles hold. A combination of checks is always more effective than each check individually. The careful addition of more redundancy improves the entire system. The marginal improvement of any check in the system improves the performance of the entire system.

The Ombudsman

Proposals to improve the bureau-monitoring capacities of each political institution will be discussed in the following section. One improvement, however, can be proposed based on redundancy alone. The United States should establish an independent ombudsman to receive complaints about bureaucratic abuse and should allow the ombudsman to act on those complaints. Given the experience of other countries with their limited ombudsmen (see Chapter 6) however, the United States requires a different type of ombudsman.

A successful ombudsman will need to circumvent two problems— the number and representativeness of complaints and the hostility of other complaint-processing institutions (for example, Congress). The representativeness of complaints is merely a matter of making sure the public knows about the ombudsman and making the procedures for complaining about bureaucratic abuse simple. Given the success of such government public relations campaigns as "Smokey the Bear" and "Electric Ant," the ombudsman could be introduced with a public service announcement campaign. These public service announcements could be supplemented by visible posters in all federal office buildings and referrals by Federal Information Centers.[5] To ensure that all people are able to use the ombudsman, the Scandinavian requirement of written complaints must be eliminated; only if nonwritten complaints are permitted will the process be representative. Verbal complaints either in person or by telephone should be sufficient to begin an investigation.

Constituents' requests to members of Congress for assistance with the bureaucracy are a second source of an ombudsman's casework. If all members of Congress referred this casework to the ombudsman, the ombudsman could process all complaints uniformly and, thus, eliminate the bias created by congressional intervention in the administrative process. Since many members of Congress correctly feel that effective casework is essential to remain in office, members of Congress should still be permitted to correspond with the constituent and send the ombudsman's answers to the constituent. In this way a member of Congress would receive the credit from a constituent for acting on a complaint, but the favoritism of the present casework system would be moderated.[6]

The United States ombudsman should have the same sanctions that most other ombudsmen have. After receiving a complaint, the ombudsman will attempt to determine the facts of the situation and informally resolve the differences between the citizen and the bureaucracy. If the ombudsman fails to resolve these differences and feels that the bureaucrat is responsible, the ombudsman may file a letter of reprimand in the bureaucrat's employment file.[7] In circumstances where a number of employees consistently act unresponsively or unethically, the ombudsman can resort to his major sanction, publicity. If the office of the ombudsman is held by a well-respected prestigious individual and if history supports the ombudsman's accuracy, then publicity is not an idle sanction. Washington, D.C. is a town that thrives on news and reputations, negative publicity especially by a reliable source is a major sanction for a rising bureaucratic politician.

Given the power of the ombudsman and the potential for abusing that power, the ombudsman and its staff must be isolated from temptation. The civil servants employed by the Office of the Ombudsman must be perceived as above temptation. The ombudsman's personnel must have an intense loyalty to the function they perform similar to the personnel in the General Accounting Office. To ensure loyalty and performance the proposed ombudsman should have a separate career system with entry based on rigorous exams covering administrative law and procedure. The high prestige, separate career system for ombudsman employees should be balanced by a ban on accepting employment with any other federal agency after leaving office so that ombudsmen do not make decisions with future careers in mind.

The advantage of the ombudsman should be speed and low cost. It is a poor person's court to protect citizens from individual bureaucrats abusing the administrative (rather than policy) functions of government. Within this limited range the ombudsman is a valuable addition to the system of bureaucratic controls.

ᕔ Strengthening Political Institutions ᕽ

Those who seek a responsive, competent, and effective bureaucracy by weakening the power of bureaucracy misperceive the problem. The United States government cannot effectively perform its governmental functions and meet the demands of the American people without a bureaucracy that has access to political resources and is quasi-autonomous. The solution is not to weaken bureaucracy but rather to strengthen other political institutions so that they can structure and check the power of bureaucracy. Only a strong presidency and a strong Congress can provide the necessary counterweight to a powerful bureaucracy. This section proposes several means of strengthening these political institutions.

The Presidency

The key to presidential control over bureaucracy is holding the president responsible for all bureaucratic actions that take place under his administration. The American people should treat presidential attacks on bureaucratic resistance and inefficiency as confessions of failure. Although contemporary presidents are clearly not responsible for all bureaucratic actions taken in the name of the president, until presidents are held responsible they will lack the motivation to devote significant resources to oversee bureaucracy.

The president's best weapon for controlling bureaucracy is his ability to appoint line administrators. Past presidential transitions have demonstrated that presidents have a significant impact on the bureaucracy if they appoint talented people with presidential confidence to policy-making positions in the bureaucracy. If the political appointees in a bureau are perceived as competent and if appeals to the president appear to be futile, the bureau's remaining major weapon is exclusive access to policymaking information. To generate independent information for political appointees, the president needs to establish a program where a number of civil servants are selected from the bureaucracy to advise bureau chiefs on policy matters. These civil servants would be exempted from civil service restrictions on pay and given special status within the bureau. The information they present could be verified by information gathered by midlevel political appointees in the bureaucracy. Currently, these schedule C appointees, some twelve hundred people in mid- and lower-level positions in the bureaucracy, are used for patronage purposes; these political loyalists need to be used for management and information purposes if political control over bureaucracy is to be achieved. To be effective, the ranks of schedule C employees must be expanded drama- tically. Currently the president can appoint only twenty-two hundred people, one political appointee for every twenty-five hundred civil servants. Taking a cue from the spoils system, which stressed responsiveness over competence, the number of schedule C employees should be at least tripled. We cannot expect a government bureau to be responsive to presidential programs if the bureau is not monitored by at least one presidential appointee.

To increase the probability that a strengthened presidency can influence the bureaucracy, two management reforms should be introduced. First, the president needs a rationalized budget system that focuses budget conflict on goals and political priorities rather than increments over last year's expenditures. Several prominent possibilities include Zero-Base Bud- geting (ZBB), Planning, Programming Budgeting (PPB), or a budgeting analogue of Management by Objectives (MBO). These procedures attempt to introduce rationality and analysis into the budget process by first defining goals and then analyzing the means to reach those goals. The purpose of a rationalized budget system is not to make the federal government more economical, rational or efficient—any system will fail if it has such ambiguous and unattainable goals—rather the purpose of rationalized budget systems is to focus conflict on policy priorities so that high level administrators can choose among bureaucratic programs on the basis of their own policy priorities. A rationalized budget system serves to centralize political decisionmaking by transferring policy decisions from the bureaucracy to the president.

Second, presidents must use their reorganization powers, recently reinstated by Congress, to structure the environment of bureaus so that by responding to its environment the bureau is responsive to the president. Despite President Carter's concern with reorganization as demonstrated by the large OMB reorganization staff, his early reorganization proposals reflect traditional preferences for functional organization rather than controlling the bureaucracy. HEW Secretary Joseph Califano's reorganization of his department (see chapter 3) is a good example of a policy-oriented reorganization. Medicare and Medicaid programs were given to a new agency in preparation for a future National Health Insurance; welfare functions were transferred to the Social Security Administration in preparation for a negative income tax welfare reform; and the services portion of the federal welfare effort were deemphasized in a temporary agency.

The purpose of both reorganization and rationalized budget systems is to break up the bureau-interest-group-subcommittee subsystems that dominate politics in noncrises times. A rationalized budget system will force budget decisions out of the subsystem into the executive office. Reorganization, if used creatively, can group unlike programs so that subsystems are not homogeneous. If conflict occurs in a subsystem, the subsystem is weaker and can be influenced by the president.

Congress

Strengthening the Congress is more difficult than strengthening the president because the major problems of congressional checks on bureaucracy are more often motivational rather than procedural. Despite the fact that Congress as a representative institution cannot be expected to control bureaucracy as well as the presidency, a hierarchical institution, some marginal improvements in congressional procedures and emphasis can be suggested.

First, many members of Congress believe that the president dominates the policy process because the president with his access to greater expertise has superior information.[8] Congress's information limitations are even greater when compared to the bureaucracy. Congress will not be able to control the bureaucracy until Congress has access to information equal that of most federal bureaus. The General Accounting Office (GAO) provides Congress with some of its best information; especially when GAO evaluates the effectiveness of bureau programs (performance audits); GAO needs to expand in this area. To avoid overburdening the bureaucracy and creating requirements that bureaucracy must meet rather than performing its stated function, the GAO should be used as the monitoring agency in a Management by Objectives (MBO) strategy. GAO's function in an MBO strategy is to take the legislative objectives of a bureau's programs and investigate how successful the agency was in meeting the goals. In short, the GAO would evaluate the policy performance of the federal bureaus. If GAO's major function were performance audits rather than financial audits, Congress would have the raw materials to check on bureaucratic policymaking.

Congress also has several other information agencies that are underused and could be improved. The Congressional Research Service of the Library of Congress is perhaps the second (GAO is first) most frequently used information agency. It provides general policy information on request. The Congressional Budget Office is a well respected, specialized information agency but its performance is hindered by its perceived Senate bias. The Office of Technology Assessment, designed to provide technical information, has been handicapped by a patronage-oriented personnel system.[9] These agencies form the basis of a good Congressional information system, but they must be reorganized and reformed to provide information about the bureaucracy.

Second, Congress' incremental response to complex problems permits it to avoid decisions about bureaucracy. Since Congress does not have the expertise to completely analyze a policy area, it tentatively establishes a policy and each year increases the effort if there are no major complaints. The press of these day-to-day incremental issues means obsolescent programs can continue to operate indefinitely. The Subversive Activities Control Board continued to exist far past any positive benefits; similar arguments can be made for the Selective Service System and the Marine Corps.

To avoid the hazards of incremental policymaking, specifically out-dated or useless bureaus, Congress should pass a comprehensive sunset law specifying that every agency in the federal government will cease to exist in a set period of years (ten, for example) unless Congress specifically acts to reinstate the agency. Through sunset laws the incremental operations of Congress and the press of daily duties will work to decrease the number of bureaus rather than to protect the older bureaus.

An adequate sunset law cannot uniformly apply to all agencies, or Congress would routinely pass extending legislation because certain agencies (for example, the Department of Defense) are essential. Forcing Congress to consider abolishing these agencies would turn the law into mere window dressing. The sunset law should apply only to bureaus and agencies, not to major departments. Thus, the question should not be whether the United States should have a Department of Agriculture, but whether it should have a Soil Conservation Service. Every department has some worthwhile bureaus and programs so that focusing debate on the department level is futile. In addition to departments, a few other organizations that are designed to operate on long term problems such as the Social Security Administration and the Bureau of Public Debt must be exempt.[10] Examining bureaus with functions based on long term fiscal obligations diverts scarce time from more worthy candidates.

The goal of sunset legislation is to focus congressional debate on bureaucratic goals rather than on how well the bureau performs its goal regardless of the goal's value. Sunset legislation means bureaus must occasionally justify their existence to Congress with the public eye focused on the process. The process will become effective and credible if, in the first years of sunset legislation, a few bureaus are publicly eliminated.

Third, Congress should enact sunshine legislation similar to the Freedom of Information Act that permits individuals to request information from the agencies' files. Current procedures need to be made simpler with few restrictions on nonsecurity data. Secrecy is a crucial element in abusing the bureaucratic authority; actions that seem logical in a bureaucratic atmosphere often appear ridiculous in the light of day.

Fourth and most difficult, Congress must break down the localism of committees and subcommittees. Bureaus are often unresponsive to public desires because they are exceptionally responsive to congressional subcommittees and the interests they represent.[11] Although breaking up a policy subsystem is difficult, some actions can help.[12] If the president uses his reorganization powers to the fullest, then the groups of agencies that each congressional committee oversees will include a more varied set of bureaus.[13] Where functions vary, interests vary so that committees and subcommittees must consider a wider range of interests. Potentially the most radical reform of Congress in recent times, the congressional budget reforms of 1974, can also tamper localisms if used properly. For the first time Congress considers the budget in its entirety and, thus, must compare agency appropriations to national fiscal needs rather than simply aggregating several appropriations bills. If the Congressional Budget Office reaches the level of skills that OMB possesses, then the entire Congress has comprehensive budget information so that it can overrule decisions made in committees.[14]

Finally, Congress could also improve its control over the bureaucracy if Congress would restructure itself administratively. The House Commission on Administrative Review suggested several ways for the House of Representatives to improve internal administration. The most important was the proposal to create a congressional administrator who would run a consolidated administrative apparatus for Congress.[15] If Congress adopted this and other commission reforms, then congressional members would be freed from administrative detail to pursue other functions including, hopefully, oversight of the bureaucracy.

The purpose of the first four suggested congressional reforms is to break up subsystem politics. If policy subsystems can be weakened, then the scope of conflict within the systems will be greater and Congress as a whole can have a greater impact on policy. When Congress reclaims its role as a policymaker, then Congress can develop the motivation along with the tools it already has to check bureaucratic power.

The Courts

Courts of law in the United States will never be an effective check on the abuse of bureaucratic power. Currently the courts are too costly for most Americans. Even if the costs of using the court system could be lowered by legislation or good management, the result would be increased court caseloads, slower court action on review of administrative actions, and the judicialization of many administrative procedures. Administrative agencies are the preferred means of implementing policy because bureaus can operate quickly with simple procedures on a wide scale. Court intervention that results in bureau action that follows court-like procedures defeats the purpose of using bureaus to implement public policy.

Some court functions will, of course, be assumed by the ombudsman; the rest may continue as they are now. If court procedures could be streamlined and better managed, then they could provide a greater check on bureaucracy. No logical reason exists why courts cannot be reformed. If administrators were given the power to allocate judges' time, if efficient scheduling were used to make sure only prepared lawyers need to appear in court, if many of the minor cases that clog the nation's courts were transferred to administrative tribunals or excluded from the system, then the courts could be a greater force in checking on bureaucracy. As the system is currently designed, however, the courts must be satisfied with only a minor role in controlling bureaucracy.

Interest Groups

American politics is pressure group politics, but pressure group politics has the normative limitations of unrepresentativeness, thus, preventing all possible viewpoints from influencing public policy. If all interests on a given policy were organized and if government responded to those organized interests, then interest groups would be an effective means to insure responsive public bureaucracy. The only problem is that all interests are not represented.

Government has played a major role in forming and developing interest groups in all policy areas. The American Farm Bureau developed under the auspices of the Department of Agriculture; the National Farmers Union rose to prominence under the Farm Security Administration.[16] The National Rifle Association grew to be a powerful lobby as the result of government assistance in the form of surplus weapons, ammunition, and government-sponsored target ranges.[17] After the Wagner Act in 1935 the federal government became an advocate for labor unions.[18]

Since the benefits of representative interest groups are obvious and since the government has never shied from assisting an interest group in its formative years, the government only needs to organize some additional groups to insure a more responsive bureaucracy. Government can bear the cost of organizing latent groups by creating bureaus charged with representing a stated interest. Recently many members of Congress recognized this means of checking bureaucracy with their attempt to create an Agency for Consumer Advocacy (ACA).[19] ACA would represent consumer interests before all other regulatory agencies; it would have no program responsibilities that might interfere with representing consumer interests. Advocacy bureaus with no more than one hundred employees are an inexpensive way to guarantee that broad unorganized interests are represented. Without additional functions that can generate clientele support, the agency will be motivated to create advisory units that can be the core of a new interest group. When the interest group reaches maturity, the agency is no longer needed and can be abolished.[20]

Advocacy agencies are possible for a variety of interests, the most obvious being consumer interests. Advocacy agencies could be created for women as some major cities have done, for nonunion labor, or for a variety of other latent groups. A separate agency is preferable to consumer advocates in every agency because a separate agency would not have divided clientele loyalties. The strength of the public interest groups in this country is strong enough to prevent the advocacy agencies from being coopted by nonconsumer interests.

꧁ Creating a True Merit System ꧂

The nation's merit system personnel processes have a major impact on the people who administer the bureaucracy and the competence and responsiveness of the bureaucracy. The merit system was designed as an attempt to maximize the goal of competence and to counter the perceived ill-effects of responsiveness. Evaluated by the standard of competence, the civil service system has made great strides since the Arthur Administration, but something is still amiss.

Every year two types of students descend on schools of public administration and public affairs. One group is the freshly-scrubbed college graduates seeking the Master of Public Administration degree. These students are young, enthusiastic, excited idealists eager to join government and fight for the public interest. In sharp contrast to the new college graduates are the midcareer people who have spent ten years or so in a bureau and are returning to school for a Master's degree or some training judged essential for their career advancement. The midcareers are pessimistic, disillusioned, and cynical; they listen to their idealistic counterparts, shake their heads, and mutter that the idealists just do not understand.

Ten years before these same cynics were also idealists off to Washington, Albany, Springfield, and Bismarck to seek the public interest. They blame their own transition on the merit system which they denigrate as a demerit system. The cynics have long since lost any belief that the merit entrance exam measures anything remotely related to job performance except for literacy, a bare minimum requirement. Once in the civil service, promotions occur on a more or less regular schedule unless the employee does something disastrous or the employee reaches the higher civil service ranks where he or she must wait for others to retire or die. The system does not reward merit according to the cynics but rather punishes "lack of merit", thus stifling initiative.[21]

Reform Entrance Procedures and Educational Training

The goal of public service training and entrance examinations is to train and select the best possible people as civil servants. For the minority of positions, the process of designing job relevant tests so that the tests measure tasks similar to those performed on the job is relatively easy. In lower level positions and technical fields, tests can be designed that accurately tap ability to perform job tasks.

For management and higher level positions, the reform of entry procedures is more difficult. To counter the cynicism about the relationship between performance and rewards, all noncompetitive entry procedures should be eliminated. One-half the current higher civil service originally entered the civil service through noncompetitive entry procedures either because they had specified occupations or because the agency specifically requested them from a list of applicants.[22] Of the 1600 midcareer (GS9 through GS12) personnel hired by the federal government each year from outside government, fully 80 percent are requests for specific individuals, the remainder are selected by the "normal" competitive entry process.[23]

If tests could be designed to tap all the needed dimensions for mid- and high-level managers, an effective merit system could be created. Although performance-related qualifications tests are nonexistent, currently some skills necessary to be an effective government manager—reasoning, problem-solving ability, and organizational ability—can be measured. The civil service needs procedures that measure performance on these criteria, but do not discriminate on the basis of irrelevant characteristics such as race, sex, religion, region, or national origin.

The procedure for establishing a performance-based exam is relatively simple. The Office of Personnel Management (OPM) should institute a national exam to replace the current PACE exam. Rather than being concerned with English usage and simple math problems, the new exam should contain a series of administrative problems. Staffing organizations, deciding organizational programs given a specified set of objectives, knowledge of government operations, and the findings of organization theory research are all possible topics. To ensure that this exam is nondiscriminatory, some core of knowledge must be offered by the schools that train potential civil servants. The National Association of Schools of Public Administration and Affairs (NASPAA), an association of schools that train many management-level civil servants, has already set standards for member schools. From standards for resources, specifying a common core for administrative studies is only a small step, especially if national exams are based on that core curriculum.

To insure that admissions to NASPAA schools is nondiscriminatory (so that civil service entry procedures become nondiscriminatory), and to provide incentives for schools of public administration to cooperate with the OPM, Congress needs to establish a large public service fellowship program. Through a series of regional competitions based on undergraduate performance, work experience, and other factors, people would be selected to receive a Civil Service Fellowship. If the fellowship is usable at any accredited NASPAA institution, the institutions have an incentive to reform curriculum because a significant number of Civil Service Fellowships could solve their tuition problems. To have an impact on the public service, the program would need to be massive with perhaps 10,000 fellowships a year at an estimated annual cost of $40 million; but $40 million is a small price to pay to see the entry procedures of the civil service rationalized.

A second order benefit of the fellowships system is that it could be used to recruit students from disadvantaged groups. A recent study of state affirmative action programs revealed that where educational backgrounds are roughly equal, minorities competed quite favorably with whites for state jobs.[24] Regional competitions plus extensive recruiting could be used to insure that fellowship recipients would be broadly representative of the American population—representative of blacks, browns, women, regions, urban areas, rural areas, and social status. Since each fellow would receive a similar education, they would have a relatively equal chance to pass the entrance exam. The end result should be a more representative civil service; representation though not a means to responsive bureaucratic policy, has some other positive benefits. By employing people from similar backgrounds as those receiving the service, representative bureaucracy enhances the competence of bureaucracy. This representation permits more open communication and a better understanding of clientele needs. A representative bureaucracy also enhances competence because administrative talent is widely distributed in the population; discrimination wastes personnel resources by limiting jobs to only one type of person.

When the examination system is fully developed, the Office of Personnel Management should offer the results of the exam to state governments so that they can also staff their government bureaus with people who pass the national exam. At this point the exam will become much like the proposed national bar exam advocated by the Educational Testing Service.

A critic of uniform exams might challenge this proposed system by arguing that a single exam encourages a uniform curriculum; and thus, a single exam would stifle creativity and innovation in public service education. A good counter example to this criticism is the nation's law schools. Although each state gives a single exam and the topics covered on the exam do not vary greatly from state to state, law schools have not become carbon copies of each other. Law schools while offering a basic core of courses provide a great number of different courses. Even within the common law core courses, the emphasis varies from school to school. Schools of public administration, anxious to guard their reputation for excellence, will probably offer different programs to attract the best of the Civil Service Fellows.

Raise the Prestige of the Civil Service

Given the public's image of the federal bureaucracy, the quality of the civil service is surprisingly high. The 10,000 people of the higher civil service probably have no peer group in the nation. Unfortunately, the public perceives civil servants as lazy, overly secure, and uncreative; as a result, many talented people never consider a career in the civil service.[25] To guarantee the best possible people to fill positions in the higher civil service, conscious efforts must be made to raise the prestige of the civil service. Two such efforts are included in this section.

First, in a nation that accepts almost without question the teachings of Adam Smith, the worth of an individual is often measured, however inappropriately, by the income of that person. Because Congress has established salary ceilings for high level positions far below those for equivalent positions in the private sector, the lower salaries reflect negatively on the civil servant's image. Congress also has refused to budget sufficient funds for the salaries authorized for higher civil servants. As a result, a GS14 is paid approximately the same salary as a GS18. Salary rewards for higher civil servants, therefore, are virtually nonexistent. Although the civil service is competitive with private industry at entry and mid-management levels, it is at a relative disadvantage at the top management level. An executive paid less than $40,000 who makes decisions worth millions of dollars would be rare to find in the private sector but very common in Washington. Many of these men and women remain in government out of loyalty or other nonmonetary incentives, but some cannot resist the financial rewards of private business. The pay ceiling needs to be lifted so that higher civil servants receive an income commensurate with their responsibilities.

Second, the visibility of the civil service should be increased. The popular perception of the civil servant as a pencil pusher or a paper shuffler does not correspond to the actual situation. For example, in 1976 Dr. Carleton Gajdusek, a federal government employee, was awarded a Nobel Prize for his work on slow viruses; Dr. William Bunney, in the same year, received the McAlpin Medal for work in mental health. Although both men were employed by a single agency, their honors were used as fillers in most newspapers. Congress should establish a series of public service awards on the order of the Rockefeller awards. Civil servants receiving these awards should be given recognition outside Washington, D.C. to insure that the civil servant's image also reflects its positive aspects.

Increase Executive Mobility

A major problem with bureaucracy is the narrow perspectives harbored by bureaucrats. The oft-quoted bureaucratic saying, where one stands on an issue depends on where one sits, is all too often true.[26] Narrow perceptions are a function of both the agency socialization process and the self-selection process whereby civil servants agree to work only for those agencies that have goals compatible with their own. To broaden bureaucrats' perceptions, a bureaucrat must be exposed to more and different experiences. Past attempts to encourage broader perceptives by increasing executive mobility have met with little success because civil servants are reluctant to leave their bureaus for extended periods of time. This reluctance is related to the belief that during a person's absence other bureaucratic politicians will divide the missing person's sphere of influence.

Congress should amend the civil service laws so that every federal executive over GS11 is required to spend one year out of every seven in another federal agency, a private organization, a university, a state agency, et cetera, or in an educational training program. If these experiences are made mandatory and prerequisites for promotion, they have a greater probability of achieving broader bureaucratic perspectives. The program can be used as an exchange program so that for every executive sent to an organization, the organization would send one of its executives to Washington for a year.

An exchange program not only increases executive mobility and, thereby, breaks down narrow viewpoints, but it also serves as an ideal recruitment mechanism. After watching a state executive function in their agency for a year, an agency may decide it would benefit by keeping the employee. If lateral entry into an agency at management levels can be increased this way, then agencies will be able to revitalize themselves by constantly adding people with new viewpoints to the agency.[27]

Awakening the American People

A country normally has an administrative apparatus no worse than it deserves. In the United States we are fortunate because the federal bureaucracy is much better than we deserve. Combining the value dimensions of responsiveness and competence, the American federal bureaucracy is clearly the best in the world.[28] No other national bureaucracy has won as many Nobel prizes, and no other bureaucracy responds to as wide an array of interests. These benefits of bureaucracy have come despite numerous obstacles posed by the American people. According to Norman J. Powell and Daniel P. Parker:

> In a country where the 'politician' is a symbol of corruption and dishonesty, if not dishonor, where a large majority of parents, as reported by the Gallup Poll, prefer not to have their children enter the public service, where the bureaucracy is regarded as a legitimate object of ridicule and even revulsion and the term 'bureaucrat' is a nasty name, how can one expect high standards of public service and responsibility? The wonder is not that we have not achieved a competent, devoted, and responsible bureaucracy, but that we have come so close to doing so.[29]

Adequate service in the past, however, is no reason to assume the bureaucracy will always be beneficent. To guarantee effective performance, a variety of beliefs and behaviors of the American citizenry must be changed.

Increase Public Awareness of Politics and Participation

Chapters 6 and 7 demonstrated a variety of ways to influence politics and control bureaucracy. Most bureaucratic controls, however, are underused. The American public needs to be shown the options they have to influence government through the ballot box, through interest groups, and through other forms of participation. If ordinary people do not control their elected leaders, then eventually bureaucracy will be responsive to an unscrupulous politician and the worst fears about bureaucracy will be realized.

Increase Public Awareness of Bureau Policymaking

Much bureaucratic power results from the secrecy of bureaucratic policymaking process. If the public has no knowledge of decisions being made, then bureaucratic decisions are presented as a *fait accompli* with no alternatives. The media bears a heavy burden to present the actual process of government and its subsystem politics at work. Few college students today know about subsystem politics and its impact on public policy, and even fewer high school graduates have this knowledge. Until the nation's students and by osmosis the majority of the voting public learns about the nature of subsystem politics and the role of bureaucracy in them, the public will remain for the most part at the mercy of bureaucracy.

Eliminate the Stereotypes of Bureaucracy

If a large group of reasonably intelligent students is informed about the quantity and quality of expertise in the federal bureaucracy discoveries of sonar, dextran, synthetic lubricants, wash and wear fabrics, and disease research contributed by these bureaucrats, the student's reaction is one of disbelief and shock. The image of the federal service is that they are lazy, unambitious, and less than competent.

The negative image of the federal service must be changed for two reasons. First, the negative image of the civil service dissuades some of the "best and brightest" from considering a career in government at a time when government needs them more than ever. Second, the negative image means that bureaucrats are consistently underestimated by the population. Underestimating bureaucrats is dangerous, because when the bureaucracy does exercise power, it comes as a surprise, thus, weakening opposition to bureaucratic influence. Most people then react by denouncing bureaucracy rather than attempting to understand it, a prerequisite for changing and controlling bureaucracy.

End Passive Acceptance of Delay

Every member of the American public has at one time in his or her life tolerated bureaucratic delays, arbitrariness, and rudeness. Although such behavior may be logical for a bureau that believes most petitioners are bending the truth and believes that little delay separates the deserving from the undeserving, the behavior is unacceptable from a systemic viewpoint. Bureaus can refuse benefits or assess costs without being rude, arbitrary, and slow. The system must be redesigned so that the public can provide feedback to the bureau chief or to his superior on the type of service they receive.

One possible way to provide feedback on service to the public is to institute a buck skip procedure. When a person enters a federal office, he or she is given a small form by the receptionist who codes the identity of the bureaucrat dealing with the client. After the citizen conducts whatever business is necessary, the citizen fills out a few questions on the slip about the contact with the bureaucracy. A summary of these slips could be placed in each person's personnel file for review when the bureaucrat is due for promotion. Bureaucrats with poor public service records should be sent to training seminars to correct the problem. Bureaucrats who show no improvement after the training seminars should be transferred to jobs where contact with the public is not necessary.

Lower People's Expectations of Government

For people in a nation established on the principle that big government is the quickest way to tyranny, we expect far too much from government today. The social security system is constantly criticized because benefits do not permit one to live adequately despite the fact the system was never designed to provide for full support. When the St. Louis police struck the city in 1975, the city's mayor immediately appealed to the federal government to do something. When Lockheed Corporation ran heavily into debt as a result of government contracting, the corporation appealed to the federal government to help it.

These are not just three isolated examples; government increasingly has been asked to intervene in the lives of its citizens. We should not be surprised that when welcomed to intervene, government does so. Responsiveness is a trait of government as well as of bureaucracy. The detrimental nature of the public's expectations cannot be overstated. As more and more tasks are shifted to the public sector in response to people's demands, the scope of government becomes too large. When government operates massive programs too complex for the private sector, it is bound to fail; when it fails, people become cynical about government.

More harmful than cynicism, however, is the effect on individuals who rely on bureaucracy. When a mayor appeals to Washington to solve a *city* problem or when a business executive appeals to Washington to solve a *business* problem, it means that these people lack the creativity and skills to handle the problems themselves. As a citizenry, we have become so dependent on bureaucracy that we have lost the ability to function without it.

Lessening our expectations of government bureaucracy does not mean that we should transfer those expectations to private sector bureaucracy. ITT is clearly no better as a *deus ex machina* than is the Social Security Administration. In fact, ITT is likely much worse because it is a private organization and does not have the formal mechanisms for public control that the public sector does.

New governmental policy must persuade citizens to depend on themselves and force other units of government and corporations to do likewise. This policy will permit the federal government to concentrate on the tasks only it can perform and will prevent major drains on federal resources that restrict effective policymaking. The days of *laissez faire*, if they ever existed, are truly gone forever; but between the poles of *laissez faire* and bureaucracy; there is ample room for a government policy that forces people to influence their own futures.

This chapter has proposed some sweeping changes in American politics and, at times, has ignored political reality to do so; but realities are alterable conditions. The American people, either directly or through their leaders, must learn to control bureaucracy, or they must resign themselves to live under its tyranny. We can harbor no expectations that bureaucracy can become completely responsive and competent overnight. Like most public policy problems, reforming the bureaucracy must be done a piece at a time, a frustrating and trying experience; but there are no other alternatives.

ᕙ Notes ᕗ

1.   Martin Landau, "Redundancy, Rationality, and the Problem of Duplication and Overlap," *Public Administration Review* 29 (July/August 1969), pp. 346–358.

2.   Herbert Simon, *Sciences of the Artificial* (Cambridge, Mass.: M.I.T. Press, 1969).

3.   Landau, "Redundancy, Rationality."

4.   The 93.6 percent figure is reached by the following calculations: Congress by being 60 percent effective is able to prevent 60 percent of the cases of administrative abuse. The president is 60 percent effective for the 40 percent that Congress lets slip through, adding another 24 percent. The courts are 60 percent effective on the 16 percent missed by both other institutions, adding another 9.6 percent for a total of 93.6. These calculations assume, of course, total overlap. The percentage effectiveness figures are arbitrary and are used only to illustrate the argument. Given the varied expectations of bureaucracy, calculating such precise figures is impossible.

5.   Federal information centers are established in most metropolitan areas to help the citizen through the maze of bureaucracy. Telephone directories prominently list this number with those of the federal bureaus in the area.

6.   A casework type ombudsman might also permit members of Congress to concentrate on other aspects of their job, resulting in better legislation and additional oversight.

7.   The procedure will of course permit the employee to appeal a letter of reprimand to a neutral party such as the Merit Systems Protection Board where the issue will be resolved administratively.

8.   The Congressional debates over the supersonic transport, the antiballistic missile system and the creation of the Office of Technology Assessment illustrates Congress' concern with executive advantages of information. The Office of Technology Assessment was created in part to counter some of the advantage.

9.   Dick Kirschten, "The Misplaced Mission of OTA," *National Journal* 9 (Nov. 12, 1977), p. 1777.

10.   Long term agencies need not live forever since they can be eliminated via the process of legislation. Continual reevaluations of such agencies divert agency time from other tasks and tend to project a frivolous image for the sunset process.

11. Lester M. Salamon and Gary L. Walmsley, "The Federal Bureaucracy—Responsive to Whom?" (Paper presented at the Annual Meeting of the Midwest Political Science Association, Chicago, 1975).

12. A. Lee Fritschler, *Smoking and Politics* (Englewood Cliffs: Prentice-Hall, 1975).

13. I assume, of course, that congressional committees will be reorganized to mirror the organization of the executive branch. This assumption is questionable since the Senate in 1977 reorganized its committees and the House considered the reorganization without knowing about any Carter reorganization proposals. Many committees oversee agencies that are not in the same department.

14. Nelson Polsby, *Congress and the Presidency* (Englewood Cliffs: Prentice-Hall, 1976).

15. Commission on Administrative Review, *Administrative Reorganization and Legislative Management* (Washington: U.S. Government Printing Office, 1977).

16. Sidney Baldwin, *Politics and Poverty* (Chapel Hill: University of North Carolina Press, 1963).

17. Robert Sherril, *The Saturday Night Special* (New York: Penquin Press, 1973).

18. Felix Nigro and Lloyd Nigro, *Modern Public Administration* (New York: Harper and Row, 1977).

19. *National Journal* 9 (Nov. 12, 1977), p. 1782.

20. Anyone who has grasped the major themes of this book will realize that even if the agency is superfluous, it cannot be abolished if it successfully organizes a latent interest group. The agency becomes a symbol of governmental concern for the latent interest; therefore, any organized elements of the interest will react strongly and negatively to its abolition. Although the benefits of advocacy agencies clearly outweigh the costs, restrictions must be placed on the agencies to prevent bureaucratic empires or to at least limit their size.

21. The midcareers and most upper level personnel do not feel that the bureaucratic superstars are not rewarded. Truly exceptional people are able to make the system work for them if they are not overly eccentric. The problem lies with the remainder of the civil service, the bright, competent but not exceptional civil servant whose contributions are not singled out either because the less competent receive the same rewards or because they are denied rewards granted to more skillful organizational politicians.

22. Lawyers are the most prominent exception to normal entry procedures. Civil service laws prevent the Office of Personnel Management and the

agencies from examining, via tests, the qualifications of lawyers. As a result, lawyers are hired by interview and noncompetitive procedures.

23. Ann Pincus, "How to Get a Government Job," *Washington Monthly* 8 (June 1976), pp. 22–28.

24. Kenneth J. Meier, "The Policy Impact of Affirmative Action" (Paper presented at the Annual Meeting of the Southwestern Social Science Association, Dallas, 1976).

25. Franklin P. Kilpatrick, Milton Cummings, M. Kent Jennings, *The Image of the Federal Service* (Washington: Brookings Institution, 1964).

26. The statement has been attributed to a variety of sources. The consensus supports Rufus Miles, former assistant secretary of HEW as the source.

27. Many critics of the State Department feel that by increasing lateral entry into the department, the staid and ineffective State Department can become again a vital force in the making of American foreign policy. See I. M. Destler, *Presidents, Bureaucrats and Foreign Policy* (Princeton: Princeton University Press, 1972).

28. The contention that the US bureaucracy is the best in the world is the author's opinion. Few bureaucracies in other countries surpass US bureaucracy on the competence dimensions. Those that may (for example, France, England, Germany) are not nearly as responsive to a wide variety of interests as the American bureaucracy is.

29. Norman J. Powell and Daniel P. Parker, *Major Aspects of American Government* (New York: McGraw-Hill, 1963), p. 362.

Index